# DATE DUE

| | | | |
|---|---|---|---|
| JE 9 '04 | | | |
| FE 10 '05 | | | |
| | | | |
| | | | |
| | | | |
| | | | |
| | | | |
| | | | |
| | | | |
| | | | |
| | | | |
| | | | |
| | | | |
| | | | |
| | | | |
| | | | |
| | | | |
| | | | |

DEMCO 38-296

# CHINA
# The Next Superpower

# CHINA
# The Next Superpower

## Dilemmas in Change and Continuity

**Geoffrey Murray**

St. Martin's Press
New York

China: The Next Superpower

Copyright © 1998 Geoffrey Murray

ɔk may be used or
ver without written permission
ìs embodied in critical articles

rence Division,
10

ʃ America in 1998

Printed in Great Britain

ISBN 0–312–21533–9

**Library of Congress Cataloging in Publication Data**
Murray, Geoffrey, 1942–
  China : the next superpower : dilemmas in change and continuity /
Geoffrey Murray.
    p. cm.
  Includes bibliographical references and index.
  ISBN 0–312–21533–9
  1. China–Economic conditions–1976-  2. China–Social
conditions–1976-  3. China–Politics and government–1976-
I. Title.
HC427.92.M87   1998
306′.0951–dc21

                                                        98-6004
                                                          CIP

# Contents

# Foreword

In a course on the human geography of China, in which I have sometimes been involved as a sessional lecturer at Liverpool John Moores University, students on the opening day are asked to fill in a questionnaire concerning their perceptions of this vast country they are about to study. The findings tend to be consistent over the years. China is perceived as an authoritarian, military-threatening but somewhat backward country with widespread poverty and poor living standards; the Chinese in general are viewed as relatively unfriendly to the outside world.

This seems to conform with some of the findings of a Gallup Poll in the United States which revealed that among Americans the five qualities most commonly associated with the Chinese were: (1) hard-working, (2) ignorant, (3) war-like, (4) sly and (5) treacherous.

Poor? Well, there are certainly many Chinese, particularly in the rural interior, who are still struggling to escape from poverty. But in the urban areas and the more successful villages, life has been transformed in less than a generation. Two decades ago, ownership of a bicycle was regarded as the pinnacle of affluence. But at least in urban China today, most households have a great many of the basic consumer items now taken for granted in the West, and are catching up fast with many of the so-called 'non-essentials' enjoyed in the West. Thus, although only two per cent of homes have running water, most are electrified.

With the evident growing affluence, increasingly the Chinese see themselves as enjoying a better quality of life than they did five years ago. The Gallup Organization's annual consumer survey , for example, in 1997 found an average nation-wide rating of 5.09 on its 10-point scale ranging from 'the best possible life one can imagine' down to the 'worst possible'; five years before, this average was only 3.09. By the turn of the century, those responding to the survey are expected to be able to give a rating of 6.73.

There is a growing confidence in China that must strike any visitor. 'Working hard to get rich' is the main criteria for two-thirds of the adult population, according to the Gallup survey. Meanwhile, in sharp contrast with the purer days of revolutionary China under Mao, only three per cent now consider the main aim of life is to 'never think of yourself but give everything in service to society'.

These numbers suggest major social changes in a very short space of time, especially when set against China's long history. And they require a major rethink of how this complex country is viewed.

In preparation for writing this book, I have spent considerable time in second-hand bookshops and libraries seeking a wide variety of writings on China from the nineteenth century up to the present day. And what is most striking is the strong emotions, for good or bad, that the Chinese seem to arouse in so many breasts. One either has to be a rabid anti-Communist, seeing a Chinese red devil under every bed, or one is at least a 'fellow traveller', seeing China as the promised land for every true Marxist, along the lines of 'I have seen the future and it works'. Whether a sinophile or a sinophobe, one is free to visit China and the likelihood is that one will see that particular view confirmed.

In the past, the Western choice of misconception of China and the Chinese seems to have depended on the individual's state of Christian devoutness or when one was born. From the agnostic of the eighteenth century comes the image of the great Confucian state moving majestically down the centuries, changeless, peaceful, inert and practically embalmed beneath the rule of its godlike emperors and the government of the wisest scholars. To the Victorian churchgoer, on the other hand, China was the nightmare of the Protestant missionary, a godless kingdom of sinful rogues and heathens. It was, after all, pious horror at the behaviour of the benighted that first gave us the image of Dr Fu Manchu and his friends, the cultivated, callous opium-smoking criminal, all long knives. Then, there are the comic laundrymen, the ship's cook, the fat greasy restaurateurs, and the most inscrutable of all, the moon-faced Mao and his fanatical coterie of sycophants waving their Little Red Books in unison. Never perhaps have a single people been so subject to stereotypical vilification for so long.

Since 1990, I have spent much of my time living and working in China, and I believe I have seen both the best and the worst in the Chinese people. They are canny, pragmatic, hard-working, sensitive, often very excitable and sometimes deplorably stupid. They can be cruelly indifferent as well as extremely warm-hearted; honest and cunning; open and close-mouthed. And I must admit that I happen to like them very much indeed. But whatever one's view is on China and the Chinese, neither can be ignored. Many pundits have expressed the view that global politics and the economy in the twenty-first century will focus on the Pacific Asia. If true, the key fact is that the Chinese dragon, asleep for a century or so, is now awakening with a vengeance.

The economic reform and opening-up policies adopted by China since 1978 have led to profound and extensive changes in its politics, economy, society and culture. The rapid rise of China's economy, its large population, strategic position and huge potential market, and its enhanced international status have made China's future development a key factor in post-Cold War world peace and order, the Oriental-Occidental cultural relationship, the North-South economic order and the Sino-US and Sino-Japanese relationships.

From this emerged the perception that China is on the verge of becoming a Superpower, if it is not already one. The superpowers that have preceded it over the ages have all significantly shaped the world of their day, and China is unlikely to be any exception – especially given its vital geopolitical location, with the Muslim states of Central Asia on its western edge, the ailing but still powerful Russian bear to the north, the once booming (now temporarily wounded) economies of Southeast Asia on the southern rim, and the developed economic powerhouses of Japan and South Korea just a short sea journey away.

∞

This book is an attempt to examine China's credentials to be regarded as a superpower and also to consider what influence it will have on its neighbours and on the world at large. It is divided up into four sections dealing with different aspects of this equation.

In the second to the fifth chapters, I consider some of the elements that will either make or break China's rise to superpower rank: the rising number of jobless in the urban areas due to the economic reforms that require enterprises to abandon the jobs-for-life featherbedding of the Maoist era; the even larger amount of rural unemployment that is creating a mass tide of jobless peasants roaming the country in search of a better life; the huge population that contributes to both the aforementioned problems; and the question of whether there will be sufficient food, from domestic or foreign sources, to feed this vast population.

The following three chapters examine some of the social implications of the economic and political reforms that have been instituted in the past two decades or so. Chapter six provides a brief overview of China's long social history as a preparation for an examination of some of the major social upheavals that have been witnessed in recent years. Finally, in chapter eight, I examine the status of women, their new-found freedoms under Communism, as well as the limitations that may still prevent them from fulfilling all their potential.

The focus then switches to China's place in the world. In Chapter nine, I consider the key international relationships for China – namely, those with the United States and Japan – that will determine whether it can be successfully integrated into the global community as a contributor to peace and harmony. In the final chapter, all these various threads are drawn together into what one could call a 'whither China?' overview.

Equally, this book is about the dilemmas that China faces in balancing continuity and change, and this theme runs like a strong thread through every chapter. There is a constant struggle between the need to preserve much of what has kept China a united country for thousands of years, while seeking to adapt to the demands of the global village in the next century.

In every facet of life, these contradictions provide real or potential sources of tension. To take one example: in order to have a modern economy, China needs to reform its entire industrial structure, which means shedding millions of existing jobs and trying to create new ones not only for the urban unemployed but also for more than 100 million peasants surplus to requirements; yet this vast jobless pool provides one of the biggest brakes on China achieving its economic goals.

Then again, with a booming population, China has embarked on a stringent birth-control policy, requiring urban families in particular to restrict themselves to one child. But this single child is over-protected and spoilt and has had none of the exposure to hardship that has enabled countless generations of Chinese to survive in a harsh world. This issue, and many others that place China on a tightrope of countless dilemmas ahead of her will be examined throughout.

At all stages, I have tried to balance current reportage with theory and historical context. Although the Chinese love to bombard any seeker after truth with endless repetitions of statistics, I have tried to keep these to the minimum. However, at times, especially in the opening chapter, I have felt the need to use more than a few figures in order to give the reader some context for assessing China's current and future strength, although I have tried to keep these to the end notes to avoid damaging the textual flow.

The research for this work was conducted in China over a year-long stay in 1996 and 1997, during which I was engaged in a training consultancy for a State-run publications company, as well as drawing on insights from previous working stays in China stretching back to 1990. I would like to thank Wang Guozhen and other colleagues at *The Beijing Review* for their encouragement and their readiness to give me access to a wide range of official documents so that I could understand the Chinese government's side of the story. The Academy of Social Sciences was also most helpful in this regard. In Britain, Ian Cook at the Centre for Pacific Studies, LJMU, provided valuable comments and advice.

Apart from on-the-spot research, I have also drawn heavily on a large library of books, some of which are mentioned in the selected bibliography at the end of this book. In this regard, I should thank Stephen Sage, who over the past few years has been assiduous in tracking down rare, out-of-print books for me which have proved valuable research tools, as well as providing endless hours of reading enjoyment.

One is staggered by the number of books that have been written about China over the past century. My excuse for adding to that mountain is that I believe the time has come for a fresh, dispassionate look at this sometimes baffling and often disquieting country that is never out of the news for long. I have tried to avoid joining the large band of 'China knockers', while equally putting aside the red-tinted glasses.

What I hope has emerged is an essentially sympathetic portrait of a great people, 'warts and all', whose history and future development has become such an important part of my life.

GEOFFREY MURRAY,
*Beijing, February 1998*

■ CHAPTER 1

# Defining a Superpower

The basic assumption of this book is that China is steadily emerging as a 'superpower' for the next century. Certainly, there can be little argument that the biggest factor for the future of Pacific Asia is the current rise of the world's most populous country in its midst.

'The emerging giant' has long since become a headline writer's cliché. Since 1979, the Chinese economy has doubled roughly every seven-and-a-half years. The World Bank expects it to become the world's largest economy by 2020, although other experts place this event towards the middle of the century. More cautiously, scientists of the Chinese Academy of Social Sciences believe it will become the world's third largest economic power, behind the United States and Japan, by 2010. Its interaction with these two powerful states economically and politically has enormous global implications.

If China is no longer the revolutionary maverick of the Maoist era, it still cannot be regarded entirely as a *status quo* power. If, for example, it concentrates on irredentism, given its boundary disputes with 10 neighbouring states, then it will become a prickly presence in East Asia, especially under a leadership that seems driven by an ancient national-cultural chauvinism demanding restoration of China's greatness and the regaining of its place at the centre of the world.

Its increasing economic weight will unavoidably bring increased political and military influence. It is a nuclear power, an increasingly important player in the space satellite-launching business, alongside the United States and Western Europe, a permanent member of the UN Security Council, and one of the world's largest arms producers and exporters. Its huge domestic market is a mouth-watering lure for businessmen the world over. Its own increasingly confident business community is now beginning to explore the world for investment opportunities emulating the Japanese and Koreans before them.

Looked at purely from the viewpoint of population, China already is a superpower; how can a country that contributes nearly a quarter of the global population be otherwise? But it should also be stressed that what is really being examined here is whether China will become a superpower again. Will it, in fact, become the first nation in history to have gone into decline after a period of greatness (examples litter history from the Greeks and Romans through to the Spanish and British empires) only to recover its former glory?[1]

Understanding contemporary China requires an appreciation of its rich historical traditions. As one of the world's oldest, geographically contiguous civilizations, history tends to loom larger in the Chinese consciousness than it does with other peoples. A deep sensitivity and respect for historical traditions meant they have had to travel down a much longer road to accommodate their culture to the demands of modernization, namely the 'panoply of forces that move a society away from old habits and customs in the direction of urbanization, industrialization and the rationalization of thought and behaviour'.[2]

While *new* China differs from *old* China in many respects, at heart it is still the same. 'Five thousand years of history' are ingrained into the Chinese character, and this creates both a great sense of pride as well as a sense of inferiority.

Surrounded by a host of the latest electronic household appliances, toting a mobile phone, and logging on to the Internet from a personal computer, today's urban residents may bear little obvious resemblance to their ancestors, even those of the early twentieth century.[3] And yet, scratch the surface, and one finds much that can be traced back to antiquity, to provide a contradictory mix of continuity and change.

Every age has had perplexing contradictions. Consider, for example, that while traditional China extolled harmony, as well as emphasizing morality and ethical precepts as the vital underpinnings for official legitimacy and authority, every imperial dynasty was founded upon military force, with victory being taken as proof of the legitimacy of the rebellion against established authority. And then, what to make of a people who invent gunpowder, but put it mainly to use making fireworks!

Historically, the giant land mass of China has cast a long shadow over its neighbours, as it does today. Imperial China exercised suzerain power, which tended to wax and wane with the vitality of the reigning dynasty, over vast swathes of territory stretching down into Southeast Asia, eastwards to Tibet, westwards into parts of Central Asia and southwards into the Korean peninsula.[4]

Chinese civilization should be seen as one of the great achievements of the human spirit. China has been both the Greece and Rome of the Far Eastern World, providing it with its arts, laws and the system of government. Although many of its ancient forms and traditions may have gone or been heavily diluted, the people most touched by it – the Chinese themselves, wherever they live in the world, the Japanese, Koreans and Vietnamese – continue to show remarkable vitality in comparison to other non-Western societies.

The tenacious martial spirit of the Vietnamese people that could triumph over the military might of both France and the United States in Indochina, for example, was first honed over many centuries struggling to hold back the southward advance of the Han Chinese. The Japanese gained their Buddhism, their written language and many of their arts from the mainland. It is also possible that the Japanese are actually of Chinese descent. The first emperor of unified China, Qin Shi Huangdi, is said to have sent a Daoist priest and 500 virgin children across the sea in search of an elixir of immortality. They never returned and legend claims the Japanese are their descendants.[5]

In examining China's restoration as a great power, we should first be aware that one of its most remarkable achievements has been in the realm of government. Most great empires have been short-lived, lasting for a few generations or at best several centuries. The Chinese, however, were able to develop a relatively efficient system of government that provided underlying political unity for over two thousand years, surviving the collapse of dynasties, invasion and conquest, civil war and disorder. 'In the world of traditional societies, Chinese civilization ranks at the forefront in enlightenment and sophistication, in artistic achievement and ethical sensitivity, and above all in the imaginative development of the arts of government and harmonious conduct of social life.'[6]

The Chinese abandoned early on in their history – at least 2,200 years ago – the traditions of aristocracy based on birth in favour of the idea that those who manage government should do so because of merit and personal attainment, largely through highly competitive examinations that became more demanding as the candidate moved from local government to seek a post at the centre of power. In doing so, they 'created a form of centralized government that the West was not to use until the nineteenth century.'[7]

3

A thousand years before Alexander the Great, the Chinese were weaving silk, carving jade, casting bronze and producing other alloys, creating durable, quality pottery, growing wheat, millet and rice, and recording events in a sophisticated written language of thousands of characters. The crossbow, used in Europe in the Middle Ages, was invented in China some fifteen centuries earlier. Its astronomers recorded the passage of Halley's Comet as long ago as the third century BC.

While Europe floundered in the Dark Ages, imperial China was at the height of its power. Three dynasties, Tang (AD618–907), Sung (960–1279) and Ming (1368–1643) witnessed a great flowering in scientific and technological development. Even before William the Conqueror landed in England, China had witnessed its own industrial revolution, with the emergence of advanced coke ovens and steel blast furnaces in Hunan and Hubei. In 1005 AD, a thousand-volume encyclopaedia was published under imperial patronage containing all the knowledge of the age.

As Kennedy (1988) observed: 'Of all the civilizations of pre-modern times, none appeared more advanced, none felt more superior, than that of China. [I]ts remarkable culture; its exceedingly fertile and irrigated plains, linked by a splendid canal system since the eleventh century; and its unified, hierarchic administration run by a well-educated Confucian bureaucracy had given a coherence and sophistication to Chinese society which was the envy of foreign visitors. Huge libraries existed from early on. Printing by moveable type had already appeared in the eleventh century.[8] Chinese cities were much larger than their equivalents in medieval Europe, and Chinese trade routes as extensive.'[9]

The technical innovations China gave the world not only included printing, paper, the magnetic compass and gunpowder, but also among other things, 'the modern horse collar, the watertight ship compartment, canal locks, suspension and segmented bridges, the crossbow and the humble but ever-so-useful wheelbarrow'.[10]

The Tang Dynasty period saw a flourishing of commerce and a growth of urban culture. In the realm of government, the Tang gave China a codified legal system and the most formal ordering of the bureaucracy. When Japan and Korea sought to adopt Chinese institutions, their model was the Tang system.

Economic experimentation that would not be out of place today was being advocated in the following Sung Dynasty, when a prime minister, Wang An-shih, proposed a state budget that would control expenditures, a system of state purchases of grain to maintain an 'ever normal granary', a system of loans to peasants, a form of graduated taxation and far-reaching land reform. The fact that the reforms proved too radical for the mandarins of his government to stomach cannot obscure the fact that such farsighted reforms could be proposed and debated at a time when Europe was still gripped by suffocating feudalism.

Although China essentially has always been a land power, its influence at the height of the empire was felt throughout the Pacific and Indian oceans. With some ships as large as the later galleons of the Spanish Armada, commerce with the Indies and Pacific islands long preceded the first appearance of the Europeans. Over a 28-year period in the early years of the fifteenth century, for example, Admiral Cheng Ho undertook seven long-distance cruises as far as the Red Sea and the East African coast down to Zanzibar, predating the Portuguese, Dutch and British incursions into the Indian Ocean. It is even possible one of his ships reached the north coast of Australia.[11]

According to historical accounts, some of the admiral's vessels were 400 feet long and displaced 1,500 tons – veritable giants for their day. It is intriguing to speculate how world history might have been changed if the admiral had continued around the African coast and 'discovered' Europe, for he certainly had the technical means to do so, rather than the Europeans finding China.[12] Sadly, this was not to be, for an imperial edict soon afterwards forbade any further voyaging of this type, banning the construction of ocean-going ships, and China turned inwards on itself, precipitating the eventual decline that was to leave it helpless in the face of the marauding European seafaring nations of the nineteenth century. The immediate justification was the need to concentrate on meeting the continuing Mongol threat on its northern border. But there were other factors.

The conservatism of the Confucian bureaucracy, with its innate dislike of commerce and private capital, eventually strangled foreign trade, especially of the maritime variety; the navy fell into disrepair, despite the fact that not only the coastline but also cities up the Yangtze River were being raided by Japanese pirates; the army was starved of money to modernize; the great canals were permitted to decay; the ironworks fell into disuse; the use of paper currency was discontinued; printing was restricted to scholarly works, thus preventing the dissemination of practical knowledge.[13] Observing this, one can only ponder on what might have been in different circumstances.

5

This attitude can be best understood by realizing that, geographically, the great land mass of China is separated from the rest of Asia either by wide deserts or very high and difficult mountain country. Eastward of China stretches the vast Pacific. The sea was the end of the world, leading nowhere and linking nothing in olden times. The Mediterranean, the central sea of the ancient world, the bond and highway of the nations, had no counterpart in the Far East.

For very many centuries, therefore, China was a world apart, even when coasting voyages brought a slight link with southern Asia, and caravans could pass the Central Asiatic deserts; even then the contacts were few and their effects delayed. The Chinese people evolved the main features of their civilization alone, adapted themselves to their peculiar environment, and it was not until the pattern was well set that foreign influences seeped in to challenge the uniform character of the Chinese culture. The only outside influence that can clearly be detected is that of Buddhism, brought in from India. But even this was to a considerable extent sinicized.

It is against this background that one sees the final Qing Dynasty presiding over the steady decline of China at a time when the European powers were beginning to flex their expansionist muscles.[14] By the mid-nineteenth century, the country was ripe for invasion, exploitation and the carving up into spheres of influence by the European powers (and, to a lesser extent), the United States. Thus, from the 1840s to the 1940s, the country experienced a hundred years of chaos. The decline of the Qing Dynasty was marked by major rebellions. In striking contrast to Meiji Japan, the Qing resisted modernization almost to the bitter end, finally accepting its necessity only after defeat by Japan in 1895. Following the dynasty's collapse in 1911, China was torn apart by fighting between rival warlords ruling different areas of the country, parts of which collapsed into banditry. By the 1930s, China had become a poor, underdeveloped country.

Under Guomindang (Nationalist) rule from 1927, the country was largely reunified, but there was a persistent civil war waged for most of the following two decades with the emerging Communists, aggravated by Japanese invasion, that resulted in virtual economic collapse. The humiliation inflicted on the Chinese by this fall from previous greatness combined with the century of confusion and despair, rankles to this day in the national psyche. It is the constant theme of speeches by the present leadership, along with reminders that it was only under Communist Party leadership that the Chinese people were, in the words of Mao able to 'stand up'[15] and become masters of their own house again.

During more than a century of violence through political upheaval, civil wars and foreign conquest, the Chinese people were experiencing profound social change. Looking beyond the surface turmoil, one can see a people grappling with deep intellectual and moral issues, perplexing questions of how they should relate their traditions to modern experiences. How can they be part of the world and yet apart from the world? These are questions that will concern us later. However, for the moment, I want to return to consider China's current credentials to be considered as a superpower-in-waiting. Apart from its massive population, what other grounds are there for considering China's claim to such status?

∞

Traditionally, military might has been an important criterion. The People's Liberation Army (PLA) is a massive force by any measurement, but a somewhat unknown quantity in fighting capability. Born in 1927, the PLA was based mainly on ordinary infantry, with only embryonic navy and air force units. After being tested in 20-odd years of revolutionary wars, it moved from small-unit hit-and-run guerrilla tactics in the early years to multi-divisional set-piece battles towards the end of the civil war against the Nationalist forces, which led to the creation of the People's Republic of China (PRC) in 1949.

Since then, it has been tested only three times in battle. The first was in the Korean War (1950–53),[16] when its sudden intervention on the side of embattled North Korea caught the United States entirely by surprise, putting paid to any hopes of an easy victory and eventually leading to a stalemate that sees the Korean peninsula still partitioned and a continuing source of regional tension. The Chinese viewed Korea as a victory, although the price paid was a heavy one in terms of the casualty list.[17]

The second foray into combat was the crushing of a rebellion in Tibet in 1959,[18] which could hardly be considered a true test given the PLA's superiority in equipment and trained troops against a motley collection of poorly-armed 'rebels'. The only other armed contest took place in 1979 when the PLA invaded Vietnam to 'teach it a lesson' for border incursions, only to suffer a bloody nose and an ignominious retreat, demonstrating just how slack and unprepared for modern combat it had become when compared to the battle-hardened North Vietnamese Army.

7

Hence, it is difficult to assess China's genuine military capabilities, if it were ever again to operate outside the national borders. But its continuing saber-rattling regarding its claim over Taiwan, and the seemingly endless disputes over bits of rock in the South China Sea with various neighbours, are a cause of concern.

Following the reduction of countervailing US power after the end of the Cold War, China's new-found strategic latitude, its growing economic strength and its military modernization are a worry, despite repeated assurances from Beijing. 'The main concern is that a strong China in the next century will reinstate its traditional suzerain role and intervene politically, acting as the regional hegemon.'[19] While many Western observers detect weakness in its air and, even more so, in its naval capabilities, China is no toothless tiger. The PLA is three million strong, down by a million from its peak strength in the 1950s following a manpower trimming exercise in the mid-1980s to reduce defence costs, and it is undergoing a modernization drive in terms of both equipment and tactics. A further manpower cut of half a million is to be achieved by 2000.[20] Maoist guerrilla strategy was long ago abandoned in favour of building up the capability to fight a high-tech conflict.

China successfully exploded its first atom bomb on 16 October 1964, having already succeeded in tests of its self-developed medium- and short-range missiles. This was followed by a gradual move into the research and manufacture of medium- and long-range guided missiles and inter-continental missiles. The strategic missile unit, or the Second Artillery Corps, established in June 1966, was a new arm engaged in strategic nuclear counter-attack. The first guided missile nuclear-weapon test was successfully conducted on 27 October 1966, the successful explosion of the first hydrogen bomb followed on 17 June 1967, the successful launch of a long-range ground-to-ground missile occurred as long ago as January 1970 and the country's first nuclear-powered submarine was launched the following December. During the 1980s, submarine-launched missiles were developed.

As early as 1980, China was testing ICBMs with a range of seven thousand nautical miles, capable of encompassing at least part of the United States. A year later, one of its rockets launched three space satellites, giving the first indication that the country possessed multiple-warhead rocket technology. This has provided a solid base for development of a civilian space industry, which foresees the possibility of a Chinese astronaut circling the earth within a few years, although the present emphasis is on making money by launching satellites for other countries. For example, a new generation Long March 3B rocket blasted off from the Xichang Satellite Launch Centre on 20 August 1997, carrying a Philippines telecommunications satellite into geo-synchronous earth orbit (about 36,000 kms above earth). In terms of payload, the 3,770 kgs Mabuhay satellite was the heaviest launched by the Chinese,[21] putting them on track to become a major carrier of space satellites for other countries.[22]

The PLA has been reorganized into groups of many specialist units. There has been a steady expansion of motorized infantry units and tank divisions, and each group has its own artillery, anti-aircraft brigade, anti-chemical war units, engineering and signal corps. The formation of group armies has boosted the proportion of the staff of the technological arms units to well over 60 per cent of the total staff of the army, surpassing that of the infantry. The naval and air forces also are simplifying and reorganizing.[23]

Training is now devoted to enhancing the capabilities of troops in coordinated operations, fast reaction, electronic counter-measures, logistic guarantee and field survival. In September 1981, the PLA held a military exercise focused on a front army defence campaign somewhere in north China. In this, it first launched an attack on the imaginary enemy by using nuclear and air-armaments, then ground troops launched a surprise attack in depth. The PLA, in turn, organized various arms and services in strong, coordinated defence and in active resistance, thus smashing the enemy's offensive attempt. According to a PLA announcement at the time, the exercise had 'demonstrated improvement in the PLA's capability for combined operations'.

Since 1990, the army has basically established an anti-tank weapon system integrating mines, rocket launchers, artillery and guided missiles; it also gained new development in tanks, armoured transport vehicles, anti-aircraft weapons, and infantry light weapons. In the mid-1990s, the navy acquired 34 home-built warships, and Russian Kilo-class submarines, along with four-tube torpedo boats, hunter-killers, large landing boats, sea patrol aircraft and anti-ship missiles, torpedoes, rockets and deep-water bombs. The air force has bought SU–27 fighter-bombers from Russia, and has various other types of modern fighters, frigates and transporters. It has acquired early-warning technology from Europe and Israel and is developing its own in-flight refuelling techniques to extend the range of its warplanes.

9

China's modest programme of nuclear test explosions provoked international protests, which in turn angered many Chinese security experts, who pointed out that China had carried out only 40 tests over the past 30-odd years, while the US had conducted more than 1,000, the Soviet Union 600 and France more than 100 tests. Japan in particular, the Chinese said, had no right to protest because it is under the American nuclear umbrella.

'From the very first day China developed a nuclear weapon, we declared we would not use it first,' government officials repeatedly asserted, adding that China only developed nuclear weapons because it saw itself under threat of nuclear attack, first by the US during the Korean War, then by Krushchev during the Sino-Soviet dispute in the 1960s. Nevertheless, the government eventually signed the comprehensive test-ban treaty along with a pledge never to use nuclear weapons first against any country.

Despite all the modernization activity, and development of nuclear weaponry, China remains modest about its military capacity. Mu Hui Min, Secretary General of the China Institute for International Strategic Studies, is ever ready to reel off statistics to demonstrate that the defence budget's proportion of GDP was halved between 1985 and 1995 to 1.2 per cent. Even if the total of $7.5 billion for 1995 understates the level of spending, as many Western analysts insist (claiming that much weapons research expenditure and other spending is disguised under other categories in the national budget),[24] it is still minuscule compared to the $260 billion spent each year by the United States, Japan's $50 billion, or roughly $30 billion each for the United Kingdom, France and Germany. But the military establishment insists the country's defences have been allowed to fall far behind, and has begun to win more money in the budget again.

Yet China does not see this as creating a threatening military presence in the region. It insists that historically it has always been the victim of aggression, never an expansionist power. The point is difficult to dispute, however, without questioning the country's present frontiers, since by and large these include the lands conquered by emperors in centuries past. Certainly, it does not see its claim to Taiwan or islets in the South China Sea, as expansionist; merely as restoring the country's territorial integrity. At the same time, it looks outward with some suspicion at the activities of both Japan and the United States, whose defence alliance to many in Beijing looks suspiciously like the old 'China containment' policy that flourished at the height of the Cold War[25]. Over the mid-term future, the United States and Japan are the only powers strong enough militarily to influence China's political evolution. And how the United States, Japan and China arrange their security relationships will dictate the Asia-Pacific area's security framework in the twenty-first century. Shifts in America's demography and overseas trade have made it a true Pacific power. It cannot tolerate a single nation dominating East Asia any more than it could in Western Europe. Japan's search for a post-Cold War role is likely to include continuing its alliance with the United States, which it sees as the fulcrum of the East Asian balance of power.

Given all these considerations, especially the continued suspicion in China of Japan's long-term peaceful intentions, there seems little doubt that China will continue to mould the PLA into a highly effective force capable of making its presence felt in the surrounding region if need be.

∞

At this point I wish to set aside the military factor for the moment in order to concentrate on the most crucial element of all in the superpower equation – namely, a powerful economy.

To the foreign visitor travelling along the seemingly endless grid of freeways in and around Beijing or past the innumerable luxury tower-block construction sites in Shanghai, the idea that China will achieve some kind of world dominance in the twenty-first century hardly seems far-fetched. The figures are impressive. In 1995, five years ahead of schedule, China had already achieved its goal of quadrupling the gross annual value of industrial and agricultural production from the 1980 level of 710 billion Yuan.[26] According to the Chinese Academy of Social Sciences (CASS), the country's gross domestic product is expected to grow at an annual average rate of nine per cent between now and the turn of the century to top 4,100 billion Yuan.[27]

Looking to the future, a team headed by renowned economist Li Jengwen reported in mid-1997 that, '[the] next 16 years will be a golden period in China's economic development. As long as we grasp the opportunity under the leadership of the [Communist] Party, we can achieve the goal of building a strong China as envisaged by the numerous martyrs of the past few hundred years'. They predicted that economic growth in the period 2001–2010 'will not be lower than 7.5 per cent', with GDP rising to 8,600 billion Yuan.[28] Vice Premier Zhu Rongji, the country's top economic official, meanwhile, predicts annual growth of eight per cent up to 2000, and seven per cent for the following decade.[29]

11

Chinese love statistics, and anyone seeking to analyse the growth of the economy will be bombarded with a bewildering array of numbers that sometimes makes one wonder who could possibly have calculated all of them. Nevertheless, a judicious selection of numbers will certainly help give a feeling for the advances that some in the international community have begun to term the 'China miracle'. 'Comprehensive national strength' is a set of indices for assessing the ability to survive as well as the development strength of a country in both material and spiritual terms. From 1992 to 1996, China moved up from eleventh place, first achieved in the 1980s, to its present rank of sixth in the world, narrowing the gap with such developed countries as the United States, Japan, Germany and France.

Looking at the results of the opening up of China to the world, Prof. Tong Dalin, vice-chairman of the Chinese Society for Research on Restructuring the Economic System, likens it to 'the discovery of a new continent'. A lot of foreign businessmen would find it hard to argue with that analogy. The great changes brought about by the dash for a market economy instituted by the late Deng Xiaoping in the late 1970s, allied with the country's huge market potential, have created a tidal wave of foreign investment which had reached $81.6 billion (with $54.8 billion actually used).

China throughout the 1990s consistently has been a world leader in utilizing foreign capital second only to the United States.[30] Latterly, the key features have been enlargement of the investment scale and investment fields, evident increase of transnational companies and capital- and technology-intensive investment, and expansion of enterprise scope.[31] Since the state enlarged the sectors open to foreign capital, infrastructure development and cooperation with, and purchase of state-owned enterprises have increasingly become the focus for foreign investment. Undoubtedly, foreign-funded enterprises in China have developed well and enjoyed good returns.[32]

Each day, through the country's airports and harbours, an average of $790 million worth of commodities flowed in and out during 1996. In that year, the total import-export volume stood at $289.9 billion, 1.7 times greater than 1992. By 2010, it is predicted that exports alone will reach $435.7 billion, quadrupling the 1994 figure. By 2020, according to a World Bank estimate,[33] China could have tripled its share of world trade to 10 per cent from the three per cent prevailing in 1996.[34] It is likely to account for 40 per cent of the increase in developing country imports between 1992 and 2020.

With so much activity in trade and investment, the country's foreign currency reserves had grown by mid-1997 to a record $120 billion, one of the highest dollar holdings of any country, and this does not take into account the $80 billion reserves of Hong Kong, now part of China again since 1 July 1997.

The World Bank says economic development has been so rapid that, if China's 30 provinces and autonomous regions were counted as individual economies, the 20 fastest growing economies in the world between 1975 and 1995 would have been Chinese. Over the next 25 years, it expects the economy to undergo a transformation which it claims took about 65 years in Latin America and 80 years in the world's most advanced economies.[35] The bank demonstrates its confidence by lending China more money than any other country.[36]

As a result, there is general confidence that China's fast developing economy will continue to see sustained growth in the foreseeable future. Readjustment of the industrial mix, changes in structure of supply and demand, and the development of the Central and West region will result in the country seeing a succession of new economic booms. In addition, a favourable labour market and the great potential for domestic market expansion remain major reasons for multinational companies to go on investing in China. Hong Kong and Macao are also regions attracting much foreign investment. Hong Kong's return to China will strengthen economic relations between it and mainland China, resulting in a further rise in investment.

It would be hard to overstate the importance of this event. The question of what Hong Kong's return will mean to China's economy in the future has largely been answered by its impact in the past. China's leaders are anticipating a further major contribution, and have stressed the advantages that the Hong Kong Special Administrative Region (HKSAR)[37] will bring to the mainland. 'Hong Kong is bound to play a more active role in increasing economic and trade relations among Asian countries and between Asia and the rest of the world,' Prime Minister Li Peng told an International Chamber of Commerce conference in Shanghai in April 1997. In an interview two months later with the Hong Kong-based *South China Morning Post*, Foreign Minister Qian Qichen declared: 'China is going to continue economic development and reform, therefore we still need Hong Kong as the bridge and window.'[38]

There is no mistaking the massive role Hong Kong has played in China's economic reforms. Since 1979, it has accounted for 60 per cent of all direct foreign investment in China. In the first 16 years, there were 150,000 Hong Kong investment projects bringing in at least $60 billion in contracted investment. According to Hong Kong figures, the territory has provided $90 billion direct and realized investment, accounting for three-fifths of all external investment in China. Take out the funds channelled through Hong Kong by the 50 million overseas Chinese (and the 'round-tripping' by enterprises based on the mainland) and it becomes apparent that China has done no better than countries like Brazil and Nigeria at attracting foreign investment.

Even these figures do not adequately highlight how central Hong Kong's contribution has been to Deng Xiaoping's open-door policy. The Special Economic Zones in southern China and the more numerous development zones in most provinces and big cities have all depended on Hong Kong for the bulk of their investment. In places like Shantou or Shenzhen (two of the SEZs) – and indeed the whole of Guangdong province, in which they are located – as much as 80 per cent of the investment has come from Hong Kong. Guangdong alone received US$50 billion of investment from Hong Kong-based firms which now directly employ five million workers. Without Hong Kong, Deng's social and economic experiments might not have worked.

Hong Kong's entrepreneurs have been the middlemen setting up factories to handle the manufacturing orders passed to them from the world's leading multinational firms. Thanks to Hong Kong, China has become a leading global exporter of textiles, garments, shoes, toys, plastic products, household goods, electrical and electronic goods. That is why little Hong Kong is mighty China's third largest trading partner after Japan and the United States. On their own, China's state-owned enterprises would never have been able to break into world markets. Most of the equipment, designs, software and management skills have been imported via Hong Kong.

Then there is the fact that 30 years of Maoism left China without adequate ports, roads and airports to cope with a vastly higher volume of goods and people being moved through it. Hong Kong swiftly became not only the biggest port in southern China but also for the whole of the mainland. While in the 1980s ships were forced to wait sometimes for months to dock at harbours like Tianjin and Shanghai, Hong Kong's handling capacity kept pace with demand, so that it has been handling up to 25 per cent of China's foreign trade and at times even more.

14

Chinese leaders now want Hong Kong to do more for mainland modernization. Li Peng has said: 'Hong Kong's prosperity and stability have a great bearing on the mainland's economic construction because the economies of the two places have become mingled. Hong Kong's capital accounts for the biggest investment on the mainland and in many cases it is a relationship between a front shop and a rear factory. Goods from the mainland have to be sold through Hong Kong because Hong Kong's trading companies, which have been in existence for a long time, have both prestige and advanced methods of settlement.'

Beijing expects Hong Kong to act as a go-between and provide the high technology which will allow China to leapfrog into the ranks of the developed countries in the next 15 years. The territory's role is to lure Western companies to set up research institutes and factories which will help introduce the latest technologies to China in much the same way that Singapore has led the way for Malaysia and Indonesia. Suffice it to say, then, that Britain bequeathed to China a veritable 'jewel in the crown' that, if handled properly, will bring even greater prosperity to the mainland than it has done in the past. The same applies to other communities of 'overseas Chinese', especially those in Southeast Asia (Singapore, Indonesia, Malaysia and Thailand), who are pouring vast amounts of money into the homeland of their forefathers, partly because of anticipation of high profits, but also to a marked extent because of a sense of pride in China's resurgence.

But amid all the optimism engendered by obvious improvements in their daily lives, to the Chinese themselves, there are sober reminders that there is still a long way to go. For them, China remains a developing country, poor and backward, still struggling to escape from centuries of foreign interference. This perspective is partly explained by the poor conditions in which so many of the country's people still live, despite many cosmetic improvements.[39] It is a subject which reappears all too often in conversations with Chinese. Zhang Wenpu, a former ambassador to Canada, for example, says it had not occurred to him that China might have a better claim than Canada to membership of the Group of Seven leading economic powers. China, suggests Mr Zhang, is 'just beginning to undergo the process of industrialization, like the US in the 1860s and 1870s, and Britain 200 years ago.' China's goal, says Mr Mu Hui Min, secretary general of the China Institute for International Strategic Studies, is to 'reach the middle level of developed countries by 2050'.

Talking to visiting Maldives President Maumoon Abdul Gayoon in 1984, Deng Xiaoping asserted: 'China is a major country as well as a minor one. When we say it is a major country, we mean it has a large population and a vast territory, and when we say it is a minor one, we mean it is still relatively poor. China is one of the permanent members of the UN Security Council. Its vote belongs firmly to the Third World, to the underdeveloped countries. We have said more than once that China belongs to the Third World. It will still belong to the Third World even in the future after it is developed. *China will never become a superpower.*'[40]

So, here is a basic contradiction, one of a number, in fact, to be considered in this book in an examination of Chinese society in a confused period of both continuity and change; of a country that says it does not want to be a superpower, but looks and sounds very much like one. But this surely is in keeping with Chinese history and the development of a unique culture. Chinese instinctively understand about the inevitably of the dilemmas, or contradictions, and the interplay of opposing forces in every aspect of their lives. It is an integral part of their culture, especially their traditional approach to medicine. A popular philosophy during the Spring and Autumn Warring States Period (722–221 BC) was an interpretation of the universe in terms of two opposing concepts of *yin* and *yang*. The Yellow Emperor's Canon of Internal Medicine[41] defined yin and yang as a universal law in the universe, the key to understanding the world, the source of all changes, and the inherent logic for the evolution of all things. In a word, yin and yang account for the evolution of the universe. In traditional Chinese medicine, it is a very important concept in diagnosis and therapy; in warfare, likewise, it is instrumental in all maneouvers from camping to deployment.

Yin and yang are mutually opposed, restrictive and balanced. Generally, anything bright, superior, active, full, superficial, hot, light, and clear is considered yang; by contrast, anything dark, subordinate, quiet, weak, inherent, cold, heavy and turbid is considered yin. For example, heaven is high above, light and clear and is therefore considered yang, whereas earth is subordinate, heavy and turbid and is therefore considered yin. The sun is bright and hot and called 'extreme yang', whereas the moon is cold and often incomplete and is therefore called 'extreme yin'. Fire is yang, while water is yin; man is yang and woman, yin.

Yin and yang, however, are not just opposites; they are also unified and interchangeable. This has two implications. One is the basis for the existence of the other; without one, the other does not exist. Cold and heat, for example, are inter-dependable; so are exterior and interior, failure and victory. The physical body (yin) is useless without *qi* or the essential spirit (yang); likewise, without the physical body, qi has no abode of existence. Because of their mutually opposing nature, yin and yang of necessity check and balance each other. Too much cold will inevitably result in insufficient heat and vice versa. Within a year, spring and summer are considered yang because the weather gets warmer daily; autumn and winter are considered yin because the heat is on the wane. If one increases, the other decreases. Thus, in the context of our theme, continuity and change both complement and contradict each other; they co-exist.

This yin-yang relationship is also closely related with the philosophical concept of the 'five elements' – wood, fire, earth, metal and water – also popular during the Spring and Autumn Warring States Period. Whereas the former is a dialectic approach about the unity of opposites, the Five Elements theory is based on the interrelationships of things. However, like yin and yang, the Five Elements beget and check one another.

Thus, said the ancients, wood begets fire, fire begets earth, earth begets metal, metal begets water, and water begets wood in an endless cycle. In turn, wood checks earth, earth checks water, water checks fire, fire checks metal, and metal checks wood. The process is never-ending. The Five Elements are inter-connected and inter-dependent. No single element is independent of the other four. Over the long course of history, however, these two schools intermingled with each other into a unified theory which was applied in such diversified areas as astronomy, geology, calendar, fine arts, agriculture, water conservancy, war, and medicine. This explanation should be borne in mind as we examine various facets of Chinese life.

The yin-yang principle can be seen in the last half century of Communist Party control over society, which repeatedly has oscillated between restriction (*shou*) and liberalization (*fang*). When one aspect became too extreme, the other aspect would act as a partial antidote. In the 1950s, the newly victorious CCP set about establishing a Stalinist-type totalitarian system, eliminating real or potential opposition, reorganizing the masses into new Party-led associations and removing from them the resources to mount autonomous activities. The Great Leap Forward was a period of intensified direct Party control over society, emerging in the wake of the 'Hundred Flowers' movement of 1956, a *fang* interlude during which intellectuals were encouraged to criticize excessively tight Party-State control. The disasters of the Great Leap Forward brought about another spell of relaxation. The decade of the Great Proletarian Cultural Revolution (1966–76) represented a renewed policy of *shou*. Following this further disaster, another period of *fang* in the economy, arts, scholarly inquiry, religious belief, personal relations and contacts with the outside world began in 1978.

Within this general trend there have been three periods of *shou*, however: namely, the 1983–4 Anti-Spiritual Pollution Campaign, the 1987 Campaign Against Bourgeois Liberalization and the 1989 Tiananmen Square incident and subsequent witch hunt of those who challenged Party rule. At the time of writing, the country would seem to be in a period of *fang* although with some *shou* undertones. This is a recurrent theme throughout the country's history, oscillating between strength and weakness, war and peace.

Such contradictions were of particular interest to the late Chairman Mao Zedong, who spoke and wrote often on the subject in the course of exploring Marxist dialectics. In August 1937, he delivered a lecture at the Anti-Japanese Military and Political College in Yaanan, the remote Shaanxi Province base of the Communist Party of China as it struggled to survive against the assaults of both the Japanese invaders and the Nationalist forces of Chiang Kaishek. This speech later became one of the crucial documents in the underlying philosophy of Chinese Communism.

Mao saw constant contradictions, in varying degrees of complexity, as both inevitable in the development of any social system and vital for social progress. He noted, for example, that, 'the law of contradiction in things, that is, the law of unity of opposites, is the most basic law in materialist dialectics. Lenin said: 'In its proper meaning, dialectics is the study of contradiction within the very essence of things.'[42]

'Changes in society are chiefly due to the development of internal contradictions in society, namely, the contradiction between the productive forces and relations of production, the contradiction between classes, and the contradiction between old and new; it is the development of these contradictions that impels society forward and starts the process of the supersession of the old society by a new one.'[43] In war, said Mao, offence and defence, advance and retreat, victory and defeat are all contradictory phenomena. Without the one, the other cannot exist. These two aspects struggle as well as unite with each other, constituting the totality of the war, impelling the war's development and solving the war's problems. Every difference in man's concepts should be regarded as reflecting objective contradictions. 'Within the Party, opposition and struggle between different ideas occur constantly; they reflect in the Party the class contradictions and the contradictions between the old and the new things in society. If in the Party, there were neither contradictions nor ideological struggles to solve them, the Party's life would come to an end.'[44]

He concluded: 'The basic contradiction in the process of development of things, and the quality of the process, is determined by this basic contradiction, [and] will not disappear until the process is completed; but the conditions of each stage in the long process of development [. . .] often differ from those of another stage. This is because, although the nature of the basic contradiction in the development of a thing or in the quality of the process has not changed, yet at the various stages in the long process of development the basic contradiction assumes an increasingly intensified form.'[45]

∞

China has entered a most profound transitional period, which consists of two kinds of social changes: institutional transition and structural transformation. The former refers to a transition from a highly-centralized planned economy to a socialist market economy, while the latter refers to a social change from an agricultural, rural and closed society to an industrial, urbanized and open one.

Though both have featured in China's reforms in the past two decades, they are entirely different in essence. The institutional transition needs to be completed fairly rapidly, despite the fact that post-Mao China favours gradual reform rather than stormy revolution, because a prolonged transition, during which the old and new systems exist side by side conflicting with each other – and the dominant social rules are absent – may result in social disorder. On the other hand, the structural transformation is a more compulsory route every state has to take on its road towards modernization. This process may be a much longer one beyond anybody's expectation, which will entail tremendous efforts over several generations.

Experiencing the two social changes in the same time-frame while at the same time trying to maintain its socialist political system, distinguishes China's reform programme from that of the former Soviet Union and other East European states, and even the newly-rising industrial states of East Asia. China's reform has moved beyond the initial stage when the old system was divided and the co-existence of market and planned prices was permitted. The remaining energy of the old system having been further released, reform has moved into a mid-term phase when the new system's initiative and creation has become the most important task. At this stage, the focal point of institutional reform has shifted from rural to urban areas aiming directly to finance, taxation, state-owned enterprises, social security and other factors which combine to constitute the so-called 'solid core' of the old system, which connects with each nerve of the society.

As the reform has come up against the 'rigid part' of the original interest pattern, it has stumbled over one problem after another. Due mainly to the change of social structure, diversification of professions, co-existence and competitiveness of different types of economic ownership, and growth of the market mechanism, the various independent interests of different social groups have emerged. Any new step inevitably will be in favour of some social groups at the expense, at least temporarily, of others, creating conflict and various social problems.

The current stage of reform, during which the new system is initiated and inaugurated, sees the structural contradictions which have gone side by side with China's long-term modernization drive. The state, which is weak in providing compensation for the loss of some social groups, has to force itself to continue the reform drive in case the situation may deteriorate as result of more social problems accumulating, which would in turn add to the cost at which the reform and social development move forward. I believe it is fair to say that were China to replicate the performance of other Asian 'miracle' economies [at least until the collapse of late 1997], such as Japan, Taiwan and South Korea, its impact would be overwhelming. China does, after all, contain 10 times as many people as Japan. The question remains whether it will do so.

There is no economic reason why a country whose real output per head lies somewhere between five and 10 per cent of that of the US should not be able to sustain economic growth at 10 per cent a year for a quarter of a century. Yet there may still be a reason for failure. For what is amazing is not that China is at last becoming richer, but that it is still so poor in many respects. If feudalism dragged China down in the nineteenth century, politics has kept it poor in the twentieth century.

The reasons for this dismal performance have been the country's inability to combine a reasonable degree of political stability with the encouragement of productive (as opposed to rent-seeking) economic initiative. Under the influence of Deng Xiaoping's 'socialism with Chinese characteristics', this combination has at last been achieved. The big question is whether it will survive his death. Optimists argue that progress is assured merely by continuing past policies. The basic assumption is that China has now reached a virtuous circle of growth. Economic success engenders further reform and further toleration of the regime. It also makes a return to old ideologies impossible. Yet, past reform has not just thrown up successes on which to build, but also erected significant obstacles.

Among the most important is the effect on political and social stability. The most immediate threats include official corruption, unrest among unemployed workers, the migration of a vast army of indigent peasants in search of work and a widening gap between rich and poor.[46] The necessity to establish affordable social security arrangements, after the breakdown of the old cradle-to-grave education, employment, health and welfare system based on work units is another daunting challenge.

Central control is also being tested by increasingly powerful provincial officials, especially those from wealthy coastal provinces, whose economic success has enabled them to carve out personal fiefdoms allowing them, on occasions, to challenge or even ignore Beijing's dictates. The fruits of economic success are the only possible basis for political stability in a country that has turned its back on Communist ideology. But they are also the source of destabilizing political and social developments. China's economic reforms have caused a dangerous decentralization of power and contributed to social decay and rising crime, a paper published by the International Institute for Strategic Studies noted in 1994.[47]

It suggests other countries need to recognize the decentralization of power and develop policies for dealing with regional powers in China.[48] But in doing so, it neither predicts nor advocates China's dissolution, because 'such dramatic dislocation would damage the prosperity of a fifth of mankind, wreck East Asian stability and lead to massive migration. Power has been devolved to a range of actors, including township and village enterprises, individuals and even overseas Chinese and other outsiders. There is no simple struggle for control between centre and province'.

The paper traces the impact on Beijing of the shift of decision-making power to the provinces. Revenue to the centre, as a proportion of the economy, has fallen sharply as richer provinces have gained muscle to rebuff successive attempts to redress the balance. At the same time, the central government failed to develop financial institutions which could exercise macroeconomic control. 'Beijing could no longer impose austerity measures on the national economy, and rich provinces could raise funds from local investment and abroad.' Provinces increasingly squabble among themselves on economic issues, sometimes seeking to exclude each other's products from their markets, with Beijing apparently powerless to prevent such internal protectionism, as I will discuss in detail in Chapter Three.

So, while the basis of an economic superpower may indeed have been created through the market reforms of the past two decades, it has also left China with much to do. The third generation of leaders with President Jiang Zemin at the core are faced with an unsettled climate of widening civil unrest, simmering demands for political and economic reform and projected unemployment figures that could eventually reach into the hundreds of millions. The present leadership also has to perform a miracle from a much weaker power-base than its predecessors – the first generation led by the towering figure of Mao Zedong, the second by the great political survivor, Deng Xiaoping – who could rely for much of their political legitimacy on participation in the great revolutionary struggle that transformed twentieth-century China.

The World Bank sees two possible future scenarios for China, one pessimistic and the other optimistic. The former, considered less likely, is of the country becoming the first significant example in East Asia of rapid economic growth followed by stagnation, which it terms as 'Sinosclerosis'. 'Impressive as China's strengths are, they do not guarantee success. The risk and challenges are strong and varied enough to threaten progress. International experience is littered with examples of economies that have enjoyed prolonged periods of growth only to be followed by setback and stagnation. China is embarked on an extraordinary voyage of change, [. . . telescoping] into one generation what other countries took centuries to achieve.

'In a country whose population exceeds those of sub-Saharan Africa and Latin America combined, this has been the most remarkable development of our time. But China is in uncharted waters. No country has tried to accomplish so much in such a short time. [The] unique attempt to complete two transitions at once – from a command to a market economy and from a rural to an urban society – is without historical precedent.'[49]

Its more optimistic scenario foresees a 'competitive, caring and confident' country in which poverty will have been eliminated.

China would be fully integrated into the world economy as a customer, supplier and investor, and with a 'greater weight and voice in international institutions'. This would be built on its own existing growing strengths: a high rate of savings, its pragmatic reforms, a disciplined and relatively well-educated work-force, and the rich overseas Chinese eager to invest in the country of their ethnic and cultural origin.

And yet, despite all the Dengist reforms and the economic transformation that they have achieved, there are new reformist voices who say that these reforms still represent only half-measures, and that something much more radical is needed. The idea that China must move towards a responsible and accountable government is no longer taboo. Lui Ji, Vice President of the Academy of Social Sciences, for example, has said: 'The idea that power must be restrained and that unrestrained power will necessarily corrupt, is right.'

The eight democratic (non-Communist) parties permitted to exist in China startled many in the government when they produced a report in 1997 based on studies and public opinion polls showing growing popular demand for quickening political reforms. Political liberalization would help defuse worsening social contradictions, they stated flatly. For all his boldness in the economic arena, Deng Xiaoping never countenanced similar liberalization on the political front. This adds a further source of tension and potential instability.

But in line with the theme of continuity and change, there are interesting parallels between China today and that existing at the time the first emperor Qin Shi Huangdi unified the nation some 2,200 years ago. The age into which he was born 'was both philosophically and religiously eclectic, a time of intellectual ferment during which rapid social mobility brought the basest forms of folk belief into the upper levels of society at the same time that their own elevated and agnostic moralism filtered gradually down into the hut of the meanest peasant. It was a time of confusion, a time when differing ideologies competed . . . when the greatest struggle was between those loyal to the past [and] those who had long tired of this 'vain and empty longing' for a long-gone utopia. And they were ready and eager to deal with present-day realities and crash headlong into the future'.[50]

On that historical note, let us now look at some of the key issues that will shape China's future.

■ CHAPTER 2

# Contradictions in Economic Reform

---

W orkers at Mianyang's Silk & Satin Dyeing Factory, which had run up debts of $20 million, were expecting the vice-mayor of the industrial town in Sichuan Province to meet them in order to explain how the factory's impending bankruptcy would affect them. When he failed to appear, some 700 workers took to the streets to block traffic with desks and chairs well into the night.[1] The next morning, tens of thousands of citizens took up the protest, erecting roadblocks and smashing bus windows. Paramilitary People's Armed Police intervened, and local reports claimed up to 100 people were injured in the ensuing clash and more than 80 arrested; the authorities insisted only nine people were detained for vandalism, and eventually released after six to 15 days in custody.

Officials blamed a misunderstanding, insisting no arrangement had been made for the vice-mayor's visit, even though a notice had been pasted up in the factory announcing it. Nevertheless, the provincial government quickly agreed to pay off the disgruntled workers until they found a new job. 'We will experience these small instabilities in exchange for rapid economic development,' said Guo Jialong, a provincial government spokesman. 'This is the sacrifice we have to make.' Even small rumblings echo loudly these days. The party leadership must come to grips with increasing unruliness among the official 'masters of the state' – the millions of workers caught in the disintegrating state sector, about two-thirds of the urban labour force.

There were widespread reports that in the first half of 1997, nearly 11 million state employees had either not been paid or were receiving lower wages. Of even more concern was the prospect of massive lay-offs of workers accustomed to the idea of lifetime

24

employment. By the end of the year, the central government expected around 14 million urban workers to be unemployed, although it thought eight million eventually would find other jobs. These numbers do not include the estimated 30 per cent considered surplus to requirements but still clinging to their jobs. If the government were really to allow state enterprises to fend for themselves, as is supposed to happen, millions of workers would have to do the same. That prospect breeds fierce resistance. In 1996, there were more than 48,000 labour disputes, a 45 per cent increase over 1995.[2]

Visitors to the industrial centre of Shenyang, capital of Liaoning Province, reported workers there had begun to protest regularly in front of government offices. More than 1,000 elderly workers staged a sit-in in late 1995 in Wuhan to protest against inflation. About 40 petitioners gathered outside Zhongnanhai, the Party headquarters in Beijing, in November 1995 to air their dissatisfaction over unemployment and falling living standards. Strikes and rallies involving tens of thousands of workers repeatedly took place in 1995 in the coal-mining town of Jixi in Heilongjiang Province.

In the first half of 1997, more than 500 such incidents were recorded. In a fairly typical week, in early September, a thousand pedicab drivers clashed with riot police in Dujingyan, Sichuan Province, over a ban on their vehicles. In Nanchong, another Sichuan City, 20,000 workers besieged the town hall for 30 hours in protest at not being paid for six months. At Beixiang, Guangdong Province, more than a thousand farmers attacked Party cadres and police saying they had been underpaid for grain. In the climate of unease and uncertainty, many rural townships have fallen under the influence of cults and clan associations connected to criminal Triad societies. More than a thousand affiliates of disparate doomsday cults, for example, were detained over a long period in Anhui Province. Police in Sichuan sought to eradicate the Society of Disciples, which at its height boasted 10,000 converts. A reading of Chinese history shows that such manifestations were common in the past as a prelude to the rural uprisings that on occasions toppled imperial dynasties.

Even though a 1995 Chinese Academy of Social Sciences report on national conditions ruled out social instability as a serious threat, there is evidence that many cadres at grassroots level think otherwise. An internal Party document revealed that 70 per cent of the nation's factories were unable to pay their workers on a regular basis. They resorted to issuing IOUs not just for basic salaries, but bonuses and medical and overtime benefits.

25

Police officers privately indicate that small-scale demonstrations involving workers in state enterprises and mines in the three north-eastern provinces, for example, have become 'routine affairs'. Industrial incidents have also spread to Hubei and Shanxi provinces, and the more remote interior areas of Shaanxi and Gansu, and have been acknowledged by the official media. As long ago as May 1989, at the height of the 'democracy' movement which led to the Tiananmen Square incident the following month, Beijing's *Economic Daily*, identified a 'contagious disease' that was spreading among workers: 'job security panic'. Epidemics of it broke out in 1992, 1993 and 1994, particularly in the north-eastern rust belt.

In fact, labour problems in China are nothing new. In 1949, within weeks of the PRC being born, prolonged worker protests broke out in Shanghai. In one incident, 700 cotton mill workers became so angry over unpaid wages that they broke into the home of a top executive and feasted on chicken, ham, and cake. Waves of labour unrest have hit China's cities, on average, once a decade. In 1989, workers joined students in the mass protests that erupted in Beijing and other cities. Though the workers played a secondary leadership role, they were punished far more harshly than student leaders.

An unusually strong police presence in Tiananmen Square on 1 May 1997 appeared to betray official fears of workers' unrest on Labour Day. In the heyday of Maoism in the 1960s and 70s, it was marked with mass parades celebrating the unity and supremacy of socialism and model workers were lauded across the nation for boosting production, working selflessly and promoting workers as the masters of society. An internal Party report in April reportedly claimed that two bombs found the previous month in the capital were the work of laid-off workers.[3] Leaders of major state enterprises in Beijing were subsequently told to pay close attention to the activities of workers who had been laid off and also warned to pay attention to jobless, demobilized soldiers. One bomb was safely defused, but the other exploded, slightly injuring one person.

The report also disclosed that phone calls warning about the bombs were made to public security departments. The callers claimed they were from the Laid-Off Workers Committee and urged authorities to help redundant workers. The Beijing city government had promised in late 1996 to give a minimum of 180 Yuan a month in financial assistance to laid-off workers. The disgruntled workers, however, were allegedly being given just over 100 Yuan a month.[4] Aware that the labour situation was more volatile than ever, the government adopted preventive measures going beyond tightened police controls. In mid-1994, the National People's Congress approved a comprehensive labour code described as 'suitable for the socialist market economy'.

While giving enterprise managers increased autonomy, the law codifies a wide-ranging protection for workers. It requires local governments to determine minimum wages based on local conditions. It guarantees workers a minimum one day off a week, limits the amount of overtime to no more than three hours beyond the standard eight-hour day, provides premium pay for overtime, permits official unions to bargain for collective contracts, reaffirms 16 years of age as the minimum for employment, and clearly defines beating, threatening and harassing workers as criminal acts.

Workers who know their rights and bring their grievances to labour arbitration committees do have a chance of winning their cases. About half of the 210,000 cases brought to arbitration in 1995 were decided in the workers' favour.[5] Most workers, however, are either ignorant of their legal rights or too intimidated to bring abuses to light. The law is also contingent on enforcement by local officials, whose financial motives are checked by neither a respect for rule-of-law nor an independent judiciary.

Another law passed by the NPC in 1992 renewed the mandate for the All-China Federation of Trade Unions and its subordinate branches as the 'mass organizations of the working class', with rights and duties in promoting 'socialist modernization'. On paper, the new law confers on unions and workers the right to participate in the 'democratic management' of enterprises. But the enterprise-level branches have an inherent weakness: they are under the thumb of the management, the party, or both. In recognition of the growing undercurrent of unrest, the chief Party newspaper, *People's Daily*, devoted its 1997 International Labour Day editorial to reiterating the high status of the worker in Chinese society but called for patience from the state work-force.

At the time of writing, China claimed an urban jobless rate of three per cent, but these figures excluded redundant state employees or its 134 million surplus farm workers. In 1998, at least four million civil servants were due to lose their jobs under a government restructuring programme for eliminating 11 of the 39 state ministries. Western analysts calculated true unemployment at anything from 11 per cent, according to the World Bank, to a high of 20 per cent. Many laid-off workers are sceptical of the official unemployment figures, believing the government understates them for fear that it would reflect badly on Communism and encourage social disorder. Many also believe the central government does more to help workers and pre-empt unrest in Beijing as the national capital, than in other, less visible cities.[6]

The scale of the problem spawned an ironic jingle about China's last three leaders: *Mao Juxi jiao women xiaxiang; Deng Xiaoping jiao women xiahai, Jiang Zemin jiao women xiagang* (Chairman Mao tells us to go to the countryside, Deng Xiaoping tells us to go into business and Jiang Zemin tells us to leave our jobs.) The worst victims of lay-offs are those who work for old, inefficient state factories, especially those making textiles, instruments and consumer goods that can no longer compete in the market with products from collectives, private companies and joint ventures, and who face enormous excess industrial capacity and massive stockpiles of goods. If laid off, a worker receives a monthly allowance from the employer – a minimum of $24 and is urged to find a new job.

Those laid off are often handicapped by their age, usually over 35, poor education, the lack of a marketable skill and the bad habits they acquired from working in a State company. According to a joint investigation in 1996 by four government organs in Wuhan, 48.5 per cent of laid-off employees were aged from 36 to 45. An investigation at the same time by the Beijing Statistics Bureau among 2,500 laid-off employees found that 52.9 per cent of them were aged from 36 to 45. According to the State Statistics Bureau (SSB), 56.8 per cent of laid-off employees had junior high school education and 13.8 per cent of them had only primary school education, or less.[7]

The number of laid-off employees is especially high in economically backward regions (the political implications of this will be considered elsewhere in this book, especially Chapter Three). For example, in West China where the economic development level is comparatively low, many laid-off employees have had difficulty finding new jobs. But in richer, coastal provinces in South and East China, there are more employment opportunities, and people are more accustomed to the challenges of the market-economy mechanism.

According to the SSB, 28.9 per cent of laid-off employees have had no job for either half a year or a year, 16.9 per cent have had no job for either one year or two years, and 14 per cent have had no job for more than two years. Many laid-off employees are in financial difficulties. According to the joint investigation in Wuhan, 50.2 per cent of the laid-off employees in the city's industrial sector lived on monthly allowances of less than $14, lower than the city's guaranteed minimum level standard of living.[8]

An official at the Job Exchange for Meter and Instrument Workers said the biggest problem was to change the mentality of the older workers from dependence on the state, and belief that employment was in no way linked to job performance. 'They are accustomed to the planned economy in which jobs were assigned by the State. They still think that only working in the State sector and being permanent workers or long-term contract workers can be considered for employment. Instead of actively looking for employment opportunities, they hope that the State will assign them jobs again.'[9]

Women are particularly hard hit. 'A few years ago, the proportion of laid-off female employees was not much higher than that of laid-off male employees. But in recent years, the proportion of laid-off females has been markedly higher than that of the males. In addition, the proportion of laid-off women who later find new jobs is lower than that of men.'[10] In Shenyang, Liaoning Province, housewives for the first time started to join the large heavy industrial labour force in the late 1950s, after Mao Zedong called on women to strive for equal status in society. They enjoyed an equal-pay-for-equal-work policy advocated by the central government. But in the era of reform, managers know overstaffing is one of their most serious problems.

According to Shenyang officials, a million workers were waiting relocation in mid-1997, of which 60 per cent were women.[11] Having been molly-coddled by the planned economy for decades with secure jobs, medical care and free housing, these women naturally now have difficulties re-adjusting to life in a free market society. Overly optimistic, many have simply waited for their former corporations to point them in the direction of a new job. But the companies, trapped in debt, cannot afford to help them. The women's plight was further aggravated by management discrimination. An iron and steel manufacturer in the province, for example, even adopted the rule of 'ladies first' to decide who should be laid off, although the male and female workers had equal skills and capabilities. Many enterprises are reluctant to hire childless workers because they know they will be forced to grant them maternity leave at some point.

For many women, the loss of a job inevitably leads to a deterioration of their marriage. The women's federation in Shenyang conducted a survey of laid-off women[12] staying at home and found most felt inferior to their husbands because they were no longer breadwinners. Other family members looked down upon them, and some were threatened with divorce. One woman thought of committing suicide when her husband wanted to leave after she lost her job. Her local neighbourhood committee women's group asked companies in the area if they could hire the woman and finally she was hired by a small neighbourhood community factory.

The official media still tends to treat unemployment somewhat gingerly, preferring to emphasize the positive side with stories about retraining and those who have made a new career after being laid off, rather than dealing with worker protests.[13] Until recent times, the only reporting of disputes involved those arising in joint venture enterprises, whose foreign managers could be blamed for strife.

In its examination of the unemployment problem, the *People's Daily* complained that work was available, but many people were unwilling to do jobs they considered beneath them and involved loss of face. 'It is not that there are no opportunities, but that people are unwilling to make use of them.' Many of the new jobs are in the service sector shops, hotels, shopping centres, restaurants, domestic help, street trading – which Beijing people have traditionally looked down upon. But given the continuing increase in the working population (see Table 2-1), it is still debatable just how much of the slack the nascent service sector can take up.

China can no longer afford to prop up failing industries merely for political reasons, which, in turn, means workers will have to face the reality of bankruptcy, job instability, mid-life career changes, part-time work and early retirement. This is the one of the major contradictions in today's China. In the early years of the PRC, everyone worked for the state, private business being considered an exploitative remnant of the capitalist system the Communists were dedicated to destroying. Under the centralized planned economy, employment was monopolized by the government. Enterprises

**Table 2-1** Changing Trend of China's Working Population (in millions)

| Year | Labouring Population | Men aged 16–59 | Women aged 16–54 |
|------|---------------------|----------------|------------------|
| 1995 | 731.12 | 387.55 | 343.57 |
| 2000 | 775.10 | 410.10 | 365.00 |
| 2010 | 851.85 | 456.92 | 394.93 |
| 2020 | 859.81 | 464.72 | 395.09 |
| 2030 | 807.52 | 439.21 | 368.31 |
| 2040 | 784.20 | 422.58 | 361.62 |
| 2050 | 729.72 | 394.25 | 335.47 |

*Source:* Population and Employment Department, State Statistics Bureau

could not recruit workers on their own, but were generally assigned a specific number of bodies each year with little or no input into the selection process.

The life-tenure employment system, in turn, prevented enterprises from divesting themselves of redundant employees. The all-embracing security and welfare system exercised by enterprises, as a form of state social welfare, covered the housing, health care and the pensions of their employees. Leaving one's work unit actually meant losing everything. These traditional practices resulted in a large amount of hidden unemployment. But now that enterprises need to calculate their input and output, lower costs, increase profit and enhance market competitiveness, the problem has been brought out into the open.

At the same time, although the Dengist reforms have encouraged the private business sector to flourish once again, the Communist Party remains dedicated to allotting the key economic role to state-run enterprises. Without a state sector, it is argued, there can no longer be socialism. Various experiments are being undertaken constantly. Those that do not produce results quickly are discarded and new ones developed in their place. Much intellectual energy has gone into trying to devise a formula that allows the state-run enterprises formed under central planning to not only continue to survive but also grow in a socialist market economy. At the time of writing, the major thrust is to create a number of state-run conglomerates that transcend the whole narrowly defined industrial boundaries of central planning – spreading not only across different sectors but also erasing provincial boundaries and even national boundaries.

The government will pump as much money as is needed in order to ensure the success of these corporate groups, while cutting adrift the smaller and medium-sized enterprises to find their own niche, perhaps through worker buyouts to form cooperatives or through acquisition of the weak by the more successful, and even by allowing foreign investors to buy into and even control them.[14] With the reforms, the rate of reduction in the proportion of the economy occupied by the State has accelerated over the past two decades. The growth rate of the non-state economy has been consistently faster than that of the State sector ever since the reforms were begun.[15] State enterprises, however, retain a very large share in raw material, heavy chemical and other basic industries. For example, they have a 70–100 per cent share in oil, metallurgy, electric power, chemical raw materials and medicine, and a 30–50

31

per cent share in food processing, machine-building, electronics and machinery, textiles, paper-making, electrical machinery.

In 1992, when the 14th Party Congress declared the introduction of the 'socialist market economy', the proportion of non-state economy exceeded 50 per cent of total industrial output value. In 1994, China introduced a series of market-oriented reforms to financial, taxation, fiscal and foreign exchange systems. Reform of the financial and taxation systems mainly involved changing the locally differentiated fiscal contract responsibility system formed since the initiation of reform into a unified system of sharing tax revenue between the central and local authorities and a new industrial and commercial tax system, pressing ahead towards a unified tax law and fair tax burden.

The modern enterprise system being tried out for the State sector mainly consists of two forms: limited liability companies and joint stock companies. Between 1984 and late 1991, 708 SOEs were restructured into share-holding enterprises. But the new system met strong opposition in the process of trial implementation. According to opponents, it would lead to division and even privatization of state-owned enterprise, the rights and interests concerning the property rights of state assets would be impaired, and speculation would emerge in the transaction of stocks. But when Deng Xiaoping made his famous South China inspection tour in 1992, during which he declared that 'we should resolutely conduct the experiment with the shareholding system', the political obstacles were immediately removed and the legal framework created through publication of the Corporate Law in December 1993.

In November 1994, the State Council selected 100 large companies to experiment with the new system,[16] and this was later followed by more than 2,000 pilot enterprises in 18 major cities for optimising the enterprise capital structure and comprehensive coordinated reform. Without getting tied up in too much detail, the reforms essentially relate to delineating the property rights and control of the fixed assets between the government and the company management, giving individual managers complete operational responsibility over the product mix, marketing and the company's profits and losses. Instead of getting government fiscal hand-outs, or so-called 'policy loans' from State banks,[17] companies now have greater freedom to raise money on their own, through bond or stock issues, borrowing domestically or on the international money markets etc. For companies in debt, including those unable to pay their taxes, the government has converted this into a State shareholding in the enterprise concerned.

Meanwhile, local governments in mid-1997 were given approval to dispose of small State enterprises by selling them to their own workers. 'Workers can volunteer to invest in the enterprises they work for and hold shares. Through holding shares, workers are also responsible for these enterprises' debts,' Xinhua News Agency reported, quoting a circular issued by the State Commission for Restructuring the Economy. All workers in small enterprises were being urged to become shareholders but no one would be forced to join the schemes. Workers would decide if the firms would keep some shares as state-owned shares, it added. However, shares owned by workers should remain the majority. Dividends would be paid to workers according to share performance.

The circular said shareholding cooperatives would hold the key to boosting the fortunes of small firms in cities. Despite the controversy over ownership rights and a reluctance to allow debt-stricken enterprises to go bankrupt, local governments have tried to relieve themselves of financial burdens by selling and renting small and medium enterprises to private investors, letting them merge or fall into bankruptcy as a last resort. The circular argued that shareholding cooperatives should practise 'democratic management' and all shareholding workers would be considered equal in the enterprise. Boards of directors would be established to look after daily operations of the company and be accountable to shareholders. Although privatization is not a word that ones hears in official circles, there is undoubtedly an ideological shift in the direction of an accelerated sell-off programmeme of state assets, which has now been given formal blessing by President Jiang Zemin:[18]

> Public ownership can and should take diversified forms. On the premise that we keep public ownership in the dominant position, that the State controls the life-blood of the national economy and that the State-owned sector has stronger control power and is more competitive, then even if [it] accounts for a smaller proportion of the economy, this will not affect the socialist nature of the country.

Jiang also tackled head-on the problem of unemployment: 'With the deepening of enterprise reforms, technological progress and readjustment of the economic structure, it would be hard to avoid the flow of personnel and lay-offs.' The Party and government would take measures and rely on all quarters of society to show concern for laid-off workers, help them with their welfare, organize job training and

33

open up new avenues of employment. But 'all workers should change their ideas about employment and improve their own quality to meet the new requirements of reform and development'.

This is a huge gamble if carried to its logical conclusion. Only a minority of State enterprises are yet fit for genuine privatization (without heavy State subsidies). But the opportunities are immense, too. Privatization could spread the dynamism already visible in the private sector throughout the economy, and, domestic savers and foreign investors will back it if conditions are right. That is a big if. It depends heavily on the government's willingness to see big changes in the way companies are run and who is running them. If the old Party hacks remain in charge, and inefficient practices remain, and new capital disappears down black holes as has occurred in many cases up to now, then investors will soon lose interest. The government will also have to further relax its controls over banking and on the free flow of information in order to ensure an inflow of sufficient capital to make the changes stick.

There is no doubt reforms carried out so far have achieved some success. But one of the most intractable problems in the State sector, remains featherbedding. Firms traditionally took on far more workers than they really needed more as a form of social welfare, safe in the knowledge that they would be subsidized by the government. There is now growing recognition that such benevolence can no longer continue if state-owned enterprises are going to prosper.[19] This is the key issue. The State sector can only prosper if the lame ducks are allowed to cease business, if the work-force is dramatically cut, or vast amounts of money injected so that millions of new jobs are continually created year after year. If the government were to carry out this programme with the ruthlessness required, millions more inevitably will be thrown out of work, with many probably remaining unemployed long-term. What then of socialism that promised so much? After all, job insecurity was one of the worst aspects of the bad old days that the Communists pledged were gone for good with the liberation of 1949.

In 1986, a groundbreaking law authorized bankruptcy for state firms – taboo in the heyday of Maoism – and ordered some closures, but the programme stalled in the conservative backlash after the 1989 upheavals, so that by the following year only 32 bankruptcies were approved. The law was only implemented with some vigour in 1992, when over 350 firms, a third of them state-owned, declared bankruptcy, resulting in 1.4 million urban workers losing their jobs. In the past, bankruptcy had only been allowed in the State sector if another company was willing to take over responsibility for the entire work-force. These days they are either transferred to service companies set up by the State-owned firms or merely given a severance package. In 1996, more than 6,000 firms failed. Observing this, economist Cao Siyuan quit his position on the State Council, the country's supreme administrative body, to start a bankruptcy-consulting firm. 'Bankruptcy is not attached to capitalism or socialism,' he says. 'As long as there's a market economy there will be bankruptcy. It's like people dying of an incurable disease: they have to die.'

One interesting new experiment in dealing with bankrupt firms is the decision taken by the State Council in late 1997 to make auctions a major means of redistributing the property of bankrupt enterprises. Zhao Jie, Deputy Director of the Market Construction and Management Department under the Internal Trade Ministry, for one, believes this is the way forward. Auctions, he said, would free buyers and sellers from the government's 'arranged marriages' of the past in favour of the modern 'face-to-face love with freedom'. In the past, 'the government sector concerned would select from a rather limited range of candidates to take over the tottering enterprise. This kind of monopoly would usually lead to an ailing combination, harmful to the enterprise reforms'. Zhao cited a deal between two enterprises in Shandong Province as a telling example. Laixi Cotton Textile Plant was auctioned off to the Qin Chang Group in Qingdao City for $614,000, $180,000 more than the appraised value. The bankrupt factory's 2.84-hectare main workshop and 8,600-square-metre building area gave a powerful boost to the enlargement plans of the latter.

Beijing, meanwhile, according to the *People's Daily*, announced plans to sell off 40 enterprises through auction at a trade fair in the capital at the end of 1997. Mostly located in suburban counties, they included machinery, chemical, electronics, food processing, building materials, auto parts, commercial, livestock and tourism companies, and had combined assets valued at almost $50 million. Officials explained that although equipped with good facilities, most of the enterprises had been out of production for about two years because of management problems, lack of competitiveness and a shortage of working funds. Some of them are heavily in debt. Beijing Voltage Regulator Factory, for example, was 47.11 million Yuan ($5.68 million) in debt, with assets of only 45.77 million Yuan ($5.51 million). Beijing Xinyao Copper Pipe Factory, another of the candidates for auction, had total debts of 110.67 million Yuan ($13.33 million) and assets of 94.77 million Yuan ($11.42 million).[20]

But whatever method is used to revive the State sector, the fact remains that millions of jobs have either gone or are in jeopardy. Twenty million out of 110 million urban state employees-production workers plus supervisory and technical staff have either lost their posts or have been temporarily laid off and are receiving token pay. For them, unemployment may mean loss not just of work but of everything else the typical state enterprise provides: housing, education, medical care, pensions, unemployment pay, and miscellaneous benefits, except to the limited extent that the enterprise or government tides them over.

In addition, there are 30 million retirees from these enterprises whose pensions are not keeping up with inflation or are not paid at all. During the period from 1978 to 1994, the ratio of the number of retirees in the state enterprises to that of employees on post changed from 1:26.2 to 1:4.8, and their total insurance and welfare fund increased from 1.63 billion Yuan to 102.2 billion Yuan representing 30 per cent of the profits and taxes they turned over to the state. This expenditure grew by 30 per cent annually before 1994 and 38.1 per cent after. In 1980 the insurance and welfare fund accounted for 19.0 per cent of the state enterprises' total wages, and the proportion rose to 31.8 per cent by 1994. Developing in this way, half of the enterprises' returns will be used to support their retirees, casting a long shadow over the interests of active workers on post.

To the dismay of reformers, the government repeatedly has backed away from wholesale downsizing, despite estimates of more than 40 per cent of state firms chronically in the red. In July 1996, the government postponed introducing a high profile 'modernization' plan until the end of 1997. Had the plan gone ahead, all state enterprises would have had clear property rights, no government control over managerial decisions and 'scientific management'. This proposal would have brought massive downsizing of the state sector's labour force. This might seem like a case of politics overruling economics, but that explanation is somewhat simplistic. For one thing, officials have depleted state assets through massive transfers of state capital and property to the non-state sector. In response to the need to modernize the economy and increase productivity, planners may have imposed some misguided reforms on the work-force. Take the much-publicized smashing of the 'iron rice bowl' (long-term job security for workers), for example.

Chinese reformers targeted eliminating 'lifetime' employment as a major objective of enterprise reform and imposed individual contracts of fixed duration as a near-universal substitute. Yet in

36

Japan, job security contributed to the country's economic success, giving workers a strong identification with their employer and its need for high productivity. It is hard to fathom how imposing nationwide job insecurity could ever be a wise move in achieving reforms. The central government continues to flinch from firmly grasping the nettle. It has tried, for a start, to cushion reality. It set aside $3.6 billion in 1997 to cover bad debts from the state sector, and sought to buy time from irate workers by subsidizing salaries, though at reduced levels.[21]

Zhou Qiren, a professor with the China Centre for Economic Research of Beijing University,[22] describes the growing dilemma in these stark terms:

Unemployment in cities may become more severe amid ongoing urbanization and the reform of state-owned enterprises. During 1985–94, the urban population grew at an annual rate of 10.23 million. The figure would reach 15.23 million if rural labourers who moved to work in the cities were included.

'The growing urban population has proven too large for state-owned urban enterprises that have been reducing their work-force through lay-offs. According to the State Statistics Bureau, in 1978 the state-owned sectors employed 3.92 million new urban labourers, which represented 72 per cent of all newly employed workers that year. But by 1994, the state sectors were employing only 2.94 million new urban labourers, representing just 41 per cent of all new jobs.

Intensifying market competition has forced many formerly over-staffed businesses to reduce the number of their employees. State-owned sectors have laid off about 15 million workers since 1990. Another 15 million to 20 million are expected to be dismissed during 1996–2000. The size of the labour force in State-owned sectors is unlikely to grow partly because the traditional preference for heavy instead of light industry has diminished the country's ability to create more jobs. Since the end of 1991, growth of heavy industry has surpassed that of light industry. Investment no longer generates jobs the way it used to. Increasing amounts of capital are creating fewer jobs.

During 1985–88, every one per cent of growth of the country's investment in fixed assets could raise the country's employment rate by 0.21 per cent. But in 1991, the rate was only 0.03 per cent. Between 1986–90, the growth of one per cent of GNP would create 1.51 million new jobs compared with 0.85 million between 1991–5.

Senior state planner Wang Dongjin[23] presents even more startling figures. According to him, more than a third of employed surplus state workers – up to 20 million people – face unemployment by the turn of the century. At least 54 million public employees – or 36 per cent of the entire state payroll – are actually considered surplus labour, but the rest could be redeployed. 'Due to population growth and economic restructuring, resolution of the unemployment issue is a difficult matter,' said Wang, a vice-minister of the State Commission for Economic Restructuring. 'It is an arduous task. But we must transform the mindset of these people to find new jobs. We must try to curb unemployment at four per cent.'

Tao Dong, a Hong Kong-based economist believes unemployment will be most acute in central provinces, where most state firms were concentrated and whose economic performance already lags behind coastal centres such as Shanghai. 'People in Shanghai are more fortunate than those in Changchun. Laid-off workers can be naturally transferred to the service sector in Shanghai, where they can work as taxi drivers and join the retail industry. That option isn't available in the interior.'

His assertion is backed up to some extent by the decision of the Beijing municipal government to specifically issue 20,000 new taxi licences in order to create jobs for workers laid off by state enterprises [there were already 80,000 taxis in Beijing in mid-1997]. The taxi programme was one of several plans by the municipal government to absorb at least 60 per cent of the 200,000 workers made redundant by the state sector in that year alone. While some of those laid off have been reassigned to other enterprises, others have taken up jobs such as cleaning. Beijing is also learning from Shanghai, which has successfully found jobs for displaced workers. 'Shanghai is more successful in the task of re-employing people laid off, and has initiated preferential treatment to encourage the jobless to become self employed,' said a Beijing city official. The Shanghai Commercial Administration Bureau, for example, has simplified its registration procedures to encourage redundant workers to start their own companies.[24]

'If a laid-off person hands in his application in the morning to set up a company, he will get his licence in the afternoon,' one bureau official promised. The Shanghai Municipal Government also granted three-year tax exemptions to small businesses. In part through such measures, it managed to relocate 800,000 redundant workers in 1996, and expected to find jobs for another 600,000 in 1997. Both Beijing and Shanghai have introduced incentives for employers willing to hire the unemployed. A company can receive 3,000 Yuan[25] from the municipal government for hiring a female displaced worker above the age of 35 and male over 40 if employed for at least two years.

But one Beijing official observed that 'it is more difficult for us to find jobs for laid-off workers than Shanghai. Some of them were departmental heads in state enterprises and they think it is losing face to be an 'ordinary' worker in other professions'. One further step taken by Beijing, however, was a regulation in April 1997 aimed specifically at the two million rural migrants who have flooded into the capital in the 1990s in search of work. The city government announced that migrant workers would henceforth be banned from working in commerce or marketing, including working as shop assistants or salesmen, accountants, secretaries, bus conductors, waiters and waitresses and lift operators, where employers would have to give priority to applicants with Beijing residency permits.[26] So, one has to acknowledge something is being done. The question yet to be answered is whether these efforts will be sufficient.

In April 1993, the State Council issued the Provisions on the Arrangement of Redundant Employees of State-Owned Enterprises, setting the principle of 'chiefly relying on enterprises concerned, making help from society secondary, and ensuring the basic living standards of redundant employees'. According to the principle, redundant workers were to be handled by three methods. First, seeking to increase available jobs by tapping the potential, and expanding the production capacity, of the enterprises concerned; second, helping firms with excess workers develop subsidiary, possibly tertiary, businesses to absorb them; third, offering training and basic living expenses to those made redundant. In 1995, the re-employment project was initiated nation-wide through a network of 're-employment service centres'. This is not an official job agency, but a public intermediate organization set up by the business community with government policy support and financial aid from other sectors of society.

∞

Mention has already been made of the re-employment programme being undertaken by Shanghai. The city experienced the most rapid economic growth and swiftest urban development between 1990–96. Along with the major readjustment of its industrial structure and the transformation of the operational mechanisms of state-owned enterprises, however, some 1.09 million workers were made redundant. Nevertheless, Shanghai claims it has kept its unemployment rate down to 2.8 per cent. The first re-employment service centres were launched by the two traditional industries, textiles and electronic meters and instruments. Shanghai's textile industry has the largest number of employees, with the maximum of 551,600 recorded in 1988. This had been reduced to 324,000 by early 1997, and was expected to be cut further to 250,000 after 1998. This suggests that one of every five Shanghai workers made redundant in recent years came from the textile industry.

The Shanghai No. 24 Bleaching and Dyeing Mill, a state-owned gauze and bandage producer, expanded its assets and was able to produce high-tech products after merging with an absorbent cotton factory and another bleaching and dyeing mill that were faced with bankruptcy. But the initial cost was high because its 400 employees had to bear the living and medical expenses of the other two factories' 400 redundant workers and 600 retirees. After the founding of the Textile Re-employment Service Centre in July 1996, the mill transferred the 400 redundant workers to the centre, which provides each member with basic living expense (the bottom line for Shanghai is 236 Yuan or $28.43 per person each month), health care and other basic social security needs. The centre also set up several dozen training bases focusing on computer operation, accounting, cooking, sewing and other skills. The No. 24 Mill, without its heavy burden, was able to develop new products. Its increased production capacity also enabled it to employ new workers from the ranks of redundant staff retrained by the centre. Within a year, all the redundant workers had found new jobs.

In 1995, the difficulty in handling the problem of existing employees prevented Shanghai's 12 textile mills in the process of bankruptcy from actually achieving their goal. Six months after the founding of the centre, however, 15 enterprises declared bankruptcy. Through the re-employment project, Shanghai's textile sector was able to make 164 loss-making enterprises either shut down, suspend production or shift to manufacturing other goods. By cutting its primary processing capacity by 30 per cent, the sector has checked its losses. Similar efforts have been made with the Beijing textile sector. Nearly 10,000 redundant spinners and weavers of the Beijing Textile Corp. found they had almost no special skills required by the re-employment market. To help them, their former units provided them with training, and the majority were quickly rehired. In 1996, some 280,000 redundant workers, newly-added labourers and unemployed people in Beijing received job training, and 80 per cent found jobs, according to an investigation of the Beijing Federation of Trade Unions.

Choices for re-employment have been concentrated on such jobs as shop assistants, waiters, bus conductors, elevator operators and government organization odd-jobmen. But, given the large numbers of job seekers, it was obvious that such positions would quickly become saturated. At the same time, the insurance, health-care, electronics and some other new industries were complaining of a shortage of trained people, suggesting the re-employment project needed to re-order its priorities to concentrate more on training professional staff.

Private businesses have become an important channel for re-employment. In Chongqing, a metropolis of some 30 million people in the south-west corner of the country, more than 150,000 of the 500,000 redundant workers from state-owned and collective enterprises either formed their own company or got employed by private businesses in 1995 and 1996. This brought about noticeable changes to the industrial city where state-owned and collective enterprises used to make up 70 per cent of the industrial sector.

In a survey of almost 800 sample enterprises conducted in 18 cities in Hunan, Jilin, Jiangsu and Sichuan provinces by the Economic Institute of the Chinese Academy of Social Sciences[27] found that 'rearrangement of jobs' was the first choice for dealing with surplus workers, with 76 per cent saying this method is very important or important. The next most popular choices were seeking voluntary early retirement (55.8 per cent) and encouraging workers to find jobs in other trades (50.7 per cent), and not paying bonuses to those deemed redundant (27.7 per cent). The least popular choice was dismissal (25.5 per cent).

In its analysis of the results, the institute commented:

Although people believe from what they have seen and heard through the mass media that enterprises are cutting down the number of employees, the results of the survey suggest that this is not exactly true. From the survey, we can see that although the rate of workers unemployed has risen year after year, which is particularly manifested in the increasing number of enterprises which have reduced their work-force, the rate of workers unemployed is small compared with the rate of workers considered excess.

In a state economic sector, enterprises will incur great political and economic risks if they plan to dismiss redundant workers. As we persist in the ideological concept that workers are the masters of the state and of enterprises, it is certain that [the latter] will meet difficulties in dismissing workers. It goes without saying that this is why enterprises discharge a small number of workers.[28]

Therefore, they would rather readjust the enterprise personnel structure. As to internal readjustment, this is only the change of internal structure among redundant workers. It cannot change the fact that there are too many workers. Persuading [them] to retire early or encouraging them to find jobs in other trades becomes a secondary choice because the two methods represent the choice of the workers

41

themselves, rather than the choice enforced by the enterprise. Workers are willing to take the risks of the choice. Even though they may have their own troubles they don't normally make trouble for the enterprise.

Many enterprises do not like to take the method of not giving bonuses to redundant workers, partly because this would meet opposition from workers and partly because bonuses do not cost the enterprises much. The more bonuses a company gives to workers, the less profits it will obtain; the less profit will mean less profits and tax the company has to pay to the state.

The CASS research found there were only 90 enterprises who considered they had no surplus in their work-force (11.3 per cent). Firms with workers surplus to requirements ranging between 1–10 per cent of the total work-force made up 29.3 per cent of the sample. Those with rates of more than 10 per cent accounted for 60 per cent, and those with more than 20 per cent were 40 per cent. There were 19 enterprises with more than 50 per cent redundant workers. Hunan Province had the highest rate and Jiangsu Province the lowest. The pattern is in line with the fact that coastal areas in the process of reform and development are growing faster than inland areas.

The government does claim some success in redeploying China's vast labour force. Some statistics frequently cited:

□ Since the reform and opening policies were first introduced in the late 1970s, various urban work units, township (cooperative) enterprises and private enterprises have created, on average, 12 million jobs annually, employing more than 200 million people altogether.

□ More than 100 million jobs were created in the decade from the mid-1980s through the development of tertiary industry. At present, the proportion of employees of the tertiary sector is double that in 1978, with the absolute number now exceeding that engaged in secondary industry. The proportion of people engaged in primary industry has dropped by 18 per cent.

□ Since 1979, more than 50 per cent of the newly added jobs have been provided by non-state economic sectors. In terms of the proportion of the number of people employed by units under different ownerships in 1978, state-owned units absorbed 23 million less people. This helped reduce the redundant personnel and promoted the reform of state-owned enterprises.

□ In the rural areas, nearly 40 per cent of the labourers are no longer farmers in the traditional sense. They are either employed by township enterprises, or run private businesses, or do odd jobs or business in towns. In 1978, the rate was less than 10 per cent.

During this period, the 84 per cent increase in the number of women employees has outstripped the 56.9 per cent growth rate for the total number of employees, while the proportion of women employees has increased from 32.9 per cent to 38.6 per cent.

China's high-growth economy may inspire awe and investment from the international business community, but to the men and women employed on the factory floor, the economic scene looks grimly different. Deng Xiaoping's economic reforms have wrought vast changes in the nation's labour force. A key innovation of Deng's 'socialism with Chinese characteristics' was that some people would 'get rich first'. But most workers, the supposed masters of the country, still seem to be awaiting their share. Some Chinese economists claim that the workers' day will come with further growth, but double-digit growth does not necessarily translate into a better life for workers. After a decided improvement in living standards during the first half of the 1980s, income inequality has widened, with workers' social status declining apace. In 1978, 27 per cent of the members of the National People's Congress were worker representatives. Their numbers declined to 15 per cent in 1983, 12 per cent in 1988 and 11 per cent today.[29]

Many so-called worker representatives are now from the managerial ranks, rather than model workers as in the Maoist days. In state enterprises, where the Communist Party has a large membership base, the emphasis has been on recruitment of managerial and technical employees, not ordinary workers.[30] In enterprise-level work councils, still promoted as prime vehicles for worker participation, worker representatives are heavily outnumbered by managers, professionals and technicians.

Reality contradicts the ideological pronouncement that managers and workers alike are members of the working class. Feng Tongqing, a teacher at Beijing's central training centre for union officials, observes in his book *Speaking Without Reservations*: 'The traditionally defined working class has split into at least three cohorts: (1) managers and other senior management staff; (2) engineers and technicians; (3) shop floor workers, each distinctive, with its own divisions of labour in production and lifestyle. Because there are great gaps between these three cohorts of individuals in terms of power, prestige, and income, conflicts between them are

43

inevitable. Here lies the root of workers' resentment about their own deteriorating status in the enterprise as well as in society.'

In pre-reform days, enterprise managers received salaries only three or four times higher than the pay of the average worker. Now, they can earn up to 300 times more, not counting wealth gained through corruption. It is not just income disparities that fuel worker resentment. In a letter published by a leading official labour newspaper,[31] 24 workers in a Guangdong Province joint venture called Zhaojie Footwear, managed by its Taiwanese partner, complained: 'The company beats, abuses and humiliates us at will.'

When the newspaper carried out its own investigation, it found that everyday punishments included forcing workers to 'hop around like a frog' and to stand facing the wall or on a stool or outdoors in the sun. Contrary to the law, the employees 'are sometimes made to work all through the night to finish a rush order'. It was alleged that under the 24-hour watch of 100 security guards, the firm's 2,700 employees, mostly women, some under the legal working age of 16, were rarely allowed to leave the combined factory-dormitory premises. One worker, his request to quit denied, climbed over the plant's wall and was crushed to death by a passing train.

Similar problems have been reported throughout the south-east coastal region, the earliest laboratory for the economic reforms, by trade unions, Hong Kong-based journalists and even China's own mass media on occasions. Some 17 million Chinese people work in coastal factories funded by foreign investors, largely from Taiwan, Hong Kong and South Korea. The workers, the great majority of them women from rural areas, make shoes, toys, garments and other products for export, often under sweatshop conditions. Low wages are not the worst of the workers' problems. The most repugnant abuse is physical punishment, involving beatings inflicted by supervisors or private guards, some carrying electric batons. As a result, even verbal threats are intimidating.

In some cases the coercive regulations that management impose on workers, during and after working hours, are unbelievably detailed: prohibition on talking, even while eating; marked routes for walking within the factory-dormitory compound, bans on leaving the compound at any time without special permission, prohibitions against getting pregnant, married or even engaged. In one factory, anyone using the toilet more than twice in a workday forfeits nearly a fifth of her monthly wage. Violating such rules can bring not just fines but also physical punishment, psychological harassment, or even dismissal with loss of at least two weeks' pay.[32]

44

Workplace health and safety in such enterprises are sometimes scandalous, In November 1993, for example, a fire at the Zhili Toy Factory in Guangdong killed 87 workers and injured more than 60, their escape blocked by barred windows and locked doors.

Because turnover rates are on the rise in southern China, many factories have become more reliant on a kind of bonded labour to retain workers. When hired, workers typically must surrender official papers (such as temporary residence permits and identity cards) and pay a substantial 'deposit' or bond. Either or both will be forfeited if a worker quits. Many of the domestic partners in joint ventures are actually government agencies or their affiliates. In the Zhaojie Footwear factory, the partner is a state-owned enterprise, China Travel. Government organs share foreign investors' desire to make money and are therefore disinclined to apply the officially set labour standards. The sweatshops recruit mainly among China's most vulnerable citizens – peasants from rural areas, who are commonly called migrants even when living in a city for years. China's apartheid-like household registration system, introduced in the 1950s, still divides the population into two distinct groups, urban and rural. To stay in urban areas, peasants must get and retain temporary residence permits, linked to employment, a dependency that exposes them to easy victimization. The justification for the abuses is that unless wages are kept down and output stepped up, China cannot compete on the international market and will lose investment to other developing countries, such as Vietnam, where labour costs are even lower.

When publicizing the worst cases of exploitation, the official Chinese media usually blame 'foreign capital', even though most of the foreign investors are ethnic Chinese who are honoured with the designation of 'compatriot'. 'Foreign capital' conjures up the image of a white big-nosed Westerner rather than a compatriot. *Outlook* magazine, for example, printed a litany of abuses suffered by workers at the hands of foreign bosses. Although the bosses in the text are described as Chinese or other Asians, the accompanying illustration featured a 'foreign devil', white, fat, smug, big-nosed, and male, standing next to two teary-eyed Chinese women. Though less publicized, sweatshop conditions have also permeated SOEs. Sociologists Zhao Minghua and Theo Nichols[33] investigated three textile mills in Henan province to describe the crushing daily routine of 20,000 workers, most of them women, involving 'exhausting work hours, no overtime pay, complex work rules, fines for breaking them, ever-increasing quotas, draconian sick leave policies and so on'.

45

The official newspaper *Yangcheng Wanbao*, meanwhile, claimed that workers in at least 11 quarries it had investigated were being treated like slaves. It said that one quarry in southern Guangdong province was 'operated like a prison where workers are forced to work like slaves and live in miserable conditions'. The labourers were recruited from unemployed rural migrants, some hired outside railway stations where they tend to congregate in many Chinese cities.[34] Quarry workers were locked in 'simple and crude dormitories' at night and were forbidden to rest or to leave the job. At least one of them had not been paid for more than a year. Those who complained were beaten by the guards and most were afraid to complain for fear of losing their jobs, the newspaper reported.

This revelation became the subject of 'Today's Hotline', a radio phone-in talk show in Guangzhou. Such programmes deal with many hitherto taboo topics such as sex and local corruption. The quarry was operated by a local township and an official of the provincial labour bureau said that 'the practice of forced labour is common across the province'. He said his department had only 284 inspectors to look after 30 million workers throughout the province. A caller to the talk show claimed that not only quarries but also many factories throughout the Pearl River delta adjacent to Hong Kong exploited their workers as if they were slaves. Another caller said that such malpractice could 'damage the prestige of the Communist Party throughout the province'.

Retaining what is salvageable from the Maoist era, many factories still make much of 'socialist emulation' campaigns, imported from the Soviet Union in the 1950s, which single out dutiful workers as models for others. A favourite method of honouring a model worker is to put his or her name and achievements on a large red poster for all to see. However, at least one Henan factory has a variation on this tactic. It uses a poster in dark green, a colour signifying bad news, to humiliate someone with conduct deemed unworthy of emulation. A typical green poster, observed by Zhao Minghua[35] at a cotton mill employing 10,000 workers, announced in large characters: 'A serious warning: 1,236 points (a third of her monthly wages) will be docked from operator Wang Xiaofeng's wages this month, due to her successive breaches of operating instructions. For example, she always failed to stand at the right position prescribed in the instructions.'

The All China Federation of Trade Unions (ACFTU), the officially approved body overseeing workers' interests, does do some good work for its members. Especially in the state-owned firms, its officials often act as ombudsmen or mediators, and they sometimes negotiate collective contracts to supplement the individual contracts of workers in state industries. At the national level, top federation officials are involved in tripartite consultations with counterparts in government and management. During extensive consultations prior to the passage of the labour code, ACFTU representatives negotiated some improvements, such as reducing the standard work week from 48 to 44 hours (and now down to 40). But their status as representatives of China's workers is marred by the fact that they are legitimized not by workers, but by the government. The ACFTU's own surveys have revealed widespread doubt among workers about the organization's credentials. Essentially, the ACFTU is just another voice within the state and party apparatus.

In the mass media, the regime has recently revived slogans hailing workers as the 'masters of the country and the enterprise'. Before faith in Communist ideology began to show signs of fading such slogans inspired a spirit of duty and self-sacrifice, now they rub salt into wounds. A 'model' worker told an ACFTU researcher: 'I strongly feel that we workers have somehow been duped.' Even the World Bank is sceptical. In its World Development Report 1996, it emphasises that nations 'in transition', such as China, must reform 'existing institutions [that] were adapted to the needs of a very different economic system'. The report cites China's trade unions as now being 'in essence part of the government apparatus'.

Over the next decade, China has three options for including working men and women in its emerging civil society. In seeking to blend capitalism and Communism, Party leaders are considered certain to avoid reforms that threaten their dominance. Today the tacit consensus, too embarrassing to be openly expressed by a regime that calls itself socialist, is that workers must be sacrificial lambs for the nation's economic development.

■ CHAPTER 3

# Contradictions in the Countryside

S ince China began to adopt the new policy of reform and opening
   to the outside world, the invisible system barrier between urban
and rural areas has gradually dissolved, due mainly to two factors:
(1) abandoning limitations on farmers working and opening
businesses in the cities; (2) bringing the price of all major foodstuffs
under market regulation.

However, the managing system separating the urban and rural
areas has by no means changed fundamentally. In cities, in
particular, people still enjoy rights in employment, housing, health
care, welfare, insurance, and education according to their permanent residence registration. While the main cities are home to the
nation's political, economic, commercial and cultural centres,
gathering most of the social wealth, they remain a dream beyond
the reach of most rural youngsters. The boom in mass media,
however, has enabled the rural population to share the same
information with their urban siblings, and it has finally begun to
occur to them how unfair the structure of existing society is with
regard to the distribution of social wealth.[1]

The reintroduction of elements of a capitalist economy during
the 1980s created inequalities which have further widened in the
1990s. Under Mao, remuneration was kept within narrow boundaries, with an emphasis on 'serving the people' rather than
acquiring wealth. The replacement of this slogan with one
declaring that 'getting rich is glorious' came as something of a
shock after the long period of Maoist egalitarianism. But even under
Mao, this was not absolute. In the 1970s, for example, 'one was still
better off as a man than a woman, as an urban worker than as a
peasant, as a state worker than as a collective worker, as a peasant
near a large city than as one in a remote area, or as a peasant with

48

many able-bodied adults in the household than as one with several young children'.[2]

At the same time, the levelling-off factor, while reducing inequality, did mean that for a long period there was extremely slow growth in living standards due to a reduction in the way people were able to use productive resources. That key inhibiting factor has now been removed, allowing those with the better means to forge ahead. In the past two decades, therefore, priority has been given to the eastern coastal regions in opening up to the outside world, with preferential government policies to encourage their rapid development. The swift boom of the regions enabled them to become magnets for not only foreign capital and technology, but also the domestic capital and skilled labour force. This inevitably resulted in an even wider east-west gap.[3]

While a growing number of Yuan millionaires lead lives of luxury in the eastern region, the central and Western regions, where the majority of the 60 million-plus officially-recognized poor live, have a tiny per capita net income of less than 500 Yuan ($60) a year. Dissatisfaction over regional disparity is a source of deep official concern. Home to most of China's poor and ethnic and religious groups, these areas are a potential block to China's social integration, national unity and social stability. Most worrying: most of the disadvantaged groups live on sensitive national borders.[4]

At the same time, the country faces an urban explosion in the next two decades with a massive population shift from rural areas to cities and new townships[5]. The Academy of Social Sciences[6] forecasts that by 2000, the urban population will grow to 50 per cent. In the mid-1990s, it was 27.6 per cent, and as recently as the early 1980s, only 10 per cent. These startling figures suggest that China, which has hitherto been predominantly an agrarian society, is undergoing a profound sociological revolution.

In order to lighten the burden of welfare expenditure in cities, the State now calls for tight control over the population increase in the urban areas, while encouraging rural industrialization under the slogan 'bidding farewell to the land but not leaving rural areas'. However, this policy has been implemented at a frightening cost, including urbanization lagging far behind industrialization, rural industry being operated at high cost especially due to inefficient project duplication in neighbouring areas, serious waste of limited financial and natural resources and serious environmental pollution. At the same time, the creation of rural industry has done little to stem the torrent of migrants flooding into overburdened cities.

The non-agricultural development mainly took place right in the rural areas before 1991, with most of the agricultural labourers bidding farewell to farming as they sought new opportunities amongst the newly-rising township enterprises. The situation has changed since 1991 when the township enterprises have developed from being labour-intensive to technology- and capital-intensive ones accommodating fewer and fewer rural labourers. Thus, the first tide of rural immigration to urban areas began.

There is a need for rapid small town development programmes to provide homes and jobs for the tens of millions of peasants leaving the land because cities have reached their limit in taking in migrants. Cities such as Beijing, Shanghai, Guangzhou and Tianjin have already been overrun, an influx blamed for an increase in crime and considered a prime source for social unrest.[7] It was the poverty afflicting the countryside which drove the government's first moves towards economic liberalization in 1979, when it freed most of the rural goods markets. Yet, the steady growth of a market economy in other sectors in the years which followed is still causing a mass migration the authorities struggle vainly to control.

> By 2000 , there will be 490 to 540 million farmers in the rural areas, about 200 million of whom will have to find new jobs outside the agricultural sector. Supposing that 10 million, a generous estimate, can find a new job each year as the country's economy develops, by the turn of the century at least 140 million labourers will remain jobless.'[8]

But although the urban population is growing rapidly, the majority of people still live in the countryside. And, if the nation is to achieve its full economic and social potential, greater efforts will have to be made to raise rural living standards.

From time immemorial, a Chinese peasant's existence has been 'bending to the yellow earth beneath the blue sky', tilling the land and doing nothing else,[9] so that rural employment was never considered a problem by the local or central authorities. Mao Zedong, visiting Hunan Province in 1927, produced a report for the party leadership expressing shock at the appalling living standards of the peasantry. In the words of one writer:

> [. . .] the poor were only peasants, passive, illiterate, abysmally ignorant, and there to be used. Lost in great tracts of land, where the only roads were rutted cart tracks, and where score on score of villages might be on land owned by one family. In 1927, few if any of them would ever have seen, let alone used, trains, radio or electric light.[. . .] They just lived the best they could trapped in the steel jaws

of Confucian orthodoxy and the network of hatreds it engendered at every level of life. Men and women from other lands who saw their plight were staggered at their apathy.[10]

By the time the Communists took control in 1949, the lot of the peasantry was not quite as bad, although still leaving much to be desired. Under the Nationalists, the land was still largely controlled by absentee landlords, whose demands often left their tenants destitute. The yoke was lifted when the landlords were amongst the first groups to be purged after the Communist take-over, many being executed. Relief, however, was tempered by the fact that under the collectivization of agriculture enforced by Mao, life in the countryside remained spartan and difficult.

Peasants worked as part of production teams, sharing the work to be done as well as the rewards through 'work points' earned during the year. There were many imperfections. Some members of the group did not work as hard as others and some did not work at all, if unsupervised. Management of the group by the team leader was sometimes poor. The day-to-day work of the team might be interfered with by higher authorities who had no knowledge of local situations but who issued detailed directives of such matters as crop varieties to be planted, output expected, planting schedules, and the methods of sowing, fertilization, irrigation and harvesting.

> It was found that as recently as the late seventies a third of the cadres in rural areas had little knowledge of management, and another third had no working experience in rural areas nor any knowledge of agriculture. Naturally, peasant enthusiasm was often low and production suffered. [Peasants] had no incentive to think much about what they were doing because they had no say in how things were done.[11]

Incompetence, and a desire to please their masters in Beijing, led local cadres in the late 1960s to grossly exaggerate annual harvests, or to switch the peasants into ill-advised industrial production – such as the grossly inefficient, virtually useless backyard steel furnaces[12] promoted at the height of the 'Great Leap Forward', which was supposed to convert China almost overnight from a poor backward country into a rich, modern industrial state, measured by its ability to catch up with Britain in industrial output within 15 years, so that crops rotted in the fields and millions of people eventually were condemned to die of starvation.

The Great Leap Forward marked the point where China diverged from the Soviet Union and was the great watershed in China's national development. It marked the final abandonment of the Soviet-oriented model of industrialization and the adoption of a bold new approach. It emerged from Chinese doubts about the suitability of Soviet methods to China's development. Although the first five-year plan, patterned on the Soviet example, resulted in highly impressive advances in the industrial sector, agricultural production had failed to keep pace. And the Chinese leadership was acutely aware that the momentum of industrial growth could not be sustained unless the agricultural surplus was greatly increased. One possible solution was to divert resources from industry to agriculture, deriving from the Soviet example of extracting a much greater surplus from the countryside without investing more resources in it. This was not acceptable, partly because rural living standards were already extremely low, and partly because the Chinese leadership, unlike Stalin, had a unique relationship with the peasantry and was unwilling to subject it to more hardships.

What the leadership had to find, therefore, was a way of increasing the agricultural surplus by increasing production, without large natural investments in the rural areas. Its solution was to achieve this increase primarily through the institutional means of collectivization which, in contrast with the Soviet Union, was intended mainly to raise agricultural output rather than increase extractions through greater regimentation. Collectivization, however, failed to provide the agricultural surplus required by the ambitious industrial goals, and this realization set the Chinese leaders off on the search for a way out of the dilemma. This search led them to the Great Leap Forward.

Adding impetus and urgency to this search was the mounting concern of Mao over the socio-political consequences of importing Soviet methods of development. 'Although the Chinese had preserved some of their unique revolutionary techniques even as they transplanted the essentials of the Soviet model, they began to perceive that, on balance, this transplantation was spawning offshoots which were sharply at variance with their revolutionary experience and post-revolutionary expectations. It was clear that under Soviet influence the Chinese revolution was becoming [. . .] bureaucratized. Mao, as well as other leaders committed to his social vision, were not prepared to accept methods of development which led to these consequences.'[13]

Mao turned to his own revolutionary experience for inspiration, and the belief in the 'human element' (properly motivated and properly mobilized masses) to overcome seemingly insuperable material obstacles. China would achieve an economic breakthrough by rapid and simultaneous development of its industry and agriculture through the maximum utilization of China's labour force in mass movements, known as 'walking on two legs'. This was based on the belief that China's masses, its most precious asset, constituted a great storehouse of productive energy which, if properly motivated, could move mountains through sheer will-power.[14] For several months after the programme got under way the entire nation seemed gripped by a spirit of determination and dedication, which seemingly moved it to achieve miraculous results. Hard-driving local cadres, caught in the euphoric mood radiated by the central leadership, spurred the masses to a feverish pitch of endeavour. On their part, the masses responding to the exhortations and pressures of the leadership, appeared to turn China into a veritable beehive of activity.

Communes were set up to facilitate the mobilization of manpower, and to bring the country closer to Mao's social vision. 'Backyard steel furnaces' were promoted throughout the nation to aid the industrial effort. Unrealistic production targets were set, and then, on the basis of exaggerated reports, were further raised. But it did not take the leadership long to realize that the gigantic effort was getting out of hand. By the summer of 1960, it was clear that the country was in the throes of a severe economic crisis, inflicting an amount of suffering on the people unknown under the Communist regime. Agricultural production plummeted and food was in short supply throughout the country. Basic commodities were extremely difficult, and, in some places, impossible to obtain. Industry plunged into recession; many plants ground to a halt, and large parts of the labour force were thrown out of work. In short, the Great Leap Forward brought disaster.[15]

This was exacerbated by natural disasters as well as the abrupt withdrawal of all Soviet aid, as a result of the sharpening of the Sino-Soviet conflict. Less spectacular than its outward manifestations, but no less severe in its implications was the crisis of confidence in the regime, which was endangered in large part by the economic hardships. For these hardships painfully demonstrated to the Chinese people that their leaders, far from being infallible, were capable of making monumental and costly blunders. Until the Great Leap Forward the regime had accumulated a vast fund of confidence as a result of its successes during the first decade of its rule, and it drew on this fund when it called upon the people to struggle and to sacrifice. The people, for their part, generally responded willingly, and were prepared to make the most strenuous efforts on behalf of the goals set forth by the regime.

'The collapse of the Great Leap Forward, however, shattered the confidence of the people in the leadership. For instead of a better tomorrow, it brought a bitter today. The result was not only physical hardships but also a mood of demoralization and distrust. This mood led to a breakdown of discipline such as had not been seen in China since the Communists came to power, as individuals struggled for survival in a climate of cynicism and lost confidence.'[16]

One writer who visited China at that time later recorded his impressions:

> Muddle, dislocation, bottlenecks and deviationist weather all helped to bring the country to the very brink of ruin in the years that followed, but one of the fundamental reasons for the spectacular failure of the great plan lay in the Chinese tendency to mistake one swallow for a summer. At the beginning of the Great Leap, I talked with cadres on cooperative farms in North and West China who assured me that thanks to 'socialist methods', which included deeper plowing, more fertilization, closer sowing, and other agricultural abuses, rice output on their land would be doubled that year, quadrupled the next, and thereafter, who knew? Anything was possible.
>
> A little earnest inquiry revealed, however, that this pipe-dream arithmetic had been inspired by increases of production already achieved by experts on small, special experimental plots of land elsewhere, whose conditions could not possibly apply to the whole country. It was nevertheless assumed [. . .] that if 400 tons of natural fertilizer had been available to produce exceptional results on one acre in Shantung [Shandong] 400 million tons would be available, for example, for one million acres in Szechwan (Sichuan). Gravely following the printed instructions, and without thought for the local environment, some cadres, inspired by reports of land reclamation in swamp areas elsewhere, drained off the water tables of such, well-irrigated paddy fields that had produced two crops of rice a year, leaving them looking like the grittier sections of the Gobi desert, and just about as productive.[17]
>
> As famine ravaged a countryside whose people were too hungry to work and pigs too hungry to stand, Mao voiced nothing but scorn for all the fussing about the shortage of vegetables, pork, grain and even umbrellas. In his eyes the much-revered masses had fallen from grace, had become 'soft' in those three years of struggle that promised a millennia of happiness. The renewed Leap of 1959–60 triggered a famine in which some 25 or perhaps even 50 million starved to death.[18]

It took some years for agricultural production to recover from that disaster, but it was not until after the change of leadership in the late 1970s that the rural sector was finally liberalized to achieve the sort of output Mao envisioned. Until then, despite endless political pressure, the full potential of the countryside could not be tapped because 'peasant families resented collective production methods on the land and egalitarian distribution both within and among local units; because low state prices and gross inadequacy in the state commercial monopolies led to very low cash incomes and low standards of consumption; and because the Maoist authorities insisted not only upon suppression of production which was not collective, but the limitation of collection to very few crops, often little more than grain (together with potatoes) and cotton.'[19]

In 1979, Deng Xiaoping launched radical farm reforms that largely ended the commune system, raised the permitted size of private plots and allowed free markets for farm products to develop. A 'household contract responsibility system' was introduced in 1985 under which families agreed to provide the government with a specified amount of produce each year at a fixed price, with any surplus then available to be sold in the 'free market'. Farmers were also encouraged to start sideline businesses to further enhance their earning potential.

Under the reforms, productivity soared. In the mid-1980s, truth finally matched the fiction of the grossly-inflated figures of three decades before. The transformation of the rural areas was once typified by Dazhai, a village in the barren hills of Shanxi province set up by Mao as a model for all Chinese farmers. With over 100 households, the village rose to national fame when its barren mountain slopes were turned into high-yielding terraced fields in the 1960s, prompting Mao to declare: 'In agriculture, learn from Dazhai', a slogan soon emblazoned across village squares across the country. Pilgrims from every corner of China flocked to the village in response to this exhortation, requiring some of the farmland to be concreted over for car parks, hotels and conference centres. Later, it transpired the wonderful crop production figures were fraudulent and the improved lifestyle was actually the result of secret government subsidies.[20]

In 1983, however, the responsibility system was brought to Dazhai. A small coal mine opened nearby followed by a chemical factory. All the men work in factories in the village, while the women are left in charge of the farmland. The town now has ambitions to be the core of an economic development zone with 22 nearby villages as satellites, based primarily on coal mines, chemical and construction materials plants, and textiles and agricultural processing factories. More than two decades after Dazhai first hit the headlines, the message in the official media seemed to be the same, only the name of the village was different. Now, it was: learn from Huaxi, a village located on the outskirts of Wuxi in southern Jiangsu Province.

Wu Renbao, veteran Party branch secretary, recalled that the tiny village originally had almost no resources to support 1,500 peasants on a plot of cultivated land less than one square kilometre in size. Over a period of three decades, he led the villagers to level the land, plant trees and build irrigation canals to ensure steadily increasing grain yields. But to Wu, the road to real prosperity could only come through establishing industrial and by-product enterprises. The first, a hardware factory which mainly repaired motorboats and agricultural machinery, was actually set up at the height of the cultural revolution, when the establishment of such an enterprise was regarded as 'taking the capitalist road'.

To ensure Huaxi was not visited by a wrathful group of teenage Red Guards, villagers kept the factory a secret. In the first year, it made profits of more than $6,000, and these soon quadrupled, creating capital for later improvements in living standards as well as knowledge in industrial development. When the political climate changed, Wu seized the chance to develop township enterprises, starting out in 1982 with three small factories manufacturing steel nets, nylon cement bags and pesticide sprayers.[21] By the mid-1990s, Huaxi had formed its own industrial framework covering metallurgy, chemicals, textiles and building materials, including a steel mill with an annual capacity of 250,000 tons, a 400,000-ton capacity rolling mill and a steel wire plant with an annual capacity of 300,000 tons.[22]

The post-1978 reforms were accompanied by a rapid reduction in absolute poverty, partially through the release of production potential in poor areas which the rural reforms made directly possible, partly through the 'trickle-down' effects to poor people from the richer areas and levels of society, especially those on the coast first opened to foreign investment, and partly through State policies to use some of the benefits of growth to help disadvantaged areas, a programme now moving into high gear in the late 1990s. The early years of the reforms saw the most rapid changes after years of political turmoil and suppression. The World Bank, for example, estimated that 'the proportion of rural population in poverty declined from 31 per cent in 1979 to 13 per cent in 1982 [. . .] the speed and scale of the improvement is probably unprecedented in human history'.[23]

The gap between the urban and rural areas could have been worse. One problem was that while almost three-quarters of all

Chinese were still farming in 1979, they produced only a quarter of the GNP. A widening productivity gap is illustrated by the fact that, whereas in 1952, an industrial worker produced 6.5 times as much gross output value as a farmer, by 1979 this difference had grown by a factor of 14.[24] With such a difference in output value, only extraordinary measures could prevent sectoral personal incomes from similarly polarizing. For two decades, this was achieved by keeping urban wages virtually unchanged (workers cushioned from any rises in the cost of living by a wide range of subsidies, especially covering food and housing costs). But this could only slow down, not stop the widening gap in incomes and living standards.

This wage freeze was certainly unpopular, perhaps helping to further discredit the idea of egalitarianism, 'everyone eating from the same pot', promoted in the Maoist era, but gradually discarded by Mao's successors, leading in the early 1990s to the promotion of the idea that it was acceptable for some people to get rich before others. There is no doubt economic reform benefited the peasants, many of whom witnessed a significant upgrading in their standard of living, once they were allowed to grow crops for commercial sale, once their commitments to the State were fulfilled, along with encouragement to develop side businesses. But in the 1990s, there was again a growing perception in rural areas that the peasantry was falling behind in the economic stakes, leading to frustration and an explosion of publicly-expressed anger.[25]

In June 1993, the Chinese authorities took the rare step of confirming that riots had occurred in Sichuan Province involving thousands of peasants said to have been angered by the heavy taxes, numerous local fees and outright bribes being demanded by rapacious officials taking the chance of the new economic freedoms to line their own pockets. The strength of the Sichuan disturbances, it seems, was sufficiently large enough to break through China's strict censorship of internal news and force the government to admit things had gone wrong. 'There were serious incidents of beating, smashing and looting', admitted an official in the Foreign Affairs Office of Sichuan, although dutifully adding that this was only the work of a handful of 'troublemakers'.

After months of simmering discontent, and occasional violence, peasants in Renshou County, about 80 kms south of the provincial capital Chengdu, ran riot over several days, beating officials, blocking traffic, destroying property, burning vehicles and holding a police officer hostage. Paramilitary police eventually dispersed the rioters with tear gas. The incident had its origins the previous year, when the government decided to build a new highway through the county and asked its relatively poor residents to shoulder about one-third of the cost. This amounted to each farmer having to pay between 30 and 50 Yuan, but according to the official accounts, even this modest amount proved too much to bear, especially as some local officials had sought to extort much more.

In one sample period of five months in 1993, peasants in Guangdong Province blocked an official motorcade to protest against their land being taken from them for industrial development, farmers in central Henan disrupted traffic on a new rail line as part of a dispute over building costs and tax collectors were attacked by hard-pressed peasants all over the country after demanding payments once too often. A letter to an official newspaper gave vent to rural anger: 'To extort the money farmers earn with their own sweat and blood will not only add to the problems of agriculture as we develop a socialist market economy, but will also sprinkle salt on the farmer's wounds.'[26]

Greed marches side by side with increased wealth and results in a collapse of egalitarian principles. Village wars with village for rights to the best land. A number of such land disputes were reported along the Yellow River in Henan, for example. In one incident, dozens of farmers, armed with clubs, beat up officials of a rival village and at least five people were injured. Paramilitary and regular police were sent and Henan authorities set up an investigation team. The land, primarily used for growing wheat, is highly valued for its fertile soil. 'Boundaries between many counties have never been clearly marked,' explained a provincial official. 'There was a bumper crop and both sides wanted to reap the profit.'

Clan wars continue to be waged largely out of sight and out of mind in many rural areas, some of them having their origins in events long before the Communists took power, and even from imperial days. In August 1993, for example, in Hunan Province, birthplace of Mao, thousands of villagers fought a pitched battle armed with home-made guns, grenades and explosives that left at least five people dead, 12 seriously wounded and several buildings in ruins. Security forces had to fire tear-gas into the crowd to split up the warring factions.[27]

Inter-regional conflicts are no longer confined to the coast-versus-hinterland syndrome. Rich provinces and cities are pitted against each other even as poor areas pummel one another with stunning ferocity. The reasons are little more than money, resources, and greed. Take the scuffles over the delineation of borders between provinces. Since 1980, more than 10 bloody clashes have taken place between the cadres and residents in Guangxi and Hunan provinces. Fifteen hundred people were allegedly killed or seriously injured in quarrels over land and water rights. Equally venomous battles have been fought between villagers living on the Qinghai-Gansu border over gold-mine rights. Two special work teams sent by the Communist Party and State Council to the area failed to solve the problem.[28] Central government arbitration has so far been required to settle disputes over ownership of some 140,000 sq. km. or about 1.5 per cent of national territory.[29]

Inter-provincial confrontations, of course, go back several centuries. Since 1949, thousands of Chinese have died in more than 1,000 armed conflicts over the imprecise demarcation of frontiers. They have worsened owing to the eclipse of central authority. For most of the new-style 'economic warlords', local development bringing tangible benefits such as wealth to close relatives and business associates is more important than heeding Beijing's call to promote national cohesiveness.[30] More significantly, the scarcity of resources – land, minerals and other resources – has become more acute as even backward areas join the craze for development. Raw material prices have soared in the world market. Such regions rich in coal and oil, such as Shanxi and Xinjiang are no longer willing to part with their products at 'brotherly' prices. Provinces in the vicinity of major mines and other natural resources often brawl over the division of spoils.[31]

A growing number of conflicts have also arisen over water resources. In the early 1980s, these conflicts were largely to do with rights regarding large rivers. Bitter struggles have since flared up between Shanxi and Inner Mongolia concerning the mid and lower reaches of the Yellow River. For example, Shanxi wants to build an artificial duct to channel water from the river, thus vastly diminishing the waterway's flow into arid Inner Mongolia. The Yangtze River is even more a subject of discord. The decision to build the Three Gorges Dam in 1992 exacerbated the enmity between Sichuan and Hubei. The latter is seen as a major beneficiary because of improved irrigation and electricity supply. Sichuan, however, opposed the project because it has to bear the environmental costs in addition to resettling a million-odd refugees displaced by higher water levels. In fact, this burden has now fallen on the city of Chongqing which in early 1997 was given an elevated status as a municipality under the direct control of the central government (following Beijing, Shanghai and Tianjin). Part of the price the city had to pay for gaining its separation from Sichuan Province was to have attached to it a large impoverished rural area, including parts where most of the resettlement of displaced peasants has to take place.

Arguments have also broken out over Yangtze tributaries, such as the Zhang River, over which Hubei and Hunan have had repeated run-ins. Practically all of the 31 provinces and directly administered cities have squared off against each other over trade barriers. Examples include one district closing its market to the goods of a rival region, or a province that will only patronize local factories. Commodities and products involved in inter-regional trade wars have ranged from cotton and silk to television sets.

The lack of cooperation between provinces is clearly demonstrated by some interesting government figures for 1990 showing the heavy dependence of most parts of the country on foreign trade, especially with Hong Kong (now, of course, part of China again), rather than dealing with each other (Table 3-1). Although it might be argued that these statistics are somewhat dated, I have no reason to believe that the situation is significantly different at the time of writing. In fact, given the country's massive export drive, one would expect to see the dependency growing even more. Data for a few key provinces such as Guangdong, Sichuan and Liaoning, collected by the Chinese Academy of Social Sciences, between 1980 and 1992, for example, demonstrates a clear decline in inter-provincial trade as the foreign element has expanded.

∞

**Table 3-1** Provincial Export Dependence in 1990

| Province | % of National Total | Dependency (%) | Main Partner |
|---|---|---|---|
| Guangdong | 18.32 | 82.66 | HK |
| Henan | 15.78 | 75.09 | HK |
| Fujian | 12.57 | 50.92 | HK |
| Liaoning | 12.53 | 47.25 | Japan |
| Hubei | 5.26 | 46.75 | HK |
| Heilongjiang | 4.24 | 41.89 | Russia |
| Gansu | 1.95 | 41.34 | HK |
| Jiangxi | 3.65 | 40.88 | HK |
| Xinjiang | 4.07 | 38.94 | Japan |
| Shaanxi | 3.24 | 35.52 | HK |
| Yunnan | 4.84 | 34.45 | Burma (Myanmar) |

Source: Almanac of Chinese Foreign Economy and Trade 1991.[32]

Turning to the social implications of the growing gap between different parts of the country, meanwhile, Wang Dongjin, Vice-Chairman of the State Commission for Restructuring the Economic System[33] has observed that prior to the introduction of the market-opening reforms in 1978, there had indeed been some gaps between urban and rural areas, and between different regions and different trades, but they had not been that great because of the egalitarian spirit that prevailed under which everyone ate a little 'from the same big rice pot'.

Low income, however, was a wet blanket to creating worker enthusiasm for production. There was a vicious cycle of 'low level productive forces-low income-egalitarianism-low enthusiasm of labourers for production-low level productivity-low level productive forces'. The introduction of the new system by Deng Xiaoping of 'distribution according to work done' led to a widening income gap. The change greatly mobilized the enthusiasm of various social sectors, emancipated and developed social productive forces and promoted prosperity and growth of the national economy, but also created new problems and contradictions.

The income distribution gap between urban and rural residents was a reality even before the introduction of reforms. In 1978, the living expenditure income for urban and rural residents averaged 316 Yuan and 134 Yuan a year respectively. The 1978–85 period witnessed fast improvement in the income for farmers and corresponding narrowing of the difference in income between urban and rural residents. In some cases, the peasants had a better lifestyle than their city cousins. But the gap began to widen again after 1986, By 1995, said Wang, the living expenditure income for urban residents on average was 2.47 times greater than that of the farmers:

> Given the natural conditions, geographical location, population distribution and many other factors, there exist differences in economic development and per capita income distribution between east, central and west China. The difference in living expenditure income between urban residents in central and west China on the one hand and urban residents in east China expanded by 19 percentage points in 1980 and 16 percentage points in 1990. From 1990 to 1995, the gap widened further (three percentage points in 1990, nine percentage points in 1995).
>
> [Meanwhile, the] per capita income for rural residents in East China was 1.7 times that for rural residents in central areas and 2.3 times that for rural residents in West China. The ratio of the per capita net income for rural residents in the central and western regions which was significant originally, widened to 1:0.74. In addition to the easily

61

found differences in income distribution for residents of the three regions, there exists a widening difference in income distribution for residents in various provinces, municipalities directly under the central government and autonomous regions outside the three economic regions, as well as for residents in lower level administrative areas in these same provinces, municipalities and autonomous regions.

From 1978 to 1996, by government calculation, the number of rural poor dropped from 250 million to 58 million. The latter live below the poverty line of 530 Yuan a year[34] are scattered in areas with inconvenient transport facilities and a poor cultural and ecological environment. The World Bank considers Beijing's definition of poverty too austere, however. It says 350 million people, just under one-third of the population, are below its international poverty standard of $1 per person per day, 5.7 times greater than the Chinese calculation. Millions of people in these remote inland areas continue to live in medieval conditions. This is no exaggeration. Chinese government officials and the media use the same expression. As the late Deng Xiaoping said on several occasions, and as his successor Jiang Zemin has reaffirmed, socialism does not equal poverty. Jiang has stated that: 'It is too embarrassing to see that there will remain several million people short of food and clothing by the end of this century when New China will have been founded for five decades.'[35]

And although there is a high profile government drive to eliminate poverty by 2000, one top legislator has suggested that in the case of the most destitute villages relocation may be the only answer if economic conditions are too harsh to improve. 'The remaining number of poor people are a real difficulty for our national poverty eradication plan because they live in extremely difficult and harsh conditions,' says National People's Congress Standing Committee member Cai Cheng. 'Villages where conditions are impossible to alter should be moved elsewhere'.[36]

One that may qualify for such treatment is the mountain village of Bapai, in south-western Guangxi Province. The rocky terrain the locals call farmland has long yielded meager crops. Bapai farmer Wu Tinghe says that ever since he can remember he had had to borrow grain every year, as the annual corn harvest his family grows on its scattered plots totalling a quarter of a hectare is only enough to feed them for nine months. His roof, like all in Bapai, is made of straw, and there is no steady water supply, let alone electricity. The village's main link with the outside world, a remote road passable only by four-wheel drive vehicles, is an hour's hike away.

Mr Wu, 34, feels he has no future in the village. Given the chance to leave, he says, 'of course I would. There is nothing I can do here'. He is not alone. When the World Bank began looking into how to stamp out poverty in the area, the first thing farmers asked for was a chance to work elsewhere, recalled senior official Alan Piazza. The bank regards helping some people find jobs in richer areas of the country as one of the easiest, most cost-effective ways to boost the prospects of Bapai and similar upland villages. The resulting labour mobility scheme, a key component of the bank's $486.4 million Southwest Poverty Reduction Project, hinges on the yawning gap between urban and rural wages and migrant workers' tendency to send earnings back home.

The average migrant working in the city sends home 2,000 Yuan a year, 10 times the average annual income in Bapai. The exodus of a few mouths to feed does little harm to poverty-hit villages. Of the 870,000 people in Guangxi covered by the project, about 400,000 are surplus labour.[37] One reason why the World Bank invested in labour mobility was because little could be done to develop upland villages, Mr Piazza said. Such areas have never been fertile and were only settled out of desperation. Anyone who has ever ridden a Chinese train during the Spring Festival (Lunar New Year) has an appreciation of the scale of migration taking place. Their belongings in a bedroll, millions of young rural workers from land-locked provinces in central and western regions clog railway-station courtyards nation-wide, often for days, and sometimes for as long as a fortnight, before they finally manage to board an overcrowded train for a city in the booming southern and coastal regions to find better paid jobs as construction workers or domestics. Their rags-to-riches dream was dramatized in a popular television series called 'Sisters From Outside', which highlighted the ups and downs of country girls working in a Shenzhen factory.

The bulk of the migrants have come from six provinces with high poverty rates and expanding pools of surplus labour: Anhui, Hunan, Hubei, Henan, Jiangxi and Sichuan. Statistics collated by these provinces indicate that in 1982 less than a million farmers left home for seasonal work in other areas; by 1993, the figure had risen to over 24 million. Sichuan has a population of 110 million, 93 million of whom live in farming communities. Provincial officials with whom I have spoken sketch out the size of the dilemma in the following statistical terms: with the population growth of recent decades, per capita land available to farmers is now less than 1 mu (one-fifteenth of a hectare). The total rural labour force at last count was 46 million, with an estimated 16 million regarded as redundant. The province only needs 20 million farmers and township enterprises and other non-agricultural sectors another 10 million. As there is less arable land than needed, a popular saying in rural Sichuan says: 'Farmers spend two months on farming, two months celebrating the Spring Festival [lunar new year] and eight months doing nothing.' In 1993, Sichuan exported five million people, two million more than the previous year. In 1994, this grew by a further 1.5 million, with the province eventually hoping to offload 10 million peasants onto other parts of China.[38]

Migration, however, remains the most controversial element in the moves to ease rural poverty and unemployment.[39] Rural job-seekers tend to be treated as second class citizens when they move to the cities, however, putting up wherever they can for the night and entitled to no welfare benefit. Such people are usually nicknamed *mangliu* (blind migrants), because they travel around the country without a definite aim, taking up any job that is going[40], and at last count there were reckoned to be 80 million of them in the major cities around the country. But despite grumbles about their presence, much of urban life now depends on 'muddy legs' building the high-rise apartments and office buildings, selling vegetables, providing the bulk of the maids and nurses, repairing shoes and collecting garbage.

It has become difficult to stop the flow since the relaxation of the system that once made it almost impossible for a Chinese citizen to move to the next village let alone to one of the big cities. In the early 1950s, peasants were free to move around the country. And as China went through a stage of rapid industrialization, large numbers of jobs were created, luring droves of peasants into the cities. But as more and more farmers settled down, the strain on the urban infrastructure increased. And mass migration affected agricultural output. In 1953, the central government issued a decree telling the rural population to stay at home. In 1957, authorities took a step further with a regulation preventing peasants from moving into the cities. The government also barred urban companies from taking on rural workers and set up special offices to repatriate farmers. In 1958 the household registration system was drawn up. From thereon, Chinese citizens were divided into urban and rural residents and the latter were forbidden to settle down in cities without approval from urban authorities.

There was a long historical tradition behind this. In the Confucian view of society, described as the 'four orders', the peasantry was actually assigned second place in terms of status, inferior only to the scholar-officials who governed the state. Social reality, however, was another matter. 'Chinese peasants lived and died in their own encapsulated world;[41] in fact, one of the most important divisions in traditional Chinese society was between the masses who lived in their villages and spent their days working the soil and the various groups who lived in the towns.'[42]

Chinese agriculture has long depended on controlling water, both in the north where inadequate and unreliable rainfall has to be supplemented by irrigation, and in the south, where rice cultivation required alternate flooding and draining of fields. Thus, prosperity, and even survival, depended on close cooperation at the everyday level of life and the mobilization of masses of people for large water-control projects. This created a value system far different than the post-Renaissance West, where individualism has been exalted as the key standard for judging social development. In China, the group was 'always paramount and the individual consistently and often mercilessly subordinated to it. Each individual had to contribute to the general welfare and do nothing to disrupt the order and stability deemed so vital to the functioning of the system on which community life depended'.[43] By and large, this same thinking justified the short-lived, abortive attempt to collectivize agriculture in the 1950s and 1960s.

Under the household registration system then prevailing, only those born in urban areas enjoy the privileged status of city dwellers. Along with their registration cards come such privileges as subsidized food, State-guaranteed employment, cheap housing, free medical care and better education opportunities. Rural families, however, have no access to these benefits. Migration to the cities required specific State approval, which was a long and arduous process. In 1984, the government issued a circular allowing farmers to seek employment in county seats and towns, and the registration system was finally abandoned in 1994. The move from countryside to the cities was also facilitated by the urban reforms which increasingly commercialized employment, the supply of housing, food and other basic commodities, as well as welfare and social securities, distributed administratively under the traditional command economy.

However, it should be stressed that the migrating peasants these days might be merely exchanging one type of hardship for another. There is now growing recognition that there is a significant amount of urban poverty which also needs to be tackled along with the moves to eradicate it in the countryside. This has led to the creation of a new social security system aimed at ensuring a minimum standard of living for urban poor throughout China which was scheduled to be in place by 1999. Permanent urban residents with a per capita income below the minimum cost of living set by local governments will benefit from the system. The decision by the State Council marked the beginning of a comprehensive reform of the social welfare system that has been taking shape since 1949, while proving inadequate to deal with the reform of the state industrial sector described in the last chapter.

Under the old centrally-planned economy, state relief policy used to be limited to helping some three million urban poor without other means of financial support. These included childless old people, orphans, the disabled or people without any income or the ability to work. With the new system, local governments provide guarantees for poverty-stricken city residents who have difficulty maintaining a basic living standard regardless of their family or work circumstances. Extensive trials begun in Shanghai in 1993 were later extended to another 206 cities, providing relief payments ranging from $8.40 $27.70 a month according to local conditions. Government statistics at the beginning of 1997 indicated that some 12 million people in 3.7 million urban families living under the locally-set poverty line. They include families with workers in loss-making state enterprises unable to meet their wage bill and those already laid off.

Faced with rising urban unemployment, and restrictions on the kind of work they can do, there are signs of a slowdown in rural migration. In 1995, six to seven per cent of the rural work-force left their villages for the city. The number fell to three to four per cent in 1996 and this trend seemed to be extending into 1997.[44] In recent years, many migrant workers from Sichuan have returned home armed with money, information and expertise they acquired while working outside their hometown and proceeded to launch their own business ventures. According to one report,[45] more than 100,000 migrant rural labourers from the province had become private merchants and entrepreneurs at home, creating 200,000 jobs.

The Ministry of Labour, Ministry of Agriculture and the State Council Development Research Centre have been working for some time to encourage this re-emigration across the country. One of the most important developments in the initial reforms was the encouragement of 'township enterprises', small factories set up by local governments and local entrepreneurs involving various forms of ownership (with cooperatives the most popular form). Township enterprises were able to recruit an average of 12.6 million workers each year from 1984 to 1988, but the numbers dropped sharply from 1989 to 1992 to an average of 2.6 million each year.[46]

In the most developed areas of the countryside, such industry now provides 80 per cent of household income. There have been many success stories reported in the State media. One such case involved the farmers of Wenzhou, in coastal Zhejiang Province, who launched a ground-breaking scheme by pooling their savings to build and run their own town. The construction of Longgang cost around $115 million, two-thirds of it on housing and the rest on infrastructure and industrial fixed assets. The entire amount was contributed by Wenzhou's residents who each contributed on average $1,550. Most were farmers-turned-salesmen/entrepreneurs who had become rich in recent years by running private and cooperative businesses.

Longgang emerged from the amalgamation of five former fishing villages that were so poor before 1979 that many residents had to beg elsewhere to survive. When the reforms began many of the fishermen turned their backs on the sea and started family businesses that quickly prospered. The result was inevitable pressure for urbanization. But the government of Cangnan County, in which Longgang is situated, did not have any budget for new construction. Instead, it contributed 6,000 Yuan as start-up funds and told everyone who wanted to build a new house that they would also have to contribute a specified amount for public facilities. The idea caught on and a new town was built on wasteland beginning in 1984. It now has a population of about 135,000.

Each of the houses on the town's main streets originally had either family-run shops or small businesses on the ground floor with residential accommodation on the upper floors. Some of the businesses (an estimated 800 turning out mainly plastic products, clothing, blankets, carpets and machinery), however, have now outgrown these small beginnings and moved into new factories. Rapid expansion was only possible because of a cooperative shareholding system. The system is practised among families in the same business when each with limited resources could no longer sustain continued growth. They pool funds, equipment and know-how as stocks and share risks and profits. The government does not interfere in the management. The system has proved its efficiency, enabling the local economy to grow by 50 per cent annually.[47]

67

In its desire to see these numbers rising again, the central government has made a major switch in its foreign investment policy. Since 1995, there has been a gradually phasing out of government incentives, such as tax reductions or exemptions, cuts in import duties and various subsidies, for coastal regions as these are no longer considered necessary to attract foreign capital; instead, the main effort is on steering would-be foreign investors to the underdeveloped interior. And the further inland one goes, the more generous they become. Inland provinces also have the right to approve overseas-funded manufacturing projects up to a value of $30 million without further reference to the central government, three times the previous ceiling.

Foreign businessman have generally been reluctant to move too far from the coast because of bad publicity about the lack of infrastructure in the interior. And it is true that until recently, the further one moved inland, the more difficult it became to make a long-distance telephone call or send a fax; the roads were bad and the railway lines inadequate to handle the efficient transport of goods; power blackouts and brownouts were a constant headache; living conditions for executives were also relatively poor – although better than the local rural populations, whose living conditions of abject poverty, were little changed from centuries earlier. But all that is changing.

The American academic A. Doak Barnett,[48] is in a unique position to make a comparison, having spent a considerable time in the region in the late 1940s, and returning in 1988 for several months of travel and study through west China. He recalls that on the first occasion, 'almost all the area was ruled by semi-autonomous warlords who controlled their own armies and ruled with an iron hand. The primary aim of these leaders was political survival not economic development. The societies they ruled were heavily militarized. Economically, the west was essentially pre-modern in every sense. Transportation and communication were still primitive. Only three railways even touched the region [. . .] the few roads were mostly unpaved. Little economic development was under way, Modern industry was almost entirely absent, and production almost everywhere was still lacking in most cities. Agriculture was based on centuries-old methods of cultivation'.[49]

The fortunes of the far interior began to change in the 1960s. With relations deteriorating with the Soviet Union, and hostility with the West undiminished, Mao decreed that the defence industry and other crucial factories should be moved to remoter parts of the country where they would be comparatively safe in case of foreign invasion. This meant investment in better transportation and communications links with the rest of the country, as well as encouraging migration from the better-off regions. As Barnett observes: 'West China entered the rail age, the motor age and the air age almost simultaneously.'[50]

New highways are linking up the various provincial capitals and being integrated into the national expressway network at a cracking pace. New railway lines are being built, typified by the new line linking Beijing with Hong Kong, and the 'Asia-Europe Continental Bridge' from the coast in Northeast China, exiting the country through Xinjiang, and then on to Rotterdam. The laying of one million kilometres of optical fiber cables, along with 130,00 kilometres of microwave lines, plus 19 satellite ground stations have revolutionized rural communications. A host of modern cities and towns have sprung up.

Between 1996 and 2000, the government said that as much as 60 per cent of the foreign preferential loans it received would be channelled to upgrade the basic facilities of the central and western regions. In seeking soft loans from foreign governments, it is also urging that these be made available not just to environmental-protection projects as at present, but also the agricultural and industrial sectors. Domestic enterprises in the interior who have a chance to cooperate with foreign investors will also be eligible for government loans to help them become more attractive to their potential partner.

This development has already had significant impact on migration patterns. In the early years of the PRC, most of those moving from east to west to work did so under compulsion rather than from choice. These were government workers and Party cadres ordered to open up the new frontier, prisoners being sent to 'reform through labour' camps and those rusticated during periods of political turmoil such as the Cultural Revolution, when it was thought that intellectuals in particular would benefit from a spell of cleaning out pigsties. Now, however, some of the peasants migrating from the countryside in search of work are heading west having discovered their are greater opportunities for employment there than in the overcrowded cities of the east. But this still remains only a trickle compared with the torrent heading for the coast described earlier.

In all these official efforts to raise rural living standards, the overriding aim is to understand the underlying causes of poverty in the country and create effective programmes to deal with it. For government officials involved in this field, the book, *China's Poverty and Anti-Poverty Strategy*, published in 1995 by Kang Xiaoguang, an economist with the Economic Research Centre of the Academy of Social Sciences, is compulsory reading.

Kang has spent many years investigating and analysing the realities of poverty, which he describes[51] as 'a structural problem, a regional problem and a classical social problem'. The so-called structural poverty problem resulted from the urban-rural disparity existing for a long time in China, in which 90 per cent or more of the people in abject poverty live in rural areas. The rural residents were put in an unequal and inferior position since they were cut off from the educational facilities, medical care, and employment opportunities available to urban people:

> Even worse, the restrictions on their free immigration to other places left them even smaller room for development. What is worth mentioning is that a general improvement of rural residents' living standards is evident as a result of the revitalizing rural economy, mushrooming township enterprises and removing the residential registration system in the recent decade. However, to substantially shorten the gap between urban and rural areas requires institutional reform.
>
> Regional poverty refers mainly to the disparity between better-developed and under-developed regions. I concentrated my research on the poor population in Guizhou,[52] Guangxi and Yunnan, three provinces in the south-west which have the lowest per-capita GDP in the country. Featured by the widespread karst (limestone) topography, the three provinces commonly have poor natural conditions either for production or for living. In addition, the social facilities and economic infrastructure are backward in comparison to other regions. There is too much agriculture and not enough industry in the economic structure which means the region has an economic baseline far behind other regions. In addition, there exists a weak social group who are put in the most unfavourable condition either in living environment, family property, employment, share of social facility and service, or food and nutrition level.

On the basis of his research, Kang said the first step in any solution was to base poverty relief action on legislation and institutions instead of merely on morality and justice. It also requires education of the bureaucrats in charge of the programmes. 'It is often a case that I hear some poverty-relief bureaucrats and those at grass-roots level in particular say in disappointment: "We have found absolutely nothing to do with these poor people. As soon as they receive the relief money, they spend it buying food and drink!" Actually, these poverty-relief officials ignore a fact that the failure of the poverty relief work in the past should be mainly attributed to the wrong belief that it is simply a matter of giving money.'

70

Kang believes that many government officials get it wrong because they have no first-hand knowledge of poverty. Before writing his book he spent several years travelling around the country and in 1994 and 1995, working as a deputy magistrate in Mashan County of Guangxi Zhuang Autonomous Region, which is one of the nation's poorest areas, in charge of working out a poverty-alleviation project with a World Bank loan. Living with the poor, and being directly exposed to their conditions, sufferings and desires exerted considerable influence on his views:

> For example, we were often puzzled that in one mountain area some families had only one pair of chopsticks, so that the several family members had to eat in turns. In addition, some families' gate doors were badly wrecked but they did not care to repair them, letting the wind and rain further tear them up. One local official commented: 'Are there any difficulties to solve these small problems? There is bamboo everywhere in the mountain, which can be used to make countless courtyard doors and chopsticks. The only conclusion is that they are too lazy to change their way of living.'
> I myself did not find a better solution for this question until the time when I was packing to return to Beijing. According to my knowledge, having enough tableware or a well-fitted gate door, the things that would bother people leading a decent life, is beyond those people's concern when they are suffering from shortage of food and clothing, the basics for survival. This is a part of the people we define as the real poor and truly needy. What is most important is that the relief work for them should be based in real understanding of the true underlying causes of the problem.

An international symposium in Beijing in 1997[53] produced the unanimous view that (1) Sustained and stable economic growth plays an important role in relieving poverty and the strategy with increase of employment as the foundation can be more beneficial to relieve poverty; (2) After selecting a suitable strategy for economic growth, it is necessary to provide the poor with public services including educational and technical training to strengthen their ability in order to use the opportunity of employment; (3) It is not sufficient to relieve poverty by only economic growth and the government has to decide policies and measures aimed at poverty relief; (4) To let the poor participate in the development relating to the stipulation and implementation of policies is very important in realizing sustained poverty relief; (5) During the course of poverty relief, we should give full play to non-governmental and grass-root organizations; and (6) Under the market economy, the poor need protection and special concern from the government, but the prerequisite is that the role of the government should not twist market mechanism and normal operation.

One of the most interesting aspects of the poverty relief programme today is the emphasis on women rather than men. For many women living in poor rural areas, the main and only concern is to manage the next meal enough for all the family. Luo Guiying, a middle-aged woman living in Gaopao Village in Guizhou Province, is typical. With three children and a tiny 0.2 hectare piece of farmland, the family did not have enough to eat by relying upon poor land with its humble yield. Luo and her husband wove bamboo baskets night and day, but the earnings were too little to entirely solve their food problem. As a wife and mother for over 10 years, Luo was always the last to sit at the dinner table. Consequently, she was physically weak through malnutrition and stomach ache.

Her bad luck came to an end in 1995 when she acquired a small loan of 2,000 Yuan. She spent all the money on buying a small number of piglets and sold them for a good profit on the market several months later. After returning the loan, she still had enough to maintain the pig raising business. For the first time, life had become manageable for Luo, who said with delight: 'Now my husband and mother-in-law smile at me often.' The loan for the piglets came from a poverty-alleviation project called the 'Programme of Happiness'. Luo is one of 10,000 rural mothers who had benefited from the programme by early 1997. Initiated in early 1995 by three organizations – The China Population Welfare Foundation, the Chinese National Family Planning Association and the Chinese Population Gazette, the charity programme was not designed to target all the people in poverty, but only poor mothers, estimated to total about one million. Being consigned to various duties at the same time such as reproduction, bread earning, preparing meals for husband, children and even parents-in-law, these women were the last to enjoy life. They have been placed in an even more inferior situation than male adults, since most are semi-illiterate, cut off from information beyond their villages that would enable them to enter the mainstream of life.

The Programme of Happiness has sought a successful way to help the poor mothers through small loans ranging from 1,000 to 5,000 Yuan. This is enough for them to run a profitable household business such as raising oxen, sheep, planting fruit trees, or making bamboo ware and embroidery. For example, nearly every farmhouse in some Guizhou Province rural areas are good at making bean curd.

By providing just a 500 Yuan loan for a poor mother can help her open a small business of her own. Sometimes, project staff will lend her the necessary materials such as oxen, sheep and feed. The loan may be repaid in one or two years, and the money she will pay off will immediately be given to the next eligible woman. This practice operating in a village or community creates pressure on the poor mother to pay off her loan on time, since her neighbours may be impatiently waiting.

The Chinese National Family Planning Association, a national organization of 1.02 million local bodies and 83 million staff, has got involved because its traditional function has been declining with the general acceptance of birth control around the country. The staff's good information about every household and friendly relationship with various government departments concerned make them a most efficient and convenient tool to carry out the task in the vast rural areas.

The Programme of Happiness has become a real part of the women's liberation movement in its implementation. Its slogans call for wiping out poverty, illiteracy and disease. After the poor mothers qualified for a loan are selected, they must attend a special school which teaches them basic reading and writing and the necessary production skills. Their school marks will determine if they eventually get a loan. Now, almost every village where the programme operates has established a 'mother's school'.

Pilot work on the programme first started in four counties: Puding in Guizhou Province, Lixian in Gansu Province, Qianshan in Anhui Province and Dali in Shaanxi Province. The organizing committee put in 100,000 Yuan for each, which was doubled by a matching donation by the county government. About 300 poor mothers in the four counties benefited and by now more than 70 per cent have returned the loan. It was extended to 15 counties in 1996 and 40 in 1997.

'Traditionally, a rural woman is a humble figure in the family, not seriously regarded as a major bread-winner despite her day and night labours. The programme has dramatically changed attitudes. When some husbands travelling far away from their village to seek seasonal jobs heard the surprising news that their wives had got a loan and were starting to run a household business, they could not wait to rush home to provide help. Rural women used to be a silent group, without a big say in family or public affairs. The programme encourages better educated women with less children by giving them priority for loans. Consequently, these women have become

73

eloquent orators in their villages often persuading others to read more while not stubbornly giving birth to too many children.'[54]

The State, meanwhile, continues to increase its funding in more high profile projects for rural poverty alleviation. In 1996, of the $1.3 billion allocated for this purpose, a little over 50 per cent came from interest-free loans. More than $480 million will be added to the figure annually. Local governments are also obliged to put aside money for use in poverty elimination in their own regions. If they fail to contribute between 30–50 per cent of the sum provided by the central government, those sums themselves will be cut accordingly.

Coastal-hinterland cooperation is also encouraged to narrow the gap between affluence and poverty. In 1996, some 2,500 cooperative projects were signed, involving the transfer of $3.6 billion in capital to township enterprises in central and Western regions. In 1996, nine eastern provinces and a number of prosperous coastal cities were directly called on for more help. Each is being held responsible for assisting one Western province or autonomous region. Beijing has been 'twinned' with the Inner Mongolia Autonomous Region, while Shanghai assists Yunnan Province, for example.

But this then raises the specter of 'internal colonialism'. The richer regions are predominantly coastal and predominantly Han (ethnic Chinese), whereas the poorer internal regions contain substantial minority populations. Moreover, it is the Han who seem to benefit most from the development within the interior/minority regions as they flood in to build new factories, mines and infrastructure. The marginalization and exclusion of other ethnic groups and provinces from the wealth of the richer regions could prove a potent brew should regional revolt ever become an issue.[55]

Hence, even while seeking to bring the interior into the mainstream in the interests of national stability, the central government also has to step carefully in this matter for the very same reasons.

# ■ CHAPTER 4

# Population Control and the Pressures of Aging

China faces three population headaches: more babies being born, an increasing number of people entering the working age group (15–64), and an increasingly aging population, as life expectancy improves. All three strain the ability of the social welfare system to support them with a decent pension and health insurance, and unemployment insurance for the jobless. One expert[1] has described this situation as 'a wolf ahead and a tiger behind'. The wolf is a third baby boom in the current decade as there are 320 million women of childbearing age (15–49 years), eight per cent more than the 1980s, including 122 million women in the prime age of 23 to 29. They will produce an estimated average 20 million babies every year. The tiger is the graying of the population. It has been calculated that the proportion of people aged 65 or more will reach 7.22 per cent by the end of this century, 11.69 per cent by 2020 and 20.6 per cent by 2040. By mid-century, a quarter of the population will be over 60. This has major social, economic and political implications (see Table 4-1).

The latest population census found only five provinces and municipalities (Shanghai, Beijing, Zhejiang, Tianjin and Liaoning) where the natural population growth has dropped below 10 per thousand. The rate in at least 10 other provinces and autonomous regions is at or above 17 per thousand, and in several areas is as high as 24 per thousand. Nearly two-thirds of the population is aged between 15 and 59.

It is estimated that by the year 2000 about 858 million Chinese will enter the working age group between 15 and 64 – about 20 million more than all the developed nations of the world put together. By

**Table 4-1** Changes in Age Structure of China's Population 1953–95(%)

| Age Group | 1953 | 1964 | 1982 | 1990 | 1995 |
|---|---|---|---|---|---|
| 0–14 | 36.3 | 40.7 | 33.6 | 27.6 | 26.6 |
| 15–59 | 56.4 | 53.2 | 58.8 | 63.8 | 64.0 |
| 60+ | 7.3 | 6.1 | 7.6 | 8.0 | 9.4 |
| 80+(Out of 60+) | 4.5 | 4.3 | 6.6 | 7.9 | 8.6 |

*Source:* China Population Today, December 1997.

then, about 233 million people expected to seek employment for the first time each year, especially in the countryside. China has done a great deal to curb its population, with the family planning programme estimated to have averted some 200 million births since 1970. But the sheer number of people involved again make it hard to produce any drastic reduction in the short term.

As an agricultural economy, China has long had to wrestle with the problem of feeding many mouths. The first national census, which might be considered generally reliable, in 1741, recorded a total population of 143,411,559. Nine years later, this had grown to just over 177 million, and by 1850, census-takers were counting a population drastically expanded to almost 430 million, mainly ascribed to favourable economic and political conditions created by a long period of peace in the reign of Emperor Qianlong (1736–95), and the introduction of foreign food staples such as maize, sweet potatoes and peanuts. Some authorities, however, think these population figures somewhat understate the total picture.[2]

But in an echo of the debate still being conducted today, the population increased faster than land acreage, causing a decline in the standard of living. Between 1661 and 1812, agricultural land increased by less than 50 per cent, the population by more than 100 per cent. 'The displaced, the poor and the unemployed often turned to banditry or became recruits for rebel outfits.'[3] Today, as was discussed in the previous chapter, they migrate to the cities.

Although there has long been a high birth-rate, in the past this was countered by a similarly high death rate, due to a low standard of living and poor sanitation, as well as frequent calamities such as famines, floods and wars. But during the 22 years of Nationalist rule (1927–49) the birth-rate was estimated at 35 per thousand and the death rate 25 per thousand, representing a yearly net gain of 10 persons per thousand. In an early study by the PRC government in the 1950s, the average annual birth-rate was put at 37 and the death-rate 17 per thousand – due to the government's successful public health work, improvement in living conditions and drastic reduction in infant mortality – for a natural increase of 20 per thousand.[4] By the mid-1970s, the death-rate was reported to have fallen as low as 6–7 per thousand.[5] The peak in the natural growth population rate was reached about this time at 25.83 per thousand, before beginning to turn down again.

At the end of the First Five Year Plan (1953–7) Ma Yinchu drew attention to the problems posed for economic development by population growth, then at 23 per thousand. He was criticized heavily and only sporadic attempts were made between 1949 to the late 1960s to reduce fertility rates. The official view for most of the time was that the growing population posed no threat to development, and, indeed, Mao himself spoke of birth-control as a 'way of killing off the Chinese people without shedding blood'[6].

Yet, within three years of his death in 1976, his successors were introducing a strict family planning policy that prevails to this day with claims of great achievements in curbing over-rapid population growth. The crude birth-rate dropped from 22.4 per thousand in 1980 to 17.2 per thousand in 1995, the rate of natural increase from 15.6 per thousand to 10.5 per thousand, and the total fertility rate (TFR) from 2.2 to 1.9 births per couple. The State Statistics Bureau in 1996 projected China's population size from 2000 to 2050 (see Table 4-2), assuming the TFR remaining stable at 1.9, showing an increase from the present 1.2 billion to 1.27 billion in 2000, peaking at 1.48 billion in 2030, and then settling back to 1.42 billion in 2050. To be on the safe side, however, most discussions take a maximum population of 1.6 billion.

The present population accounts for 22 per cent of the world's total, but provided with only seven per cent of global arable land. In addition, it has only one-quarter of the world average of per-capita freshwater resources, less than a sixth of the per capita share of forested areas, less than 50 per cent of grasslands, and its proven mineral resources are only a quarter of the global average. This will be considered in more detail later in respect to the country's ability to feed itself. Although national income has grown rapidly, a quarter of the annual increase has been eaten up by new population growth, resulting in reduced fund accumulation and delayed economic construction. A fast growing population is also a burden on employment, education, housing, transportation and health care. Family planning, therefore, is vital not only to the existence and development of the Chinese people, but also to the stabilization and prosperity of the entire human race.

77

According to Peng Yu, Vice Minister of the State Family Planning Commission,[7] the core of this policy is 'a preference for late marriage and child-bearing, fewer and better births, and advocating one child per couple in the urban areas'. It also incorporates persuading rural couples who are officially allowed to have two children to space births appropriately. Ethnic minorities, although under few, if any, restrictions, are also encouraged to implement family planning.

The key measures of the programme are:

☐ Responsibility and leadership by local authorities. Each year the State Council convenes a family planning work meeting of provincial, autonomous regional and municipal leaders. Each local government brings population planning into line with its own comprehensive economic and social development scheme, places family planning on the government agenda and coordinates all relevant departments in implementing the programme and providing labour, financial and material guarantees.

☐ Widespread and persistent publicity on the advantages of family planning to raise public awareness and scientific knowledge. Training classes for different age groups of different conditions have been conducted in both rural and urban areas to give wide-ranging education to adolescents, newly-weds and women facing pregnancy, childbearing, child-rearing and menopause. Non-governmental organs such as women's federations, trade unions, youth leagues, and family planning and population associations also play a great role in birth control.

☐ Efforts to provide contraceptives and birth-control technical services.

☐ Advancement of all aspects of family planning. It recent years, with the development of a socialist market economy, endeavours have been made to combine family planning with economic progress, poverty aid, enhancement of women's status and establishment of cultured and happy families.

☐ Enhancing the social welfare system, especially in commercializing life insurance and pension schemes, and encouraging farmers in particular to buy them.

In a developing country such as China, the focal point of family planning must lie in the countryside. Government officials and family planning workers have made unremitting efforts to show couples this is in the interests of themselves and their children, fewer births being equated with faster prosperity. In the past, couples had a large number of children due to the need to have someone to care for them in their old age, along with an assumption that some of the offspring would die in childhood.

Some provinces, such as Sichuan and Hunan, have published preferential policy for families that practice birth control. The main aspects are: priority in arrangements of wealth-creating projects; funding assistance for production activities and related loans; employment in township enterprises; and land supply for production contracts. In addition, families with one child enjoy receive endowment, insurance, social security insurance and related policies for the their children. Children from one-child families might attend nurseries and primary schools free of charge. The current population of Sichuan exceeds 110 million, equivalent to the combined population of Britain and France, and it continues to grow at an annual rate of 1.1 million. But family planning awareness is growing.

In Daba, a mountainous area in northern Sichuan, for example, a large population and limited land mean most people subsist in dire poverty. As a result, they depend on economic aid provided by the state civil affairs departments and provincial government. Maying, a township located 2,800 metres above sea level, is linked with county seat some 40 km away by a twisting mountain highway. Small patches of crops cling precariously to the mountain slopes. Local farmers treasure every inch of land, planting crops on every available plot that can possibly be cultivated.

Before family planning was introduced, local couples typically had three to four children, and some had as many as 10. Today, even though the government encourages each couple to have only one child, many families still wish for more, as the difficult terrain requires greater labour intensity and thus more labourers. Lu Quande, a 30-year-old farmer, has a son and has decided not to have a second child. His family is one of the 35 families in his village which benefit from the local government's plan to assist those who practise family planning. The county science commission has invested heavily to help the households build methane-generating pits for cooking and lighting.

Wang Shufa, a township enterprise manager, only has a daughter. His parents gave birth to seven children and four have survived, of which three are illiterate. The whole family supported him to complete a higher middle school education. His willingness to practise family planning is also a result of government policies. He received a preferential loan of 680,000 Yuan for the establishment of his factory, and his daughter is receiving a free primary school education as promised by the government when he applied for the only child card. Lu Zehua's parents had seven girls. The family has to rely on the state's relief grain to survive, and all the girls are illiterate. Lu is determined not to follow her parent's examples into a tragic cycle of giving birth to more children because of poverty, and becoming poorer due to more mouths to feed. She understands family planning is essential for those who seek to escape poverty.

The status of women has improved step by step with the implementation of family planning, helping to free them from the virtual slavery of frequent births (and high maternal mortality) and given them more chances of participating in state and social affairs management, economic activities and studies of scientific, technological and cultural knowledge. Meanwhile, women's status in the family has changed greatly.[8]

In many areas, poverty relief and birth control are promoted jointly. The government and international aid organizations have both come to favour giving financial aid only to the woman of the family, rather than her husband, encouraging the former to start her own business. This not only brings in much needed cash, but also improves the status of the woman within the family.[9] In recent years, no family in the Daba area has seen the birth of a third child. In 1994, the township's birth-rate was 9.29 per thousand, with the natural population growth rate standing at 7.02 per thousand, a figure lower than the 10 per thousand characteristic of the province.[10]

One of the most controversial questions regarding the Chinese family planning programme is whether there is any coercion involved in promoting birth-control. The Western media has frequently carried stories of forced abortion, even forced sterilization; at the very least, it is suggested, those who violate the one-child policy face social ostracism, punitive fines and even loss of their jobs. So, what is the Chinese response to these allegations of compulsion? After extensive conversations with various government officials in Beijing, the various responses can be crystallized as follows:

> Whether or not a pregnant woman has a sterilization or abortion depends totally on her own wish. If she refuses to do so, no coercive action will work. In fact, each year there are some non-planned births.[11] China does not advocate induced abortion as a means of birth-control. Instead, it has always stressed putting education and preventive measures first when implementing family planning as day-to-day work. Now, 75 per cent of childbearing couples nation-wide

have adopted contraceptive measures. The Chinese government promotes voluntary adoption of birth control on the basis of extensive education and opposes forced imposition of it.

However, we don't deny that shortcomings and mistakes occur. China is very vast, with over 3,000 counties and the standard of officials varies. In some areas, coercion may happen in the initial phases of family planning activity. On finding such actions we resolve them resolutely.

But, there are some in the West who still hold that China's population control violates human rights and personal freedom. So how do officials respond to that belief?

The issue of population, fundamentally speaking, is an issue of development. For developing countries to seek subsistence and progress is the most basic and imminent task. Only by proceeding from our population features and national conditions, and formulating and exercising population policies and goals that conform to national, community, family and individual interests in the effort to seek economic development, can we find a way for solving the population problem. In the practice of family planning, we are always opposed to coercion. But, this does not imply a *laissez-faire* attitude, because traditional concepts such as the idea that a son is essential to carry on the family line still exist, so education is required. The majority of farmers still face difficulties in production and living. In addition, the reduction of the high birth-rate in some areas will greatly hinge on raising the status of women, improving adequate care for the elderly and developing consultative services and technical guidance. The implementation of family planning in China follows the principle of respecting and safeguarding the wishes of individuals and couples with regard to birth, whilst also encouraging them to fulfil their duties for society and children.

Of all the affronts a man can offer his parents, the most serious is to fail to have a child to carry on the family line: such is the philosophy that has influenced the Chinese people for more than 2,000 years. But nowadays, in some of the larger cities, a growing number of young couples prefer not to have children at all.

A survey of voluntarily childless couples in Beijing found that almost 74 per cent of them were officials and intellectuals.[12] Another placed childless couples in five groups. The first were afraid children might stand in their way of achieving professional goals. The second type did not want to see their love for each other buried in the household chores inseparable from bringing up children. As some of them aptly put it: 'Once a couple have a child, there is a mass of trifling matters to attend to, like washing milk bottles and diapers and, with the wife naturally turning her mind to the child, less exchange of affection between the two but more conflict and quarrels.' The third group considered having a child irrelevant to the happiness of a family, while a fourth group preferred not to have children due to lack of money and a desire not to further depress their already modest living standards. The fifth group preferred to be childless because they had been 'bitterly disappointed to see the way many parents were forsaken by their children when they grew old, after all the hardships they suffered to bring them up'.[13]

While this may help to bring down the Chinese birth-rate, it is not necessarily good for the country. Demographer Yang Wihui, for example, calls the phenomenon 'inversive growth', by which he means a population increase in an undesirable way: well-educated, urban people who did not want children, while poorly-educated rural people gave birth one after another. According to Yang: 'This will hinder the improvement of our population quality.' Table 4-2 shows the implications of the declining birth-rate on the country's future educational structure, with shrinking numbers, particularly for all levels of education from primary to tertiary.

Although population growth has slowed down over the past two decades of birth-control efforts, it also being influenced by another phenomenon: an increased number of Chinese living longer lives. It is reckoned that the Chinese mainland currently has more than 20,000 people celebrating their 60th birthday every 24 hours. Those in the age group of 60 and above has exceeded 100 million, growing to 130 million by 2002, or more than over 10 per cent of the population.[14] The aging of the population will approach its peak period by the middle of the next century, with the percentage of people aged beyond 60 making up 27.4 per cent of the total. The key issues created by this development are reckoned to be:

**Table 4-2** Changes in School-Age Population (in millions)

| Year | Primary | Junior and Secondary | University |
|------|---------|----------------------|------------|
| 1995 | 130.12 | 117.03 | 106.24 |
| 2000 | 132.99 | 127.16 | 97.47 |
| 2010 | 113.38 | 122.85 | 111.50 |
| 2020 | 112.48 | 107.82 | 94.68 |
| 2030 | 106.59 | 112.30 | 92.96 |
| 2040 | 96.35 | 100.83 | 88.92 |
| 2050 | 94.69 | 97.27 | 79.88 |

Source: Population and Employment Department, State Statistics Bureau.

The fast rate of aging is due to a sharp fall in births and mortality. The variation of population structure has evolved over many generations, or as long as a 100 years, in some countries, while it took only 21 years in China, giving it less time to prepare.

A dual economy composed of traditional agriculture and modern industry is still in place in China. There are gaps between urban and rural areas, and between different regions in economic and cultural development. They also vary regarding the aging process. Therefore, a unitary national policy will fail to meet the needs of all regions and sections. Industrialization and urbanization have accompanied the population's aging in developed countries. Economic growth has presented these countries with a needed material foundation. In contrast, the aging of population in China results from the successful implementation of family planning, but has not been synchronized with national economic progress. Economic under-development will make it more difficult to cope with problems associated with aging.[15]

The Chinese have been noted for their traditional values of respect for the elderly and the habit of caring for elderly parents at home. One reason that the elderly were so treasured was that with such a low life expectancy, they were in fact a rare commodity and like other scarce resources were much valued. In a peasant society whose members were frequently illiterate, an old person would be a repository for much useful practical knowledge about crops, weather, religious practices, childbirth and medicine, to say nothing of gossip and history. This tied in with the traditional large and extended nature of the Chinese family, with several generations living under the same roof.

This made sense in a basically territorially stable, agrarian society where much labour was needed on the farm. But there have been many changes since 1949. As life expectancy has increased the numbers of the proportion of the aged in China have also grown. While they are still very much respected, sheer weight of numbers has diluted their rarity to the extent that care of them is perceived as presenting problems rather than encouraging the family to carry out their traditional responsibilities. By the third decade of the next century, 100 working-age people will have to support 40 of their elders and 30 children. With the dependency ratio at its peak, the burden may prove intolerable, especially as the working-age population is also aging (see Table 4-3).

To further confound the traditional picture, it appears that the family structure increasingly is moving towards the nuclear pattern.

**Table 4-3** Trend of the Dependency Ratio of China's population 1991–2050

| Year | Total Pop. (b) | 0–14(%) | 15–59 | 60+ | 65+ | Child D/dency Ration Ratio | Aged D/dency Ratio | Total D/dency Ratio |
|------|------|------|------|------|------|------|------|------|
| 1991 | 1.161 | 27.55 | 63.70 | 8.75 | 5.69 | 43.24 | 13.74 | 56.98 |
| 1995 | 1.231 | 27.78 | 62.92 | 9.30 | 6.11 | 44.16 | 14.79 | 58.94 |
| 2000 | 1.304 | 27.08 | 63.03 | 9.84 | 6.71 | 42.94 | 15.60 | 58.54 |
| 2005 | 1.357 | 24.51 | 65.07 | 10.42 | 7.21 | 37.66 | 16.02 | 53.68 |
| 2010 | 1.400 | 21.40 | 66.82 | 11.77 | 7.71 | 32.03 | 17.62 | 49.65 |
| 2015 | 1.442 | 19.51 | 66.37 | 14.12 | 8.84 | 29.40 | 21.77 | 50.67 |
| 2020 | 1.483 | 19.04 | 65.41 | 15.55 | 10.85 | 29.10 | 23.77 | 52.88 |
| 2025 | 1.513 | 18.83 | 62.70 | 18.47 | 12.06 | 30.04 | 29.46 | 59.50 |
| 2030 | 1.529 | 18.04 | 60.03 | 21.93 | 14.64 | 30.05 | 36.54 | 66.59 |
| 2035 | 1.532 | 16.84 | 58.79 | 24.37 | 17.63 | 28.65 | 41.45 | 70.11 |
| 2040 | 1.528 | 16.07 | 58.81 | 26.11 | 19.57 | 27.33 | 42.70 | 70.03 |
| 2045 | 1.519 | 59.94 | 58.19 | 26.87 | 19.97 | 27.39 | 44.46 | 71.84 |
| 2050 | 1.502 | 16.01 | 56.56 | 27.43 | 20.43 | 28.31 | 48.49 | 76.80 |

Source: Du Peng, 'A Study on the Aging Process of China's Population' (1997).

Some surveys suggest as many as 45 per cent of families are of this type, although it is more common in the cities than the rural areas. Clearly, much of the care of the elderly remains family-based, as it has been for centuries. There are signs, however, that the easy assumption that families will automatically look after their aged members may no longer be relied upon. The declining size of family and the escalating pace of life are destined to make it increasingly difficult for families to adequately care for aged members. The problem will be particularly severe for one-child families. As a result care for the aged is destined to become one of China's most significant social problems.

In the cities, the problem of family care for the aged has become increasingly complicated. Only a small number of senior citizens have so far moved into the convalescent homes now springing up in urban areas, most still preferring to be looked after by family members. Unfortunately, this tradition is being challenged as the introduction of the market economy has dramatically accelerated the pace of life and altered family relationships. Many people, though feeling duty-bound to show filial piety to their parents, lack time or energy to look after them.[16] Furthermore, the urban housing shortage prevents many retirees from living with their children. Moreover, owing to the generation gap, many elders complain that they have little rapport with their children, leading to conflict.[17]

The Marriage Law states: 'Children have the duty to support and assist their parents. Parents who have lost the ability to work or have difficulties in providing for themselves have the right to demand that their children pay for their support.' This provision extends to include grandparents and maternal grandparents whose children have died. If children refuse to pay up then 'in cases where the relevant party refuses to execute judgement or rulings regarding the cost of support, the people's court has the power to enforce the execution in accordance with the law'. The Criminal Law takes this even further when it states 'whoever, having responsibility for the support of an aged person, flagrantly refuses to support that person, shall be sentenced to imprisonment for not more than five years or to detention or to public surveillance'.[18]

A system of support contracts was first introduced in Jiangsu Province in 1986 and they have become popular in Hunan, Hubei, Beijing and Tianjin. These are agreements witnessed by local government officials between a child, or children, and the parents. The contract specifies what support the parents may expect from the child and if there is more than one child which one will provide food, which one clothing and fuel etc. In return, the parents have to specify how their possessions will be divided on their deaths. A son or daughter breaking the agreement would first be spoken to in an attempt to change their attitude. Should this fail, it is possible for support payments to be deducted from their salaries at source and paid directly to the parents.

But in the final analysis, China has to deal with the problems associated with an aging population by combining features of traditional culture with an active programme of socio-economic development level. Above all, it needs to step up the current efforts to perfect the social welfare system, especially with regard to old-age pensions which currently cover less than a third of the elderly either through work-related or voluntary schemes, as well as considering the offer of subsidies or the exemption of certain taxes to encourage family support of the aged.

Prior to 1966, the central government paid out pensions to enterprise workers under a unified plan, a system that was cancelled during the tumultuous years of the Cultural Revolution. At the time, employers were asked to take over the burden. Because of poor economic conditions, however, some firms had to reduce or even halt payments. Older enterprises suffered more than newer ones because of the greater percentage of aging workers. Pensions for retired silk and textile workers in Wuxi, Jiangsu Province, for example, were equivalent to 40 per cent of the total salaries for active workers, while in the grain industry, it was almost 50 per cent.

But, as pensions were paid out of profits retained by the enterprises, enthusiasm for hard work amongst the remaining work-force was considerably diminished.[19]

In fact, the establishment of a sound pension system may resolve many problems faced by China in its economic transition. Between the late 1990s and 2020, more than 70 million people will retire. Payments for their pensions will amount to more than $96 billion by then.[20] The State Council has decided that the effective solution to the challenges posed is the creation of a national unified multi-level pension system funded by State finances, enterprises and individuals. At present, the old-age pension plan covers 78 per cent of the work-force; in State enterprises, coverage rises to 95 per cent.[21] But, as discussed in an earlier chapter, the state industrial sector has found the burden of having to support a large number of retired workers extremely onerous, and this is often the key factor in the large debt levels many companies are now faced with.

However, the establishment of an effective pension fund system will also require the creation of a more diverse range of financial institutions. The specialized State banks and credit cooperatives in the countryside now play a dominant role in the domestic financial market. In developed countries, however, such financial institutions as savings banks, building societies, government or private pension funds, and life insurance companies usually act as economic engines.

In 1995, around 95 per cent of all Chinese citizens' savings flowed into banks, but the bulk of it[22] was then disbursed as loans to State enterprises, who, due to their long-term deficits often struggled to make the necessary payments and created an endless debt chain. This raises the specter of savings insecurity. By the end of 1995, outstanding savings deposits stood at the equivalent of $357.37 Billion, that is 51.4 per cent of the gross national product (GNP), rising to $427.20 billion. An important reason why people have deposited such large amounts is that they want to use them for old-age care. Because of the lack of alternative financial institutions, they are obliged to accept the meager interest returns offered by the banks of around three or four per cent. Another alternative is to speculate on the securities market, which runs counter to the principles of safe pension management.

# CHAPTER 5

# Who Will Feed China?

Having considered the two key contributors to a growing population in more births and longer life expectancy, it is now necessary to place this within a wider context of whether China has the ability to continue feeding itself in the twenty-first century. Amid all the predictions that it will eventually possess the world's largest economy, how is this going to impact on the world food situation in general? A figure repeatedly used by the Chinese themselves shows that although China accounts for at least 22 per cent of the world's population it has only seven per cent of its allocation of arable land. In addition, per capita arable land is one-third lower than the world average. Compounding the problem, its water resources account for a mere seven per cent of the world total, with per capita figures significantly lower than the world average.

It was Lester Brown, Director of the Worldwatch Institute in Washington, who raised the issue of 'who will feed China in 2030', and in a number of his writings he has created somewhat of a grim scenario of Chinese eating their way through the world's diminishing food supplies as their own ability to produce enough food is eroded by the growing demands of industrialization. Brown argues that with their incomes rising, the Chinese are quickly diversifying their diets, shifting from heavy dependence on a single starchy staple, such as rice, to one that contains more livestock products. Consumption of pork has quadrupled to 30 million tonnes in 1994, making China the world's leading consumer of red meat. Consumption of poultry in the 1990s doubled to 6.6 million tonnes in 1994. During this period, China also moved rapidly from being a net grain exporter to an importer in the mid-1990s. Its overnight emergence as a leading importer of grain, second only to Japan, drove up world grain prices, promising to raise food prices everywhere. The need for more grain is also influenced by the official goal of doubling egg consumption to 200 a year per person by 2000.

Meanwhile, the industrialization that is raising incomes is simultaneously undermining food production with its claims on cropland. In the southern coastal provinces where industrialization is most rapid, land that was until recently producing two or three crops of rice a year is now occupied by industrial parks. This loss of some of China's most productive land has reduced the mainland's rice harvest by seven per cent since 1990. In recent years, an estimated 100 million workers have left the countryside to seek jobs in the cities. Since each factory in the private sector employs just over 100 workers, creating the 100 million jobs needed to absorb this flow of migrants will require roughly one million factories. Building a million factories and the associated warehouses and access roads will take a vast area of land, much of it cropland. The factories have to be sited where the people are, and most of the population are concentrated in a 1,600-km strip along the eastern and southern coasts, where the cropland is.[1] More land will be lost through the country's commitment to developing its vehicle manufacturing industry as a powerful engine of economic growth, leading to the need for far more roads, especially expressways, to house the increased factory output.

'Water may be even more scarce than land,' says Brown. 'With the demand for water increasing six-fold since 1949, the northern half of the country has become a water-deficit region. The water table under Beijing has fallen from 4.5 metres below the surface to 45 metres below since 1950. Eventually, these aquifers will be depleted. At that point, pumping will necessarily reduce the rate of aquifer recharge, reducing the irrigated area accordingly. As well as these coming cutbacks in irrigation, farmers are losing water to the cities, some 300 of which face acute water shortages. In early 1994, farmers in the agricultural regions surrounding Beijing were banned from water reservoirs. All the water is now needed for residential and industrial uses in the city, thus forcing farmers to return to less productive rain-fed farming.'[2]

If, as conjectured, China continues to import huge amounts of grain, can it afford to do so? The answer would seem to be yes given the healthy foreign reserves. But, more important: can the world supply China's needs? Brown thinks not. 'If China's rapid industrialization continues, its import demand will soon overwhelm the export capacity of the United States and other grain-exporting countries. More than 100 countries depend on the United States for grain as well as China, including many whose needs are also rising rapidly.' He concludes:

> With its grain imports climbing, China's rising grain prices are now becoming the world's rising grain prices. As the slack goes out of the world food economy, China's land scarcity will become everyone's land scarcity. As irrigation water losses force it to import more grain, its water scarcity will become the world's water scarcity. [This] is a wake-up call telling leaders everywhere that the world is on an economic and demographic path that is not environmentally sustainable.

Leading China's response to this dark scenario, Nong Ruan, a member of the Soft Science Committee of the Ministry of Agriculture,[3] says:

> Older generations may still remember that just before the founding of New China in 1949, some predicted the Chinese government might not be able to solve the problem of feeding its people. But the fact is that over the past 45 years, China's grain output has increased dramatically. Although the per capita cultivated land has decreased from 2.7 mu to 1.2 mu,[4] the per capita consumption of grain has grown from 209 kg to 380 kg in the past two decades. Admittedly, China will still be plagued in the coming decades by the pressure of population growth and reduction of farmland as industrialization continues to accelerate. But the inferences that China's grain output will significantly decline, and the assertion that the Chinese are unable to support themselves do not tally with the actual situation in China and lack a scientific basis.

Nong argues that the conclusions of Western analysts like Brown are based on the experiences of Japan and the Republic of Korea, who both imported large amounts of grain due to the reduction of domestic output during their period of industrialization. 'It is impossible for China to rely on others to feed its huge population. The Chinese government has long followed a basic policy for being basically self-sufficient in grain, and it will continue to make unremitting efforts in this regard.

'Brown and others have predicted that the grain output in China will decline by at least one-fifth during the 1990–2030 period because as it turns rapidly from an agricultural country into an industrial one, vast tracts of farmland are taken over and per unit grain yield may not see significant growth. According to their calculations, the cultivated area in China will decline from 1.435 billion mu in 1990 to 1.148 billion mu in 2030. Although this is too alarmist, the fact is that the loss of current arable land can be offset by better methods of crop production, and the potential for utilizing land presently considered as marginal.'

Jian Song, Chairman of the State Science and Technology Commission,[5] adds his reassuring voice. For a population that may in a worst case scenario reach 1.6 billion in the mid-twenty-first century, he anticipates a need to produce 640 million tons of grain annually to meet basic needs based on per capita annual consumption of 400 kg:

> A study of the present food situation and the potentials of cultivable land resources and grain production indicates that the target to produce 640 million tons of grain annually is both indispensable and attainable. Therefore, great efforts must be made to guarantee an additional increase of grain output by 160 million tons or 30 per cent in the coming 30 to 40 years. That means China's grain output should increase one per cent annually.
>
> The extensive application of the genetic technique will substantially contribute to the national grain output. China has a great potential of arable land resources to be tapped. It is reported that there are 20 million hectares of cultivable wasteland and 250 million hectares of grassland not fully made use of. These lands can either be reclaimed for crop growing or for raising more domestic animals. It is estimated that China can easily produce 818 million tons of grain annually if farming techniques, irrigation in particular, record a substantial improvement in the coming decades. Theoretically, the country can turn out 1,026 million tons at the maximum each year, according to an estimate by the Academy of Sciences.

One authoritative analysis[6] insists that self-reliance in agricultural products did not mean a 100 per cent rate of self-sufficiency. In fact, China was too self-reliant and should be importing more! It recommended progressive reductions, with the self-sufficiency rate in the near term lowered from the present 98 per cent to 95 per cent. In the intermediate term, a further reduction to 90 per cent could be aimed for, with a figure of below 90 per cent the long-term goal.

The analysis insisted this was still a very high rate, but a distinction had to drawn between basic foodstuff consumed by the population and feed consumed by the animal husbandry and various other industries. For rice and wheat, two major staple foods, a high level of self-sufficiency is necessary, but for feed and industrial grain, more dependence on imports was acceptable. 'Judging from the present supply and demand of food, in the next 30–40 years demand for food will overtake supply along with increases in the total population and per capita consumption of farm products. While self-reliance and self-sufficiency are the strategic, long-term goals, an adequate level of imports and food trading are tactical options.'

The analysis noted that for years China had been both an importer and exporter of grain. During 1991–3, China was the largest importer of wheat, the second largest exporter of corn and the fourth largest exporter of rice. In the future, it should gradually reduce exports of grain while drastically increasing exports of non-grain products, so as to realize a surplus in China's foreign trade of farm products:[7]

> In fact, China can not only feed itself, but can also help feed the world. In international trade (including grain and farm products) a system based on mutual exchange of commodities, there is no such thing as who feeds whom. There is no need to dodge the international resources and markets just because Mr Brown has raised the question of who will feed China. We should not be taken in by Mr Brown's pessimism and stick to the 100 per cent rate of self-sufficiency. The Chinese are fully capable and competent of feeding themselves. This means that the Chinese have the capacity to both produce grain and to trade for grain. As the country's per capita income and overall national power rise steadily so is the Chinese people's capability to feed themselves.
>
> China and the United States are the only two countries in the world able to feed more than one billion. Yet China, with only half of the arable land of the United States and much more backward farming technology, produces 114 per cent of food Americans produce and feeds a population 4.58 times the size of the American population. This fact represents a major contribution China makes in the world in feeding the world's inhabitants.

This all seems very reassuring. But, let us examine the grounds for this optimism in more detail. First, there must be some concern at the continuing loss of land used for agricultural production. In the 1990s alone, a half a million hectares of farmland has been lost annually so far, equal to the decrease of production capacity of 25 million tons of grain.[8] The reasons for the decrease are threefold: 1) The adjustment of agricultural structure. Government officials argue there is no need to be over-worried, because this kind of land occupation is reversible and is still mainly used in producing other kinds of food; 2) Natural disasters which may or may not be possible to prevent or to mitigate; 3) Non-agricultural construction. This kind of land occupation is basically not reversible. If land for construction of key projects (e.g. infrastructure) is under strict control, that for construction of industrial development zones, villages and new townships is not. This kind of land occupation causes anxiety and stems from an incomplete land control system in which contradictions between the central government and localities are relatively conspicuous.[9]

Overgrazing and erosion, meanwhile, are turning vast swathes of China's farmland barren and costing billions of dollars each year. Every winter challenges the patience of inhabitants in China's north and, in particular, northwest regions, who suffer from incessant bad weather featuring gale-blown sand. As the wind from Siberia begins howling over the cities and villages, it picks up sand from the deserts in the northwest and, soon, every inch of the living space is filled with dirt.

On 5 May 1993, a catastrophic sandstorm swept over the region, turning daytime into night for three hours. Seventy-two counties in Xinjiang Uygur Autonomous Region, Gansu Province, Ningxia Hui Autonomous Region and Inner Mongolia suffered heavily. There were over 100 casualties, some 370,000 hectares of farmland were destroyed and the total economic loss was put at $65.4 million. On the afternoon of 16 May 1995, another disastrous sandstorm raided Yinchuan, capital of Ningxia Hui Autonomous Region. Vehicles on the roads ground to a halt as visibility was reduced to one metre. House windows were smashed and power lines were snapped. All factories had to suspend production; much grain was destroyed.

According to environmental experts, the vast region covering Gansu Province, Ningxia Hui and Inner Mongolia suffered more sandstorm damage in the past 50 years than the long period from the third century BC to the fifteenth century AD. Records show that about 1,000 years ago, such serious sandstorm as those in 1993 and 1995 took place once every 100 years on average. Now, they occur every two or three years. A scientist with Ningxia Environmental Protection Bureau explained the area was a green land about 1,000 years ago; now, three-quarters is desert.

China is one of the countries in the world most seriously prone to desertification. Geographically, its arid, semi-arid and dry sub-humid areas lie well inland. The long distance to oceans and the intersected mountain ranges, particularly the uplifting of the Qinghai-Tibet Plateau, block the movement of vapour from the oceans. Consequently, these areas have been turned into the driest zones with fragile eco-environment characterized by the least precipitation and the highest evaporation at the same latitude in the world. Surveys show about 80 per cent of the land in the affected areas have become desert to some extent.

The Forestry Ministry says the desert-affected land totals 1.68 million square km accounting for 17.6 per cent of national territory.

Using United Nations criteria, however, the situation is far worse: an affected area of 2.62 million square km accounting for 27.3 per cent of the territory, with 400 million population. Addressing a conference in Beijing[10] on the issue, Vice-Premier Jiang Chunyun said soil erosion had affected over one-third of national territory. Although during the past four decades, more than 700,000 sq.km. of eroded land had been prevented from further erosion, Jiang said that there had been an increase in total affected land from 150,000 sq.km. in the 1950s to 180,000 sq.km., with another 2,100 sq.km. lost annually. He blamed random tree-felling and large-scale reclamation projects destroying forests and grasslands. 'Soil is either damaged or washed away by construction projects. In the past few years, three billion tons of earth and stones from mining and road construction have been piling up with about 20 per cent being washed into rivers, lakes and reservoirs. The rest covers large sections of arable land making it useless for farming. If not controlled, this could threaten the existence and development of the nation.'

Gao Shangwu, an expert in deserts with the Academy of Forestry, cited blind reclamation and cultivation, over-grazing of grasslands, excessive collection of firewood and undue cutting down of forests, unplanned mining, and irrational utilization of water resources as the major human factors resulting in the continuous land deterioration. The 74-year-old scientist said some local governments ignorant about science and the environment had made many mistakes by merely emphasizing agricultural expansion at the cost of the environment.

Inner Mongolia is a place short of water resources and most of the land there is not suitable for farming. But the local government encouraged more land to be brought under cultivation by giving subsidies in the 1960s and 1970s. Consequently, the land opened up is soon abandoned because of poor irrigation.

The Tarim River is the longest inland river in China, running for 2,200 km in Xinjiang Uygur Autonomous Region. Because of its abundant water and dense forest of populus euphratica growing on its banks, the whole drainage area, which covers 198,000 square km, creates a valuable oasis in desert. Unfortunately, human activity since the 1960s such as blind cultivation and lumber activities on its upper reaches caused large-scale drying up of the lower reaches. As a result, the river has shortened by 300 km in the past three decades and the eco-environment in the valley has been swiftly deteriorating. In the past few years alone, the Kuruk Desert has moved 60 km pressing on towards the valley and some sections of the valley are now just two km away from the Taklamakan Desert, the largest drifting desert in the world. Environmental experts say the Tarim River would have disappeared completely in a short time had the desert continued to encroach.

China, however, is also among the countries which has worked hard to develop techniques to combat desertification, including dune fixation and sand stabilization with biological complex and mechanical measures along railways, highways and mining facilities, enlarging farmland by pumping flood water in the rainy season to flatten sand dunes, air-seeding of bushes and grasses to re-vegetate shifting sand areas and so forth. Teams of scientists, with experts of the Academy of Sciences and the Academy of Forestry as the backbone, have created many desert experimental bases for demonstrating the possibilities of turning sand into green land again. During the period from 1991 to 1995 alone, more than 4.29 million hectares of desertified land were said to have been rehabilitated.

A large-scale afforestation project carried out since 1979 by scientists of the Academy of Forestry has had some success. Covering sand land of over 1,400 hectares in the northeastern part of the Ulanboh Desert in Inner Mongolia, it is regarded as the largest desert oasis in the world. As a general-purpose experimental site, it not only has vast stretches of shelterbelt system, but also farmland and orchard. Constant checks for years show that because of the existence of the oasis, local climate and environment quality have enormously improved.

Wushen county, lying in the Maowusu Desert, for example, used to be a poor area. Living on barren land, local people would dig up every bush and even grass root they found for either eating or selling. When they went to bed at night the only thing bothering them was whether or not the dunes would move onto their doorstep and prevent the door from opening. Now, Wushen has become a green land famous for growing various fruits. Solar and wind energy are widely used for generating household power. A national project, called 'Three North' Protective Shelterbelts System, to combat desertification and protect farmland is creating a forest defence line from northwest to northeast. Started from the 1970s, the 'green Great Wall' has increased the forest coverage in the region from a previous 5.05 per cent to 9 per cent.

In 1991, the State Council approved 'The Outlines of the National Overall Plan to Combat Desertification, 1991–2000' for inclusion in the national economic and social development plan. In 1994, the China National Committee for the Implementation of the

United Nations Convention to Combat Desertification was established. Headed by the Minister of Forestry, the group consists of senior officials of 16 ministries such as State Planning Commission, Ministry of Finance, Ministry of Water Resources, Ministry of Agriculture and Ministry of Foreign Affairs. Related to the advance of the deserts is the fact that China is a water-deficient country. Uneven precipitation and water distribution worsen the situation.

The Yellow River is both the great cradle of Chinese civilization and also its sorrow. Historically, the Chinese have always worried about its floods. Records indicate between BC206 and 1949, the banks collapsed in the lower reaches of the Yellow River more than 1,500 times, claiming millions of lives. There is also worry about the heavy volume of mud it carries down to the sea. Each year, the river displaces 1.6 billion tons of soil, leaving a quarter on the riverbed which constantly rises. Through the protective dykes built along some stretches, the river level has risen so that it now flows many metres above the surrounding land.

But now the fear of flooding has been replaced by a fresh concern: that the river is dying, threatening millions of hectares of crops.[11] This might put an end to other worries, but has not made people any happier. The river ran dry in its lower reaches in February 1997, a new record. And in 1996, the drought lasted a record 136 days. Since 1972, the river has run short of water along its 786-km lower reaches 20 times. The situation has become especially acute in the 1990s, as droughts began earlier and affected increasingly wider regions. This worrying trend prompted some experts to predict the river may ultimately become a continental river: one that never reaches the sea.

'This is an exaggeration,' says Ren Guangzhou, senior engineer and deputy director of the Department of Water Resources Administration and Policy at the Ministry of Water Resources.[12] Ren points out the drying-up only happens in certain months and in certain regions. But he admits it is a real problem.[13] According to Ren, the drought tendency can be traced to four causes. First, rainfall in the Yellow River Basin has been on the decline, especially in the 1990s. Meanwhile, demand for water has been increasing through rapid economic development. To prepare for the dry spring season – the sowing season that demands a lot of water – regions have started diverting water from the river into their reservoirs even in winter. As a result, the river carried only 8.8 billion cubic metres of water between January and July 1997, down 50 per cent from previous years.

'Decreasing rainfall is not the main reason for the river drying,' insists Ren. 'We have yet to work out a mechanism to effectively manage the water resources of the Yellow River.' It is true that in 1987, the central government, together with the 10 provinces, autonomous regions and Tianjin Municipality that lie along the Yellow River, mapped out a distribution plan for the river's available water runoff (rain flow from the land into the river). Precautionary measures have been taken to guarantee each year at least 20 billion cubic metres of water go to the sea after diversion – in part to reduce the silt deposits on the river bed. But the plan failed to address distribution of water during severe droughts. Each year, as each region takes its annual share of the water, problems arise if they all rush to take water at the same time.

'The third cause of the problem is the rampant waste of water whether it occurs in the upper, middle or lower reaches of the river,' the official says. Nearly 90 per cent of the water diverted is for irrigation. The waste is worsened by outdated irrigation facilities and methods. In Ningxia and Inner Mongolia, one hectare of land uses up to 15 tons of water, three times higher than the standard amount. The fourth cause of the problem is insufficient flood control facilities in the middle reaches of the river. 'Sixty per cent of the river's annual runoff is concentrated in July, August and September. The figure for April, May and June, the traditional peak seasons for water use, only accounts for less than one-fifth of its annual runoff.'

If there were enough reservoirs in the middle reaches to store water in the flood seasons in readiness for the dry seasons, then the problem of the lower reaches would be greatly reduced. In the upper reaches, there are several large reservoirs, but they can hardly help regions in the lower reaches that are too far away. The Yellow River problem has helped to revive interest in a plan first mooted in the Maoist era to divert the abundant water resources available in south China to irrigate the arid farmland in the north. Essentially, the idea is to draw off water from the Yangtze – up to 70 billion cubic metres a year – and channel it through one of three possible routes to the Yellow River.

A proposed western route will start from the upper reaches of the Yangtze, run through the Qinghai-Tibet Plateau and end up in the upper reaches of the Yellow River. This takes advantage of the fact that at this point the two rivers are only a few hundred kilometres apart, before diverging and reaching the sea very far apart. The eastern route starts from Jiangsu Province in east China, runs through Shandong and Hebei and ends up at Tianjin via the 1,500 year-old Grand Canal. The central route seems to be the most practicable and workable at present. It will divert the water from the Hanshui River, one of the largest tributaries on the middle reaches of the Yangtze River.

The project, however, is still in the discussion stage and is unlikely to see fruition before the second decade of the next century. There are major engineering problems to be overcome. On the proposed western route, for example, the water would have to be channelled through hundreds of kilometres of tunnels through the vast mountains on the Qinghai-Tibet Plateau. It does, however, have the additional merit of also helping to boost economic development in the poor, water-short areas of northwest China.

Looking at the various problems so far discussed, it would seem fair to say that agricultural modernization has begun from a very weak foundation. Overall, it is estimated that about two-thirds of the available farmland involves medium- and low-yield fields faced with industrial pollution and soil erosion, so that the agricultural ecological situation on the surface does not seem too optimistic. And yet, successes are being claimed. In the Yucheng area of Shandong Province, on the lower reaches of the Yellow River, for example, even the most able farmers used to shake their heads with doubt. More than 6,700 hectares had become salt and alkaline wasteland over the past millennium causing farmers to leave. Some tried to plough a few mu, but never turned a profit.

Faced with this challenge, the Academy of Sciences and the Academy of Agricultural Sciences formulated a development plan for the Yuxi Agricultural Development Zone, now hailed as 'as a magnificent feat in changing the world'. The people of Yucheng shifted millions of cubic metres of earth to fill the low-lying salt and alkaline land, turning it into terraced fields for crop-growing, which now boast profitable, fertile soil.

This type of ecological agricultural zone has now begun to spread to other parts of the country, with a coverage so far of an estimated three per cent of land converted from low- to high-yield, and from environmental destruction to good ecological cycles. Thus, for China, the global 'green revolution' of the 1970s has now been replaced by the more broader policy of 'sustainable agriculture', which is regarded as the best route for the country to modernize its farming sector – even though this suffers from the fact that China's overall scientific and technological level remains 15 to 20 years behind the West.[14] To narrow the gap, the government set aside $500 million to 'introduce 1,000 suitable advanced agricultural technology items before 2000'. Zhang Hongbiao, a researcher with the Academy of Agricultural Sciences, however, says[15] that while it is not difficult to introduce advanced foreign agricultural technology, the problem is how to popularize the ideas and ensure that more farmers can gain benefit from them.

'In China today, the use of science and technology for agricultural growth is not even 35 per cent. There are more than 6,000 achievements recorded by Chinese agricultural scientists each year, but only a third are really put into operation. An American farm owner will first consider putting all his agricultural products on the market to earn the largest profit after harvest. When he needs bread, he will buy it. But a Chinese farmer will first put aside one year's grain and fodder after harvest and then sell the rest on the market.'

This is the different psychological habit of farmers under different economic situations. Chinese farmers are not concerned about agricultural import and export taxes or whether the government will cancel agricultural subsidies like French farmers. To many Chinese farmers, 'market economy' perhaps only means going to market. Less than 50 per cent of Chinese agricultural production is marketed. Most of the produce is for the use of their own families. Under inadequate marketization, most farmers can live on meager earnings from selling cheap raw material and agricultural products. Being well off is one of the important symbols for China's agricultural modernization.

In recent years, many enterprises and companies have become another important bridge linking farmers and markets. Shatu Township, Heze City, in Shandong Province, had abundant wild cabbages, but for years locals showed little interest, their attitude summed up by young farmer Zhao Zhongyun, who said: 'Nobody wants them, if I grow them it is awkward to transport outside. So, I don't grow them.' That attitude quickly changed when a food group built a vegetable-processing factory in Shatu Town and signed an agreement with local farmers to grow wild cabbages. The factory provides local farmers with seeds, technological services and even loans. After harvesting, the factory purchases the wild cabbages at a previously fixed price, dehydrates and processes them for export to Japan. Such arrangements are seen as an important way forward in enhancing rural incomes and developing the full potential of the rural economy.

Agriculture is not only the foundation for the national economy, but also is a major precondition for its political and social stability. So long as China produces enough food to feed its people, then chaos and instability will be kept at bay, is the government's basic belief. This can only be achieved, it argues, by ensuring a basic level of national self-sufficiency well into the next century. The State posture towards agriculture, despite the significant reforms in the sector, continue in one important way to resemble that of the past: i.e. the State still hopes that, with the right institutions, agriculture will develop on its own and not be a burden on the national budget. The proportion of capital construction investment devoted to agriculture and the food-grain growth rate went from around eight per cent of the total in the early to mid-1950s to a high of around 18 per cent in the mid-1960s, as a reaction to the emergency conditions created by the famine of the preceding years, before steadily declining as normality returned to around four per cent by the mid-1980s.[16] In the 1950s also the Party thought that institutional change – at the time collectivization and communes – would provide a growing farm output and surplus without the need for diversion of major state investment resources to agriculture.

'Despite the governing slogan of "agriculture as the foundation" and the nominal priority given to the sector in the 1960s and 1970s, its actual priority in claiming State investment resources was relatively low [. . .] while the long-term growth rate of grain production drifted downwards. In absolute terms, the State invested 20 per cent less in agriculture during 1981–5 than it had during 1976–80. [T]he fact that the growth of grain production rose sharply between 1976–80 and 1981–4 because of institutional change, and despite the absolute drop in agricultural investment, gave the government an excuse to continue and even intensify its policy of benign neglect.'[17]

Getting it right in agriculture is crucial to the overall fate of China's reform programme. The luxury of being able to experiment, of having room to make mistakes like those made over the years, can be afforded only in conditions of thriving agriculture. The confident predictions that China can feed itself now and up to the middle of the next century stems in part from a succession of bumper harvests in the mid-1990s. Should something go wrong in the future, if food supply becomes a serious problem again, the outlook for industrial and commercial reform in turn becomes gloomier.

# CHAPTER 6

# Chinese Society: Dealing with a 2,500-year-old Legacy

Who are the Chinese? According to one authority, writing in both exasperation and admiration after many years of experience in dealing with them, they are 'admirable, infuriating, humorous, priggish, modest, overweening, mendacious, loyal, mercenary, ethereal, sadistic and tender'.[1] A darker view was provided by an extraordinary pamphlet circulating in China in 1986. *The Ugly Chinaman*, written in 1984 by a Taiwan-Chinese using the pseudonym of Bo Yang, attacked the Chinese for their failures and self-inflicted degradations with great energy and bitterness.

'What makes the Chinese people so cruel and base?' asked Bo Yang. 'What makes the Chinese people so prone to self-inflation?' His answers were harsh: 'Narrow-mindedness and a lack of altruism can produce an unbalanced personality which constantly wavers between two extremes: a chronic feeling of inferiority and extreme arrogance. In his inferiority, a Chinese person is a slave; in his arrogance, he is a tyrant. Rarely does he or she have a healthy sense of self-respect. In the inferiority mode, everyone else is better than he is, and the closer he gets to people with influence, the wider his smile becomes. Similarly, in the arrogant mode, no other human being on earth is worth the time of day. The result of these extremes is a strange animal with a split personality.'[2]

This catalogue of good and bad personal traits reveals some of the difficulty of typecasting a people whose cultural and ethnic roots are so diverse and which reflect such a broad sweep of human history. Lin Yutang, the noted author and commentator of the Republican Era, wrote a portrait of the Chinese people in the mid-1930s in which he identified 15 key national characteristics: (1) sanity, (2) simplicity, (3) love of nature, (4) patience, (5) indifference, (6) old roguery, (7) fecundity, (8) industry, (9) frugality, (10) love of family life, (11) pacifism, (12) contentment, (13) humour, (14) conservatism and (15) sensuality.[3] He sums up all the qualities with the word, 'mellowness', a mellow understanding of life and human nature with all its potential strengths and weaknesses. Many Chinese whom I have consulted assure me that Lin's description remains valid today, and so I would like to explore a few of these characteristics in more detail.

They are, Lin contended, passive qualities, 'suggestive of calm and passive strength rather than as youthful vigour and romance [. . .] a civilization built for strength and endurance, rather than progress and conquest,' where one can find peace under any circumstance.[4] To him, the three most striking elements of the Chinese character are patience, indifference and 'old roguery'. In a society where legal protection for personal rights is not strongly established – certainly not in Lin's day and hardly even now despite efforts to establish the rule-of-law, indifference is a safe and attractive characteristic to nurture. Patience is certainly a most noble virtue which has been inculcated in Chinese from time immemorial. 'There is so much of this virtue that it has almost become a vice. The Chinese people have put up with more tyranny, anarchy and misrule than any Western people will ever have to put up with, and seem to regard them as part of the laws of nature.'[5]

But it takes a lot to rile up a Chinese to physical violence, although loud public shouting matches can be seen any day of the week in the cities frequented by foreign visitors. I do not believe we Westerners could accept a tenth of the daily frustrations of life as experienced by the Chinese without exploding into violent rage (e.g. 'road rage' killings). As the Chinese saying declares: 'A man who cannot tolerate small ills can never accomplish great things.'

The best training school for patience over the centuries has certainly been the large families, where numerous daughters-in-law, brothers-in-law, fathers and sons, daily had to learn the virtue of enduring each other. In the big family, where the closed door is an offence, and where there is little elbow room for the individual, one learns by necessity and parental instruction from early childhood the need for mutual toleration and adjustments in human relationships. With the twentieth century population explosion and the growth of urban sprawl, with people living on top of each other with little or no privacy, this virtue remains as important as ever.

'The Chinese people take to indifference[. . .] because the political weather always looks a little ominous to the individual who ventures a little too far out alone.' Indifference has a distinct 'survival value'. Some learn this by native intelligence, others by getting their fingers burned. 'One can be public-spirited when there is a guarantee for personal rights, and one's only look-out is the libel law. When these rights are not protected, however, our instinct of self-preservation tells us that indifference is the best constitutional guarantee for personal liberty.'[6]

This would seem to explain the Chinese apathetic gaze that one often encounters. Thus, a large crowd would certainly gather round a road accident victim to gaze impassively at the blood and gore, but it is unlikely anyone will venture to offer assistance because one would then become somehow 'responsible' with endless repercussions for self and family. And, only the most deeply committed, or foolhardy, meddle in politics, with all its possibilities of being on the wrong side and punished for disloyalty.

As regards 'old roguery', Lin admitted that, while he considers it the most 'striking quality' of the Chinese, it is difficult to explain to Westerners because it stems from a different philosophy of life. Essentially, however, it is an outgrowth of Daoism, which I will discuss later in this chapter, which decries all the bustle and restlessness of spirit, self-assertion, struggle and war and hotheaded nationalism, and instead opts for the easy life. 'An old rogue is a man who has seen a lot of life, and who is materialistic, nonchalant and skeptical of progress. At its best, old roguery gives us mellowness and good temper [and] kindliness stemming from a profound observation and a knowledge of the vicissitudes of life.' And further: 'At its worst, this old roguery works against idealism and action. It shatters all desire for reform, laughs at the futility of human effort and renders the Chinese people incapable of idealism and action.'[7] Mencius, the great interpreter of Confucian thought, is seen as an 'old rogue' for declaring that the chief desires of mankind were alimentation and reproduction.

The Chinese, declared Lin, are a 'hard-boiled lot. There is no nonsense about them. They have an indomitable patience, an indefatigable industry, a sense of duty, a level-headed common sense, cheerfulness, humanity, tolerance, and that unequalled genius for finding happiness in hard environments [. . .] that make this commonplace life enjoyable to them.'[8]

The mellow, old-roguish philosophy that teaches patience and passive resistance in times of trouble, also provides against momentary pride and assertion at the moment of success. When fortune comes, do not enjoy all of it; when advantage comes, do not take all of it. To be over-assertive and take full advantage of one's position is a mark of vulgarity and an omen of downfall. Above all, the Chinese can see the funny side of any situation, even where a Westerner might see none. 'Life is a huge farce, and we humans are mere puppets in it. The man who takes life too seriously, who obeys library reading-room rules too honestly, who actually keeps off the lawn because the sign says so, always makes a fool of himself, and is usually subject to laughter from [others], and since laughter is contagious, very soon he becomes a humourist, too. This humourist farcicality then results in the inability of the Chinese to take anything seriously, from the most serious political reform to a dog's funeral.'[9]

At the same time, because of the dominance over the millennia of rule by man, rather than rule by law, and despite the moralistic overtones of Confucianism, the Chinese do not seem to have a strong sense of guilt. Shame, yes, but guilt, no. For many Chinese, it is not so much a matter of whether something is morally right or wrong, but of whether I can get away with it; and if I get caught, what shame will this bring on me and my family? Hence, is it worth the risk? This is the main constraint that keeps them on the straight and narrow.

When a Chinese is arrested, whether rightly or wrongly, the first instinct of his relatives is often not to go charging off to law to seek protection and redress, but to find a 'back channel': someone who knows the judge or magistrate and can intercede in his favour. With the high regard for personal relationships, and the importance attached to 'face', the person who intervenes can often succeed if his 'face' is big enough. This provides the essential oil that has long kept the wheels turning in Chinese society.

Honour can be described as an affair of conscience and reality, but face is more a matter of reputation and appearance. 'A man of honour may only give a blind man a penny, but he does not rob him; a man who is concerned about his "face" may rob the blind man if no one is looking but will ostentatiously give him a dime once people are. A Chinese may perform an honourable action not because it is dictated by honour, but because it will give him face.'[10] A man's face is considered his fortune. Thus, have numerous generations been ready to bankrupt themselves in order to give their sons impressive weddings and their parents impressive funerals. Unsuccessful businessmen have been known to leave their shop or office lights on at night to give the impression that business is booming.

A Chinese will lie if this is the best way out of a tricky social situation, and if caught in that lie, will laugh out of embarrassment not out of contempt for the person being lied to. The lie, after all, has been used to try and avoid conflict and to help the other side save 'face'; the other side, equally, should play the game by avoiding open confrontation concerning the lie. In a sense, it is hypocrisy, but when living in a society where overcrowding and lack of privacy are inevitable, a little hypocrisy can help keep the lid on the cauldron.

The social rules were set in part in the warring states period more than two millennia ago when a book appeared known as the 36 Stratagems[11] which provided various overt and covert means of successfully waging war. The common theme is admiration for the wily strategist who uses subtlety and subterfuge to gain his ends; a warrior who was forced to actually engage in mortal combat was considered to be a failure, while he who gained the day by lying and cheating and sleight of hand, thus avoiding bloodshed on both sides, was much praised.

In ancient battles, one common tactic, if one appeared to be outnumbered, was to make an appalling row to convince the enemy that he faced a much larger force and should decamp from the battlefield forthwith – and Chinese literature is full of examples of this tactic working superbly. One can see much the same today in the inevitable street arguments that break out in overcrowded cities where constant jostling can fray the tempers. The noise will be tremendous, but that is usually all it is: noise, designed to save face.

This also comes into play with the Chinese love of semantics, and their great attachment to the well-turned euphemism. In ancient times, the Confucian scholar Han Fei commented sardonically on the way that a man who put old pals before the public interest would be described as a 'staunch friend', and officials who make exceptions to the law for kinsmen as people of 'loyal principles'. Drowning a baby at birth to avoid future expense, or if it was a useless female, was known as 'bathing the infant'. But my favourite story is of the Dowager Empress, who presided over the collapse of the Qing Dynasty, when she wanted a provincial governor to commit suicide and simply told him: 'The price of coffins is rising'. He took the hint.

In more recent times, a warlord in the 1920s referred to his percentage from narcotic sales as a 'tax to discourage opium', while others in the same business who imposed crushing taxes to pay their thuggish armies described this as a 'goodwill tax', on the principle that it was to be used to pay mercenaries who would otherwise create ill will by robbing the peasantry if they were not paid. It may be this that has enabled post-Liberation generations to fit so comfortably into chanting the latest slogan-of-the-day at the Party's behest, for example during the xenophobic days of the cultural revolution, without giving too much thought to the reality behind the words.

Having considered some of the essential characteristics of individual Chinese, it is necessary now to probe further into the make-up of Chinese society today by examining its cultural and ethical roots. The four major influences have been Confucianism, Legalism, Daoism and Maoism (although some three decades after the departure of The Great Helmsman, this can only be seen in a somewhat watered down version). The history of China has been built on social order, and that remains true to this day. The ethical system first laid down in the Sixth Century BC by Confucius emphasizing personal virtue, devotion to the family and justice – still retains merit. Mao may have elevated devotion to the 'people' or State above the family, but the fact is the ancient sage, having been much denigrated during the Cultural Revolution, is again being invoked by the Party leadership in the interests of national stability.

For Confucians, the central concept of justice was the notion of righteousness. Social order was maintained through specific role positions in a hierarchical relationship, governed by a code of conduct. Regarding the functional organization of a good society, Confucius declared that 'the master should master, the servant should serve, the father should father and the son should son. The amount of one's virtue determined one's place in the hierarchy and anyone's virtue could be increased by self-control'.[12]

Through self-restraint the individual demonstrated virtue and so paved the way for greater things. Keeping faithful and sincere while meeting the obligations of one's rightful position in society gave increased vigour to personal virtue. There was mobility in a Confucian social scheme, but no matter where individuals found themselves in the hierarchy they were expected to conform to the role associated with that position. There was an intermediate stage between common man and sage Known as 'Chun-tzu'. The fundamental meaning of *Chun* is a prince or ruler, while *tzu* means viscount or baron, and the whole term originally indicated those people with official power or rank. Confucius, however, gave it a broader meaning and the English terms 'Princely Man' 'Kingly Man' of 'Superior Man' have all been suggested at one time or another, with the latter now generally considered to be the one that best sums up what he had in mind.

'The Superior Man does what is proper to the station in which he is; he does not desire to go beyond this. In a position of wealth and honour, he does what is proper to a position of wealth and honour. In a poor and low position, he does what is proper to a low and poor position. Situated among barbarous tribes, he does what is proper to a situation among barbarous tribes. In a position of sorrow and difficulty, he does what is proper to a position of sorrow and difficulty.'[13] If everyone behaved properly in their station in life, and adhered to the precept of 'do unto others as you would have them do unto you', there would be social order. There are 30 mentions of the term in *The Analects*, the work of Confucian teachings studied by scholars and rulers for more than 2,000 years, and closely perused by Mao himself. In cultivating himself with reverential carefulness, so as to give peace to himself and to others, the Superior Man should be careful in all the moral, intellectual and physical aspects of his training.

But in the teaching of Confucius the moral aim was always predominant. 'The Superior Man holds righteousness to be of highest importance. A man in his superior position, having valour without righteousness will be guilty of insubordination, one of the lower people, having valour without righteousness, will commit robbery.'[14] The Superior Man was frugal and virtuous; not covetous of securing money or power. 'He who aims to be a Superior Man in his food does not seek to gratify his appetite, nor in his dwelling-place does he seek the appliances of ease.'[15] And further: 'The Superior Man thinks of virtue; the small man thinks of comfort. The Superior Man thinks of the sanctions of law, the small man of the favours which he may receive.'[16]

Confucius set out further requirements:

The Superior Man has nine things which are subjects with him of thoughtful consideration. In regard to the use of his eyes, he is anxious to see clearly. In regard to the use of his ears, he is anxious to hear distinctly. In regard to his countenance, he is anxious that it should be benign. In regard to his demeanour, he is anxious that it should be respectful. In regard to his speech, he is anxious that he should be sincere. In regard to his doing business, he is anxious he should be reverently careful. In regard to what he has doubts about, he is anxious to question others. When he is angry, he thinks of the difficulties (his anger may involve him in). When he sees gain to be got, he thinks of righteousness.[17]

Confucianism, in the eyes of contemporary Chinese, has good and bad points. In representing the Chinese spirit and culture for so long, it is credited with helping the country survive numerous trials and difficulties. As a result, some still favour it in the belief its teachings are compatible with modern thought, political, social, economic or moral. For example, 'the ethics which Confucius extolled have been regarded as the virtues which are in great need of being popularized today: courtesy, justice, honesty and honour.'[18]

Others, however, argue Confucianism was the strongest bulwark of the monarchy, used time and again as an instrument to subdue and exploit the people. For example, the Mongolian invaders, after their conquest of China, advocated Confucianism. The Manchus did the same when they conquered China, and such was the case in Manchuria under Japanese control. 'There was a strong belief among Chinese political reformers in the period 1917–27 that Confucianism was opposed to the Republican form of government and a stumbling block in the way of the nation's advancement.'[19] Equally, it was blamed for the country's inability to cope with the incursions of the rising Western powers in the nineteenth century,[20] as I will discuss in more detail in Chapter Nine.

For Confucians, government had a limited role in social life because the interaction of individuals motivated by benevolence, dedicated to righteousness, and committed to dealing with each other in accordance with propriety would see to it that maximum social tranquillity and harmony would automatically prevail. Confucius and Mencius argued for light taxes, minimal punishment and generally mild rule. The Legalists, who had their brief moment of glory at the time of Emperor Qin Shi Huangdi's reunification of the divided land in 211 BC, had a less charitable view of human nature and the potential for individuals to achieve social order on their own.

'Legalists set down techniques for rulers to mobilize the full resources of all those under them for the purposes of State aggrandizement. Man-made law created duties for the people in order that they could serve the state. Justice for the Legalists was any scheme of social organization set out by the holders of political power.'[21] Man was essentially born sinful and only the full force of arbitrary law ruthlessly applied could quell his baser impulses.

Confucians, essentially, saw the good in man, which could be brought out through self-education and training.

Meanwhile, Daoism, the naturalistic, quietist philosophy enunciated by Zhou imperial court archivist and sage Lao Zi (born about 570 BC), rejected both the righteousness of Confucianism and the laws of legalism as products of social contrivance and as leading to hypocrisy or to exploitation. The Daoists sought for justice in nature alone. By creating society, they believed, man had only created evil. They asserted that unlike Confucian gentlemen, heaven knows not benevolence; it treats all things as straw dogs. Yet, in nature things do prosper according to a rule. No striving or contrivance is necessary for each to receive its due. This is natural justice.

Men should realize there is no alternative to their acting as they do and they should 'rest' in the place where they find themselves because such a place constitutes the life that has been appointed for them. Since all men receive a similar fate in being destined for some end, each man was equally a son of Heaven. Distinctions, other than natural ones, were sources of evil and were unjust. 'For Daoists, Confucian social distinctions merely brought out envy and strife, while Legalist rewards for meritorious service and punishments for infractions of man-made laws brought about competitive self-seeking and oppression of man by man.'[22]

Lin Yutang claimed that 'if there is one book that can claim to interpret for us the spirit of the Chinese, or that is necessary to the understanding the characteristic Chinese behaviour, including literally 'the ways that are dark' it is the 5,000-character *Dao De Jing* (The Way and Its Virtue). [It] contains the first enunciated philosophy of camouflage in the world; it teaches the wisdom of appearing foolish, the success of appearing to fail, the strength of weakness and the advantage of lying low, the benefits of yielding to your adversary and the futility of contention for power.'[23] The message is simple, contained in a dozen ideas repeated in epigrammatic form again and again. Briefly, these are: the rhythm of life, the unity of all the world and human phenomena, the importance of keeping the original simplicity of human nature, the danger of over-government and interference with the simple life of the people, the doctrine of *wu-wei* or inaction, or perhaps non-interference (i.e. laissez faire), and the pervading influence of the spirit, the lessons of humility, quietude and calm, and the folly of force, of pride, and of self-assertion. All these will be understood if one understands the rhythm of life.[24]

A couple of brief extracts will illustrate the sage's teaching. Thus, under the heading of 'Action Without Deeds', one finds the following: 'Exalt not the wise,[25] so that people shall not scheme and contend; prize not rare objects, so that people shall not steal; shut out from sight things of desire, so that people's hearts shall not be disturbed. Therefore in the government of the Sage: He keeps empty their hearts [meaning open-minded or humble in Chinese], makes full their bellies, discourages their ambitions, strengthens their frames; so that the people may be purified of their thoughts and desires. And the cunning ones shall not presume to interfere. By action without deeds may all live in peace.'[26]

And again, this homily on 'The Danger of Overweening Success' declares: 'Stretch a bow to the very full, and you will wish you had stopped in time [fullness, again, meaning pride, as the opposite of emptiness, or humility]. Temper a sword edge to its very sharpest, and the edge will not last long. When gold and jade fill your hall, you will not be able to keep them safe. To be proud with wealth and honour is to sow the seeds of one's downfall. Retire when your work is done, such is Heaven's way.'[27]

Two hundred years after Lao Zi another philosopher, Zhuang Zi (who died about 275 BC) took up the same themes as the master and sought to develop them further, just as Mencius had done with the teachings of Confucius. As with the Confucians, he also took up the task of defining the Superior Man, although in Zhuang Zi's case, it was 'The Perfect Man', who would be a 'spiritual being. Were the ocean itself scorched up, he would not feel hot. Were the great rivers frozen hard, he would not feel cold. Were the mountains to be cleft by thunder, and the deep to be thrown up by storm, he would not tremble with fear. Thus, he would mount upon the clouds of heaven, and driving the sun and the moon before him, pass beyond the limits of this mundane existence. Death and life have no more victory over him. How much less should he concern himself with the distinctions of profit and loss.'[28]

It seems to me that in all the words of Confucius and Lao Zi/ Zhuang Zi, there are close parallels with Biblical teachings, the latter perhaps more akin to the Psalms, the former to the Sermon on the Mount.[29] At the same time, in all the Communist literature, and the major speeches of Party leaders, there is a great emphasis on a better world that will be created by adherence to socialism, just as Confucius and Lao Zi painted a picture of an ideal world that would follow from adherence to their rules for social behaviour. Confucian ethics demanded the sacrifice of the individual to social obligations. The traditional Chinese practised a type of selflessness that tied him very tightly into the narrow, local world of family and friends, patrons and clients – a world anchored in respect for the past.

The good Communist is supposed to devote his life to 'serving the people' and his reward for doing so will be the achievement of ultimate meaning in life, in the Communist parlance 'revolutionary glory' – a glory that will come from having played a significant part in the progress of history towards its Communist goal even at the cost of one's life. The people whom a good Communist is supposed to serve are not, however, concrete individuals, 'but the abstract people in general (all Chinese people, with the exception of class enemies, and indeed, all of the oppressed people of the world). A good Maoist is supposed to subordinate all "natural" obligations to family, associates, and friends to the cause of the Chinese revolution'.[30]

The Communist Party also kept alive the tradition of the superior or perfect man, although now calling him a 'new man' in a 'new society'. The 'old society'[everything pre-dating Communist rule and particularly the Nationalist period] was evil and corrupt. This was because it was dominated by the 'exploiting classes' – landowners, bourgeoisie, and intellectuals – all of whom had to be either eliminated or given the opportunity to purge themselves of the old 'ideological poisons'. Mao compared the process to a medical problem, referring to 'diseases in thoughts and politics' which require an 'attitude of saving men by curing their diseases'.[31] What the West saw as a set of coercive manoeuvers, or brainwashing, the Communists presented as a morally uplifting, harmonizing and therapeutic experience in the best traditions of Confucius and Lao Zi etc.

Another writer on this theme has noted that, in the first two decades or so of Communist rule at least, 'one is struck at first glance with thought reform's bold attack on traditional cultural forms: the open denunciation of the father in a culture steeped in filial piety, the lack of consideration of face in the humiliating public demonstrations and the violations of codes of loyalty in criticizing family and friends. But it is important to point out that the traditions violated had been under steady assault for more than 50 years, and in this sense the Communists have been riding the wave of the broad intellectual rebellion of modern China. There are also aspects of the process that are quite consistent with the Confucian tradition, in particular its thesis that man can and should be re-educated, its emphasis upon following the "correct" ideological path as a guide to human conduct, its stress upon "self-cultivation".'[32]

Disillusionment with the existing social structure was evident long before the final collapse of the Qing Dynasty. Sun Yat-sen, the first leader of Nationalist China, when founding the Progressive China Society in 1894, issued a treatise in the preamble of which he wrote: 'Affairs in China are going wrong. The old loyalties and virtues are corrupted every day. Our strong neighbours look down on us and despise us for the reason that we are not one at heart. Our people are striving for selfish and immediate ends, and are neglectful of the situation at large. They do not realize that when China is one day dismembered by other people, their sons and grandsons will be enslaved and their families will go unprotected. There can be no urgency more urgent than this. Selfishness was never more selfish. The whole nation is confused. Nobody understands. There is nobody to save the situation. How then is the calamity to be averted. If we do not make an effort to hold our own, if we do not rouse ourselves in time, our thousands of years of fame and culture, our many generations of traditions and morals will be destroyed, utterly ruined.'[33]

The Communist regime came to power, therefore, with broad support from the intelligentsia. This reflected not only political desperation but cultural disenchantment: both traditional Chinese assumptions and their Western liberal challengers were equally challenged. In a dialectical sense, a socialist 'people' might be released equally from a restrictive Confucian past (feudal) and in intrusive Western present (imperialist). This formulation appealed to intellectuals who were seeking new departures yet Chinese continuity. The Chineseness of the Confucian order could not redeem its moribund aspects in a modern context. At the same time, the renovating force of the Western influence could not redeem its alien aspects. Men felt a passionate need, cultural as well as political, both to clear the ground and to own the ground they stood on.

But ask anyone in China about cultural values these days and the answer is likely to boil down to money – ways to make it and spend it. In the new China, the way of Deng Xiaoping was described as *ren ren xia hai jingshang* (everyone plunges into the sea of commerce) but in common parlance is more often known as *ren ren chuchu zhuan qian* (everyone is out to make a buck). Either way, it is not an uplifting way of looking at the world. Yet for most people in China the arrival of the 'economic man' at the end of the twentieth century is something of a relief. This was after all the nation that tried to abolish money altogether in pursuit of the infinitely difficult task of creating 'new socialist man'. Serving Mammon is a lot easier than trying to live up to Mao Zedong's woolly rhetoric about serving the people. Besides, this way there is a lot more to eat and drink.

Like many other Asian countries, China is now enjoying the sort of economic boom which has prompted some regional politicians and thinkers to argue that a set of unique values is driving Asia to new heights of prosperity, while a morally bankrupt West is riddled with social problems and is losing its economic momentum. However, interviews with Chinese indicates the values underpinning China's economic success are related less to traditional Confucian concepts than to a scramble for anything that works to fuel the economy. In the process, China finds itself in a moral vacuum.

In the 1980s, as society rapidly developed into the haves and have-nots, jealousy, known by Chinese as the 'red-eyed disease', became endemic. At first the city-dwellers were consumed with jealousy of the newfound wealth of the peasants who had already benefited from the reforms. Then, as the reforms started in the industrial sector, the white-collar workers became envious of the increased wages and bonuses of the factory workers. The new rich then became the small traders in the cities at their market stalls, hard-eyed young men and women with fashionable clothes and hairstyles.

When the stalls first appeared everyone was delighted. They offered better goods in greater variety than the state shops. This soon turned sour. The red-eyed disease began blinding people to the benefits. Nowadays, all they do is quote the scandal stories: the dumpling seller who poisoned a hundred people by using meat which the meat inspectors had already condemned in the state market, the clothes that fell apart after two washings, the shoes which wore through in a week, the gadget that promised to make a person grow five centimetres a year, but in reality burnt the skin and brought the gullible purchaser out in spots. The Communist Party professes to be appalled at the selfish cynicism that has gripped the nation. Party leaders believe they are confronted with a real problem: the absence of a state ideology. Without a philosophy to bind its millions of subjects together, the Communist Party fears that China will become nothing more than 'a loose heap of sand', in the memorable words of Deng Xiaoping to describe the chaotic situation after it became a republic.

'Without leadership by the Communist Party, without socialism, there is no future for China,' Deng told cadres.[34] 'We cannot do without dictatorship. We must not only affirm the need for it, but also exercise it when necessary. Of course, we must be cautious about resorting to dictatorial means and make as few arrests as possible. The struggle against bourgeois liberalization will last for at least 20 years. Democracy can develop only gradually, and we cannot copy Western systems. If we did, that would only make a mess of things. Our socialist construction can only be carried out under the leadership, in an orderly way and in an environment of stability and unity. Bourgeois liberalization means rejection of the party leadership, and there would be nothing to unite our billion people and the party itself would lose all power to fight.'

On another occasion, Deng repeated his belief that China's greatest battle was to create a bulwark against Western bourgeois culture. 'All our workers on the ideological front should serve as "engineers of the soul". What attitude should we take towards the bourgeois culture of the modern West. With regard to economic exchanges, however, we are following a dual policy: we keep our door open, but we are selective. We don't introduce anything without a purpose and a plan and we firmly control all corrupting bourgeois influence. Spiritual pollution can be so damaging to us to bring disaster upon the country and the people. It blurs the distinction between right and wrong, leading to passivity, laxity and disunity, corrupting the mind and eroding the will. It encourages the spread of all kinds of individualism and causes people to doubt or even reject socialism and the party leadership.'[35]

Scholars have attempted to provide the leadership with various alternatives to traditional Marxism. Among the various ideologies that have been debated at one time of another are 'socialism with Chinese characteristics', old-fashioned Maoism, neo-Confucianism, Legalism, neo-authoritarianism, bourgeois liberalism and Western democracy. The trouble is that none of them really fit the bill, so there is much talk inside and outside the party of a crisis. As Xinhua news agency complained: 'The disappearance of social norms, the death of morals and the disintegration of traditional values has brought about a moral crisis.'

Soon after the 4 June 1989 fiasco, Deng admitted his major shortcoming in the previous decade had been the neglect of 'education', meaning ideological and political work, or indoctrination in Marxist norms. Hence, his successors have stepped up the campaign against bourgeois liberalization. During study sessions for Party cadres, the emphasis has been on 'preventing the infiltration of corrupt capitalistic thoughts'. In mid-1997, leftist elements in the leadership circulated a 10,000-character letter entitled 'The Trend and Characteristics of Bourgeois Liberalization since 1992' among senior cadres, warning against the deep penetration of Western influences, and saying the trend was worse than in 1989. It violently attacked provincial leaders, senior party cadres, state officials and intellectuals and accuses them of promoting and practicing bourgeois liberalization.

The letter argued that bourgeois liberalization had mainly influenced scholars, journalists, cultural workers and young intellectuals in the past, but it had now spread to most Party and state units. 'Some provincial governors have suggested that we must give more promotion for a privatized economy. They even strongly advocate preferential treatment for private enterprises. Some municipal party secretaries have urged government departments to give the green light to facilitate 'unconventional' high growth for privately-owned enterprises. They hope their cities can give birth to more millionaires and billionaires. Many of these senior cadres believe only capitalists can save China.'

Reacting to the penetration of these Western influences, President and Party General Secretary Jiang Zemin has tackled the problem by resorting to what he is most familiar with: Maoist-style exhortation. Extolling what he called the leitmotifs of the times, meaning 'patriotism, socialism and collectivism', Jiang has sponsored an elaborate revival of Confucianism and traditional Chinese ethos. The masses are once again told to emulate models: model cadres, model workers, model farmers, model soldiers, model mothers etc.

This is somewhat reminiscent of earlier days, when to many Western visitors in particular, the country seemed to be a virtual cultural wasteland. The few novels and short stories available were about heroic commune leaders or army men, and the style in which they were written was extremely simple and used a minimal number of Chinese characters. The heroes and heroines were all created in the best socialist tradition – self-sacrificing, hard working and incorruptible. The individual was of no importance, only the society in which the individual existed. State property counted for more than people and one often read in the official media accounts heavily laced with extravagant praise for a hero who had sacrificed himself to save state property. The property in question might have been a couple of telegraph poles about to fall into a river or a horse about to be run over by a truck. In each case the property was saved and the man died.

In October 1996, a central committee meeting released the blueprint for 'spiritual civilization', Jiang's signature campaign, denoting capitalism minus capitalist excess, strong central control, a Confucian respect for authority, a citizenry that competes in the marketplace like Adam Smith, but behaves like a troop of boy scouts. The principal document insisted 'literature and art should adhere to the direction of serving the people and socialism.' Since then, the quest for ideological purity has been largely proscriptive: strict censorship of anything controversial, critical or bawdy.

In these campaigns, role models are once again extremely important. When the Party's prestige dipped to its lowest levels after 30 million people starved to death in the Great Leap Forward, Mao's propaganda chiefs elevated to virtual sainthood a selfless model soldier whose greatest virtue was the unthinking obedience and devotion to the people. In 1963, Qiao Anshan backed his truck into a clothesline pole (others say telegraph pole) which toppled onto the head of the soldier, 22-year-old Lei Feng, killing him. Despite this somewhat unheroic death, the PLA man eventually emerged as a model hero, a virtual a saint of Communism. Every adult urban Chinese at some time has studied the 'Lei Feng spirit', sung the lyrics to Study Lei Feng, Our Great Model and chanted his name as an 'unrusting screw' in the socialist machinery. Essentially, the 'Lei Feng spirit' is the Communist spirit, 'the spirit of serving the people wholeheartedly, and the spirit of warmly loving the mother-land and socialism, of studying painstakingly, of waging arduous struggle, of being selfless, and of taking pleasure in helping others'.

As part of his strategy to regain control after the disaster of the Great Leap Forward, Mao ordered the country to 'learn from Lei Feng'. Overnight, Lei was transformed into a national hero beyond normal human dimensions. A diary, which cynics allege was actually written by army propagandists, was 'discovered' after his death, and it immediately entered the Chinese Communist canon as a weapon against waning revolutionary ardour. The Lei Feng campaign was a key step on the road to the Cultural Revolution. In 1989, the Party once again trotted out Lei Feng for public veneration after the Tiananmen Square disturbances. Embattled leaders needed an example of unswerving, even superhuman zest for the Commu-nist case and Lei fitted the bill. In the late 1990s, his name resurfaces with a new message. Instead of presenting Lei as the avatar of Maoist virtue, a film about the man who kills him reinterprets Lei in the context of the new 'spiritual civilization' campaign.

'People had oversimplified Lei Feng,' says Wang Zhu, President of the Beijing Film Corp., which produced the 1997 blockbuster *My Time After Lei Feng*. 'In the 1960s, we needed a message of social unity, now people feel less attachment to the common cause, so Lei can teach us how to behave individually within society.' The film attempted to show how things should be. *My Time After Lei Feng* documents how Qiao Anshan internalizes the Lei Feng spirit in today's China. It opens in black-and-white, with upright party officials clearing Qiao of wrongdoing for the mishap and he vows to assume Lei's rectitude as his own. The scenes represent a China that the leadership would like to see today, which is unified by common cause, with black-and-white values and effective leadership.

The Cultural Revolution is not depicted. Suddenly, it is 1978, the first year of Deng Xiaoping's reforms and the film is in colour, all the better to illuminate the peeling paint and Qiao Anshan's tattered coat. He has become a bus driver seeking a route through the darker aspects of China's reforms. A corrupt bus dispatcher tries to sneak his family aboard early. A pickpocket snatches an old man's wallet. A ticket collector finds a peasant woman's lost ring and plans to keep it. When Qiao tries to rush a poor pregnant woman to the hospital to give birth, a heedless toll guard blocks his way. The driver donates blood to save the woman and her baby. But despite his selfless deeds, his superiors criticize him for disregarding orders. He also faces a family that tries to fleece him after he rescues an old man run down by a Volkswagen, knife-wielding thugs who try to commandeer his truck, and avaricious fellow travellers who demand cash to pull his stranded vehicle from a sinkhole.

At stake is Qaio's loyalty to the Lei Feng spirit, and, by extension, the Communist Party. Qiao's son repeatedly pleads with him to forget all this Lei Feng stuff. Yet Qiao perseveres to the unambiguous conclusion: an army of schoolchildren in red hats arrive to heave his truck out of the mud. Qiao is vindicated. 'You see,' he tells his son, 'people say the Lei Feng spirit is dead, but it lives.' But while Lei Feng continues to appear on centre stage on occasions, Jiang has also created an updated version in the shape of Kong Fansen, whose virtuous life the whole country is urged to emulate. Kong was a low-ranking party cadre from Shandong who went to work in an obscure part of Tibet and died in a car accident. His most exceptional characteristic seems to be he was not corrupt.

Seeking to regain the moral high ground, Jiang, in a speech to Eighth Plenary Session of the CPC Central Commission for Discipline Inspection[36], called for a revival of the Party's fine traditions of hard work and thrift, and an end to excessive indulgence in luxuries. 'In the course of reform and opening up, for various reasons the Party's fine tradition and style of hard work and thrift have faded from the memories of quite a number of Party members and officials. Some people wallow in material comforts, luxury and dissipation,' he said, adding that the situation was deplorable.

Jiang said some leading officials regularly frequented expensive entertainment spots such as luxury hotels and nightclubs, spending money like water. Money was wasted building luxury office buildings and spending huge sums of public funds on buying or furnishing leading officials' residential quarters. He condemned commemorative events where money was wasted buying unnecessarily large numbers of souvenirs and gifts. China still faced a host of difficulties and new problems on its road of advancement because of its vast population and a weak economic basis. 'Facing this situation, our leading organs at all levels and leading officials and the masses of cadres should all the more conscientiously adhere to the spirit of hard work and thrift.'

In response, the Special Economic Zones, set up by Deng to pioneer economic reform in the 1980s, pledged to halt 'the decline of moral and social order'. Shenzhen, Zhuhai, Xiamen, Shantou and Hainan had long been criticized by the Beijing authorities for neglecting to combat crime and corruption in the pursuit of wealth.

Fujian province, meanwhile, drew up a 'civilized citizens pledge' which set standards for citizens, showing their love for the country and province: abiding by the law, improving services and enhancing social politeness. Local officials said 10 key tasks needed to be completed in the province, including efforts to combat group gambling, superstitious activities, luxurious weddings and extravagant funerals. 'Those who discard garbage carelessly, post advertising without approval, park cars illegally, squeeze into public transport impolitely and operate as street vendors without licence will be punished', declared a provincial official in an interview with Xinhua news agency.

Will it work? Lin Yutang would no doubt be cynical about the prospects. Old roguery would come to the fore, he would insist, with everyone playing along with the campaign during the initial white heat of enthusiasm, ready to slip back into old ways as soon as it seemed safe to do so. In fact, having spent many years in Japan, I see some interesting parallels between this and the Japanese concepts of *honne* and *tatemae*: the ideal that one professes to live up to set against the reality which is at a much lower level of personal performance, the two constantly struggling for dominance in the individual soul.

# CHAPTER 7

# The Cement Begins to Crumble

H an Qing graduated from a well known university in Sichuan
Province in the 1980s and was assigned to work in an
electronics company, full of dreams of a bright future. She came
from an intellectual's family, her father being a factory chief
engineer of a factory, and there seemed no reason to doubt she
would do well. On a business trip to Beijing in 1986 she visited a
former university classmate in Beijing. 'I was on a scholarship,
earning 76 Yuan a month, while she was obviously so much better
off and fashionably dressed. I remember her joking in a kindly way
about my modest clothes. I suppose the factory was doing well,
then,' recalls the classmate.

As with many other state-run factories, however, the electronics
company is now struggling to survive. For Han Qing, things have
gone downhill fast, compounded by the fact that her husband, also
a former university classmate, works for the same factory. In a state
of semi-unemployment, they earn 400 Yuan a month which
compounds their problems finding decent housing and raising a
young son. The classmate, now earning 12,000 Yuan a month in a
Sino-foreign joint venture in Beijing, says sadly:

> It's all gone badly wrong for them and it's so sad. Han Qing spends her
> time smoking and playing mahjong. She used to be so proud and full
> of dreams, and now she is filled with dismay and cannot see any light
> in the future. I asked why she didn't move to another city and look for
> a better job, but it seems neither she or her husband have the courage
> to throw away their golden bowl, which I would have thought is
> pretty tarnished now.
>
> I know the hardest thing for her to bear is that those of her old
> classmates who were poor in their academic performance or choosing
> to major in arts instead of science, were once looked down upon by
> people like her, treated as less intelligent etc., but are now doing better

in life. There are many like her, who once had what they thought was a wonderful job, who were admired by their peers, and have now lost all their glamour and style.

It seems to me that they are in a much worse position than the rural poor. They may not live in areas regarded as more affluent, but I think they're happier and more satisfied with life than my classmates. They have reached middle age with family responsibilities, and just when life should be richest they are losing jobs. They have high education, which in a way hinders them to look at other development opportunities. Their eyes are blinded.

The cement which has held post-war Chinese society together, whether party edicts from the centre, blind faith in Maoism or a sense of hope in a brighter tomorrow under Communism, has begun to crumble. Although they still talk the language of Marxist-Leninism – or its local equivalent Maoism/Dengism – the real legitimacy of the present leadership lies in the progress they can achieve by putting more money into peoples' pockets through open-door policies and free-market reforms. And not everyone is benefiting.

Grumbles can be heard that the revolutionary ideals upon which a Chinese spiritual civilization should be founded have been betrayed wholesale in recent years. Even as they rush to make money, the people see all around them the collapse of the old moral standards and the dishonesty and selfishness that have become the norm in the moral vacuum left by rejection of pure Maoism. In the words of one Chinese author,[1] the country has moved from 'utopianism to hedonism'.

Whilst Mao Zedong was alive, China was poor and austere, yet remained a byword for honesty and integrity. Lost property was returned, theft was uncommon. Such a state of affairs may partly have been due to the repressive policies of the time, but there is no doubt that many believed that in a socialist society people did not steal from or cheat each other. But the economic reforms have given rise to what seems at times an almost obsessive desire for wealth and material possessions. This is the criteria that now counts for everything.

There is much intellectual debate about aspects of what are seen as unhealthy Western influences invading Chinese society and how they can be combated. In particular, there is a concern for the great stresses imposed on the Chinese family which is creating funda-mental change, none of it seemingly for the better. Individual Chinese lament the soaring divorce rate[2] in a country where the practice was rarely known until modern times; they agonize over the perceived selfishness of 'little emperors' – the only children, a by-product of the national birth control programme, who demand everything and yet still aren't satisfied when they get it[3] – and they wonder what is happening to a society built on the concept of filial piety that now sees children having to be forced to take care of their aging parents.[4]

But this also operates in the opposite direction. Just as in Japan with the famed *kyoiku mama* ('education mother'), Chinese parents are becoming obsessed with the need for their offspring to do well in life from a very early age. This is placing great strain on the young, leading to child abuse linked to excessive parental expectations and an increasing incidence of child suicide. Hu Dandan, a three year-old boy from Nanjing, was kicked to death by his father because he could not remember a verse of poetry he was supposed to be memorizing. A local court was told the father, a steel plant worker, had recently divorced and put all his hopes for the future on his young son, who was treated with great strictness. Then, there was the case of Xia Lihan from Wuhan, who bound his 11-year-old son by the waist and hung him from a beam for playing truant. The boy died. An eight-year-old boy in Shenyang City suffered a similar fate for not meeting his father's strict demands.

While such cases may still be isolated, physical punishment in the home is common.[5] Sociologists suggest that as the majority or urban families only have one child, he or she is burdened with the expectations of the whole family. Parents set very high standards that make no allowance for personal ability. According to Lu Qin, who runs an advice column for the newspaper *Chinese Children's Daily*, parents never seem content with their child's achievements, so that good pupils as well as backward ones are beaten. 'I once received a call from a little girl who cried for a long time before saying that although she was an excellent student she was still beaten by her mother for failing a foreign language exam. The child felt life was meaningless, and I know of several cases in Beijing where that attitude led to suicide,' she said.

'Children aren't allowed to play after school. Besides homework assigned by their teachers, they get extra assignments from their parents. Even on Sunday, it's common for them to have to practice a musical instrument, art or English. If they show reluctance they are beaten. One little girl was learning to play an electronic keyboard with her teacher who noticed that her fingers were red and swollen. She'd been beaten so severely she couldn't play.'

According to her analysis, many parents whose children are now primary or junior middle school students were deprived of schooling themselves during the Cultural Revolution, when the education system was virtually closed down and bands of 'Red Guards' roamed the country on rampages of destruction or where sent to live in remote rural areas to 'learn from the peasants'. They are now working under worse conditions than some of their peers for this reason. Hence, they hope their offspring will have a bright future and make up for their own loss. Some parents satisfy every material desire of their children, and only demand one thing in return: good marks and acceptance by a key school that can virtually guarantee a good job at the end of the road.

This is reinforced by the one-child policy in urban areas. Aware that the first child will be their only one, parents become over-protective as well as extremely demanding. A whole generation is growing that is living in a cocoon, cut off from the harsher realities of life and therefore unable to cope with unexpected difficulties which may arise. They are also more self-centred and selfish – hence the nickname 'little emperors' with all its negative connotations.

Walk down any street in Shanghai or Beijing today and you stare into the face of China's future: young people wearing name-brand clothes, armed with cellular phones and pagers. Stop a few on the street and ask them what freedom is and they are more likely to point to their bulging wallets than to politics. I often read laments by American journalists and writers about the perceived political apathy among China's younger generation, which they somehow see as a disturbing trend. Where, they ask in anguish, are the democracy activists who were so prominent in 1989, seeking to loosen the Communist Party's grip on politics and society? Well, some at least are now more intent on making money than disturbing the political *status quo*. The most prominent leader of the 1989 movement in Tiananmen Square, who emotionally assured the world she was willing to die for her beliefs, is now living comfortably in the United States studying for her MBA.

For most young Chinese, superficially at least, freedom is narrowly defined as economic success and the ability to spend money on things that have long been available to Westerners – fast food, the latest fashions and new technological products, as well as club-hopping and rock n'roll. Of course, one aspect of freedom is the ability to eat, dress and live as one pleases. There was little room for individual preferences or consumerism in Mao's more restrictive era, when Versace jeans or an air-conditioned apartment would have been condemned as 'bourgeois' and anti-Communist. The progress made under Deng Xiaoping in these areas has been widely documented. But today's young Chinese do not seem to mind that there have been no similar reforms regarding the other side of freedom: political freedom, including the right to choose one's leaders and express one's thoughts and opinions freely.

And, while this may not be something for Western political analysts to lament, I find it hard to blame young Chinese for wanting to get away from the obsession with politics that ruined the lives of their parents. At the same time, while quite happy to buy Western products, many young Chinese are now more ready to join their government in criticizing the West for its hypocrisy and double standards, even if they may not have a clear understanding of what they are criticizing.

A typical comment, usually by people who have never been to the United States, for example, is to condemn Americans as bossy, simple-minded and too critical of a country that they have little understanding of. 'They're simply scared that China is becoming too powerful,' they say, referring to Washington's penchant for criticizing China's politics and human rights. Political apathy, of course, is not unique to China's young, but equally prevalent in the West. But, as one American writer anxiously asserted:[6]

> Political laziness is not as dangerous in the US, where democracy is carved into the Constitution, as it is in China. Traditionally, young people and students – with their idealism, intelligence and courage – have been a driving force behind political change. Unfortunately, today's young Chinese have shrugged off this role at a key point in the country's development.
>
> Very few young people are willing to risk giving up their BMWs,[7] spacious air-conditioned apartments, and fancy clothes for marches, demonstrations and hunger strikes. In a sense, the Communist government has bought their silence on political issues with economic reforms that allow them to lead comfortable lives. Now they seem to have no allegiances to anything but cash.
>
> Alas the next generation doesn't look hopeful either. China's youth, the 413.7 million little emperors and empresses under 21 years old, have the same materialistic habits as their big brothers and sisters.
>
> In a recent Roper Starch survey, 30 per cent of Chinese children put watching TV on top of their favourites list. Although their brains, talent and brilliance are sure to put China on an economic pedestal in the next century, they are being brought up in an atmosphere where silence and submission are valued over critical thinking. If they do question the government and push for the freedoms that Chinese citizens have yet to enjoy, they won't be able to ask the current generation for advice.

The writer of these words was a Chinese American, with the American genes predominant along with a strong tinge of youthful idealism, it seems. Actually, the Chinese government shares some of her concerns about the loss of political idealism – although in the cause of communism not Western democracy. But when Americans and Chinese talk about 'democracy', they are not necessarily referring to the same animal. Democracy as it is known in the West is the product of Roman Law, the Magna Carta, the Boston Tea Party, the Fall of the Bastille, the Industrial Revolution, and the intellectual contributions of many great thinkers, such as Rousseau, Locke and Jefferson. The Chinese are coming from an entirely different tradition.

The great virtues that the Chinese traditionally have valued so highly are tolerance, patience and non-interference in others' affairs. There is also the strong individualism of the Chinese, which may seem a contradiction when one is taught that it is the 'group' not the individual that is important in China. But loyalty to the 'group' is still on a family or clan basis, rather than the vaguer concept of nation. Chinese do not particularly like to interfere in what they see as 'idle affairs'. Public spirit and civic pride are difficult to grow in this type of soil, and that mitigates against the planting of democratic ideals.

Secondly, the parental concept of government that has evolved over millennia and survives to this day means government of the people, for the people but not by the people. Essentially, the average Chinese simply wants to be left alone to get on with daily life without outside interference from *anyone*. Democracy is the plaything of intellectuals, and China essentially is still a peasant society which traditionally has shown little interest in voting, paying income tax or helping to run the country.

This society, however, is now locked into an ideological debate involving a battle of values that reflect the fundamental changes that have taken place in the balance between China and the rest of the world since the nineteenth century, and that have yet to be fully worked out. Looking back, one can see that as the West began battering at the door of a closed China in the middle of that century, Chinese society began to experience the first stirrings of profound change which inevitably accompany the decline of a traditional order and its replacement by something more modern, technologically-oriented. After centuries of being hermetically sealed off from outside ideas, largely through the smugness of a closed mind, the Chinese were ill prepared for change. The old order was crumbling, but nobody quite new what should take its place.

By the end of the nineteenth century, human relations under-went 'wave after wave of upheaval as new forms of urbanization pulled people in from the countryside and as rural life reacted to a broadening of a [monetary] economy.'[8] That pretty much also describes the situation prevailing at the close of the twentieth century, as China again opens its doors to outside influences after a period of being sealed off during the Maoist era. And again: 'Members of such once-despised classes as soldiers and merchants were to find new opportunities, while such obviously secure classes as scholars and gentry were to have their most basic values and their self-esteem threatened.'[9] One of the biggest sources of class tension today is the emergence of a class of post-socialist *nouveau riche* determined to flaunt their wealth with lavish restaurant meals, flashy clothes and mobile phones. The dedicated, hard-working and poorly paid Party cadre is treated with scorn for his or her naïvete.

Many writers and film directors in China are now exploring this issue. A typical genre is the loyal bureaucrat who refuses to cut corners and earn some 'black' income, despite coming under intense pressure from family members using the argument that 'everyone does it, so why be so stupid and miss out on the opportunity?'

As discussed elsewhere, there is today an increasing income disparity between urban and rural areas, different regions, different trades, and units of different types of ownership. Deng Xiaoping first abandoned the egalitarian principle of everyone dining from the same communal pot in favour of allowing some people to 'get rich first' in the belief that this was the best short-cut to overall prosperity for the country. And it is certainly true that it had become essential to find a way to relate rewards more closely to work done, thus encouraging workers to strive harder to promote the well-being of the enterprise employing them. However, even though the varied income level between urban and rural areas, agricultural and non-agricultural sectors and different regions are main factors contribut-ing to the social problem as a whole, there are other factors needing attention. The wage system regulated by government and that adjusted by market differ to a great extent. The disparity between income derived from capital and that from working is widening to become a serious problem.

The idea that you do not have to slave away at a factory workbench for decades in order to make a living is spreading. Confidence tricksters have found a rich vein of gullible and greedy people ready to listen to their get-rich-quick schemes. The stock market has become a magnet for private savings, even though many of the people buying and selling had little knowledge of how such markets work. The idea prevailed for a long time that share prices only went one way – up. When gravity took over, as had to happen, many investors lost heavily, some their entire life savings.

Stock exchanges were abolished soon after Chairman Mao took power in 1949 because he saw them as the hotbeds of capitalist profiteering. But all that was forgotten when the central leadership in its reform-minded phase during the 1980s realized what a handy device bond and share issues could be in raising capital for financially hard-pressed State enterprises and relieving the central government of the funding responsibility. The first experiments met a very cautious public response, understandable after decades of being bombarded with propaganda about the evils of capitalism. Faced with such reluctance, staff of the first enterprises offering shares had to go from door to door trying to promote them, but were still only able to sell about half the total issues.

In 1988, the authorities gave the green light to the trading of securities at officially controlled exchanges. Shanghai, which typified the twin sins of speculation and profiteering more than any other city in China under the old regime, was first in the field with its own stock exchange, growing big enough by August 1991 to launch its own index, followed soon after by Shenzhen. In 1992–3, the price index of the two exchanges reached a high point of 1500 and 3400 respectively. But, in the following three years, there were more falls than rises. By February 1996, the price index came down to around 500 points in Shanghai and 900 points in Shenzhen. But on 1 April of that year, the People's Bank of China announced a halt to inflation-proof deposits which it had been implementing for over a year. Interest rates on savings deposits and loans were lowered on 1 May and again on 23 August. As a result, about 150 billion Yuan of private capital flowed from banks into stock markets. By the end of November 1996, the price index in Shanghai had exceeded 1250 points, while Shenzhen was up to 4500. The number of individual investors shot up from 12 to 21 million. Zhang Li, 39, owner of a private restaurant in Beijing, once bought a small amount of stock in Shenzhen in 1992, but lost. From then on, he kept away from stocks. But when the bank interest rates slumped Zhang was so sure the stock market tide had turned that he sold his slow restaurant business and began trading in shares.

The stock he held increased rapidly. Within a mere half year, his 900,000 Yuan investment turned into over three million Yuan.

Amazed by his luck, Zhang decided prudence was called for, so he eventually sold his stocks to wait and see. Just when he decided to leave the market, however, people from all walks of life were flocking in. In Beijing alone, an average 2,000 people a day queued up to register. Stock prices soared day by day under the continuous injection of new capital. Public demand was so heavy that any stock that came on the market was snapped up at ridiculous prices regardless of whether the company concerned was financially sound – which many were not.[10] Zhang could not resist the siren song and hurried back to the stock market.

But in December 1996, both Shenzhen and Shanghai stock exchanges declined 30–40 per cent, with the value of their shares dropping over 300 billion Yuan. Several junk shares Zhang had bought came dramatically down by over 60 per cent. Within less than a year, his money was gone. He was not alone, despite a government campaign launched three months earlier by a worried government warning against rash stock trading.

There should have been no need for such warnings if the public had heeded the lesson of misplaced confidence in get-rich schemes provided by the so-called 'Great Wall Scandal' in mid-1993, when an estimated 100,000 investors were swindled over the issue of junk bonds by the Great Wall Machinery and Electronics High Technology Corporation, whose promises of a staggering 24 per cent return on investment proved illusory – except to the company's founder. What aroused even more bitterness among those who lost money, however, was that both the mass media and even some senior politicians had for a long time lauded Great Wall as an excellent investment.[11] Adding to the general headlong pursuit of wealth at any cost are widespread tax evasion, coupled with the universality of invisible income from moonlighting, and corruption. 'Existence of these problems is even monstrous in the public's psychological reflection, tarnishing the dream of social fairness in their mind.'[12]

It is considered a must, therefore, to re-establish the social fairness accepted by the majority through adopting various institutional measures which include establishment of a unified market-oriented income system, rigorous enforcement of levying individual income tax by progressively increased rates, adjustment of the remuneration order to make it in accordance with social status, and establishment of unemployment insurance system, minimum wage system and the bottom-line living guarantee system.

For while most people seem take the change of income level and the existence of income disparity for granted at present since the society is enjoying a universal improvement of living standards, it is also possible that public reaction to social unfairness will eventually become radicalized when the contrast is shown more clearly – that while a great part of the people are suffering from declining living conditions, a tiny proportion are able to become millionaires overnight. These disparities encourage attempts to cut corners through bribery and under-the-table dealings.

The rampant government corruption in recent years[13] is challenging China's legal system, with an increasing number of government officials and huge amounts of money involved. In addition, the deteriorating social order is characterized by increasing economic crimes, prostitution, and drug-trafficking. This is seen as due mainly to the absence of a commonly-recognized concept of values, or ethical standards. Nevertheless, what is actually even more urgently needed is a check-and-balance system based on government institutions.

One legacy of the country's long history is that behaviour is based on the rule of man, not the rule of law. A complex body of nationally-enforced law was not considered necessary in traditional society because society had built in powerful forces of self-regulation. Government intervention was rarely needed because social order could normally be maintained through the family or clan, or other associations and occupational groupings. With the whole family liable to be blamed for the wrongdoing of an individual member, this was a powerful force to keep everyone in line. With the weakening of such links, however, especially under the pressures of mass migration around the country, it has been recognized within government that something more is needed, and this can be seen in the flurry of legislative activity in recent years and the government's propaganda campaigns to encourage the population to understand the law and obey it.

Under the imperial system, officials (known as *guan*, from which comes the expression *guanxi*, or connections, the essential lubricating oil for business relations) were often classed simply as 'greedy' and 'clean', their selfish side exemplified in their standard form of greeting each other: *sheng guan* (promotion) or *fa cai* (getting wealthy). Essentially, the dream of every *guan* at whatever level was harmony below to keep those above them in the pecking order satisfied. 'Model magistrates were those who could keep the people from complaining or disturbing the peace while they were passing to those above them gratifying amounts of revenue.'[14] For this, however, they were paid a pitiful wage, hence the need to find ways to quietly meet their own needs and satisfy the demands of a growing entourage of family and hangers-on.

After the founding of the People's Republic in 1949, this network of *guan* was largely undermined by the land reform movement in rural areas and the anti-despot campaigns in the towns. However, the age-old maxim of 'those who work with their brain rule, and those who work with their muscles are ruled' could not be wiped out overnight. The cadres of the 1950s, who should have been servants of the people, were regarded by some as rulers, because they still exercised great power. With the advent of the market economy there emerged a scarcity of materials and capital; some officials fell into the pit of bribery and corruption. Abuses of power returned with a vengeance.

The corruption before the reform related mostly to abuse of power by officials getting their own or their relatives and friends' offspring into the army, university, a good job, gaining promotion, or purchasing some highly-desired consumption goods in short supply through the 'back door'.[15] But the present situation is different, even though many of these same activities continue to occur, they have now been 'commercialized', with executive power traded for cash. Some Chinese fear the result will be even more catastrophic now that executive bodies, state-monopolized organs such as banks and railway systems, public service departments such as hospitals and schools, and even judicial bodies and army are all devoted to 'creating profit' under official instruction to ease the budgetary burden on the central government.

The worsening situation in 1994 made Jiang Zemin comment: 'If the upper beam is not straight, the lower ones will slant; but if the middle beam is not straight, the whole structure will fall'. His remarks, intended for civil servants who were then dabbling in business, reflected a fear of the political price that would have to be paid in a tarnished image for the Party.

In 1995 and 1996, the various judicial departments investigated and adjudicated a number of serious corruption and bribery cases. According to an official report, these included that of 'Li Xiaoshi, former vice-minister of the State Science and Technology Commission, who abused power to embezzle public funds and solicit bribes; the bribery case of Ouyang De, vice-chairman of the People's Congress of Guangdong Province; the cases of Yan Jianhong, former president of the International Trust and Investment Co. of Guizhou Province, and Xue Gen, an accountant for the office of Haikou Branch of the Bank of China, who embezzled huge amounts of public funds; the case of Zhou Beifang, president of Beijing Great

Wall Mechanical and Electronics Scientific and Technological Industrial Co.; and the bribery case of Li Shanyou, former deputy secretary-general of the People's Government of Hainan Province.'[16]
On 4 April 1995, Wang Baosen, former standing committee member of the Beijing Municipal Party Committee and deputy mayor of Beijing, shot himself by a lonely lake north of the capital after being informed that he was under investigation. Officials later said that he faced months of investigation and humiliation for his family with execution inevitable at the end. The CPC Central Commission for Discipline Inspection found Wang guilty of 'grave economic crimes. During his term of office, he abused his power to embezzle, squander and divert large sums of public funds, which he then used to lead a dissolute life. Property deals and investment activities were investigated'. The commission's work was helped by a huge number of denunciation letters detailing corruption not only in the granting of building permits but also in job offers. Building-site selection and authorization procedures were also investigated.

At the same time, Beijing secretary general Chen Xitong lost his job and was placed under house arrest, eventually being expelled from the Party. His son, Chen Xiaotong, president of Beijing's New Century Sino-Japanese joint venture hotel, was jailed. Caught in the corruption net were not only municipality leaders, but also Chinese corporations such as Beijing Shougang (Capital Iron and Steel Works), whose former head in Hong Kong, Zhou Beifang, son of the company president, was detained for corruption – allegedly the illegal export of funds from China, and involvement with Hong Kong property companies which are rumored to have cleared the way for building permits by offering 'incentives'. His father quickly announced his own retirement.

According to the commission's report, city leaders were offered trips to other Asian capitals, their children's education at overseas universities was taken care of and gifts like luxury cars were commonplace. 'Gratitude payments' and commissions were allegedly paid into secret bank accounts in Hong Kong and Europe. Hong Kong businessmen were said to have arrived for restaurant meetings with Chinese officials carrying the keys to expensive new cars, which were then left on the table after the meal. In this way, deals for property development were smoothed.

This should be seen against the background of a rush by Beijing and other cities to raze picturesque old residential quarters allegedly without consultation or visible concern for the citizens who live there. Public protests against developers have taken place in

Shanghai and elsewhere. Commercial interests of developers, who openly brag of their *guanxi* have been pursued without any consideration either for residents or for the aesthetics of city development. And officials in charge of licenses and building permits are accused of behaving like feudal rulers.

At the fifth plenary session of the Central Discipline Inspection Commission in January 1996, 'ultra-individualism and corrosive lifestyles' were criticized, with Jiang Zemin declaring: 'Some of our people have lost their ability to distinguish and resist decadent lifestyle and values. They have been poisoned and refuse to come to their senses.' He said party comrades should avoid 'red lanterns and green wine places of debauchery', and he banned all leading cadres from using luxury imported sedans or from borrowing such cars from "business friends"'.

In November 1995, meanwhile, Deng Bin, general manager of Xinxing Co of Wuxi City, Jiangsu Province, was accused of 'conspiring with accomplices under the ruse of trading certain products to lure investors with offers of exorbitant annual interest rates of 60–120 per cent. They illegally amassed 3.23 billion Yuan [$389 million) and eventually entailed losses of 1.2 billion Yuan ($144.6 million). Deng was executed along with five others. An additional 123 Party members and officials were subjected to Party and administrative disciplinary punishment.

More recently, in August 1997, two high-ranking officials with Beijing's legislature and political advisory body were imprisoned for taking bribes. Tie Ying, former vice-chairwoman of the Standing Committee of the Municipal People's Congress was sentenced to 15 years in prison for accepting 430,000 Yuan ($51,800) between 1982 and 1995 from a Hong Kong businessman to allow him to participate in joint ventures under the control of the municipal government. During that period she served as secretary-general of the municipal government of Beijing and director of the General Office, director of the Legal Affairs office and vice-chairwoman of the municipal legislature. Her property was confiscated. Huang Jicheng, who had been assistant to the mayor, vice-chairman of the Beijing People's Political Consultative Conference and adviser to the municipal government in 1992–4, was sentenced to 10 years for taking bribes totaling 220,000 Yuan ($26,500).

In Shenzhen Special Economic Zone, a senior bank executive was sentenced to life imprisonment, and four accomplices received sentences from three to 15 years, for taking bribes and misspending. Zhang Juxi, head of the Bank of China, Shekou branch, and his accomplices were convicted of accepting a total of 690,000 Yuan ($83,000) in bribes and embezzling more than three million Yuan ($361,000) in public funds. In February 1995, 11 people were executed and 112 sent to prison of labour education camps in a national crackdown on fake invoices and receipts. The campaign led to the closure of 198 illegal printing shops, the seizure of more than 81 million fake receipts and invoices and 1,078 arrests. Counterfeit invoices are used to avoid taxes and to claim money from private and public firms and government agencies. Among the fake items seized 660,000 involved receipts for value added tax introduced in 1994. A number of local government bureaucrats around the country were implicated in the scam.

Officials say some 80 per cent of corruption cases handled are based on public tips. At present, there are 2,929 reporting centres which receive an average 1.5 million tips annually. The public are encouraged to report offenders by telephone, telegram, letter or in person, as well as entrusting the task to others. In his report to the fourth session of the 10th People's Congress of the Shanghai Municipality at the end of 1995, Ni Hongfu, chief procurator of the Shanghai People's Procuratorate said the city had paid 80,000 Yuan ($9,640) in rewards to 223 citizens for their reports during the year.[17] From September 1993 to June 1995, the government reported that 237,627 party members were disciplined for financial irregularity, 35 of them equivalent to minister or provincial governor. In 1996, the central government examined more than 61,099 allegations of bribery, embezzlement of public funds and cases of 'sums of money from unclear origins' were recorded. About 7.7 billion Yuan was said to be involved in the allegations, which implicated 13,530 Communist Party cadres and public servants.[18]

In a separate report, it was claimed that that between October 1992 and June 1997, disciplinary or administrative action was taken against 669,300 Party members for some form of corruption, of which 121,500 were expelled and 37,492 'were punished for their criminal acts'.[19] And at a national meeting of chief procurators in November 1997, Procurator-General Zhang Siqing, said that between January 1993 and October 1997, more than 290,000 cases of corruption and bribery involving government employees had been investigated, along with more than 80,000 dereliction of duty cases and violations of citizens' personal and democratic rights. As a result, 29.4 billion Yuan ($3.54 billion), considered to be direct economic losses, were recovered.[20] One government organ commented that 'what is most remarkable is the similarity between these malpractices in the 1990s with the age-old feudal vices such as the selling of office and exhorting gifts from people on the occasions of birthdays, weddings and funerals'.[21]

The public suffers in many ways due to the endemic corruption, but the results can sometimes be lethal, as was demonstrated by a 1994 case in which greedy officials turned a blind eye to medical fraud. Antibiotics made of starch, talc and pigments and 'injections' made of tap water with monosodium glutamate dissolved in it were a winning formula for Wang Zhiqiang, former military officer and head of the Zhoukou No.1 Veterinary Medicine Factory based in Henan Province. Wang made three million Yuan from his fake medicine in five years while being lauded as an 'advanced worker' and awarded a 1 May Labour Medal by local authorities. The victims were not dumb and the authorities were not deaf. But local officials time and again covered up his crimes by giving certificates and even using armed police to thwart investigations and suppress accusations. Wang was only arrested after intervention by central authorities.

According to the official organ[22] which reported the case, 'there are many cases of rampant manufacturing of fake products in China which have turned out to have the strong backing of the local governments. With the administrative and economic decentralization under the market reforms, the powers of local authorities have increased and they have a higher stake in local enterprises. Subsequent financial reforms made income taxes from local enterprises a major source of local government revenues.

Since the amount of local government turnover made to their superiors is pre-determined by a contract between the two, the more they earn the more they retain. The strategy succeeded in achieving its aim of strengthening the link between local economic development and local governments' immediate interests, but it also fuelled local protectionism. 'On the other hand, some local governments have tried all means to develop and protect profitable enterprises, giving little care to what they produce and how they are managed. This partly explains why the authorities of Renqiu County went so far as to shelter a maker of fake medicine, for Wang was a big money-maker and a contributor to local finance. In the meantime, judicial independence is vulnerable to administrative influence.

'Since the budgets and personnel arrangements of law enforcement departments largely depend on local governments, they have developed many common interests. The convergence of interests has made it even more difficult to execute court decisions over cross-regional economic disputes. Some local governments resist court verdicts. In other places, local courts refuse to cooperate with non-local counterparts in investigations out of fear of "hurting local interests".'

Wang's confession illuminated his intimate relations with local officials. In his own words, he was 'a water tap in the eyes of local officials', who used his money like tap water. He spent 200,000 Yuan at one time to help a brother-in-law of the county's Party secretary repay a debt of 400,000 Yuan incurred in buying cars to please the county magistrate and Party secretary. Many other leading officials in the county also received Wang's bribes. He was even asked to supply bonuses to officials at the county's bureau of agriculture and buy equipment for the bureau of public security. He might have begrudged such forced 'contributions' but he could not back down as he indicated. That was an explicit exchange. He had to pay for the protection he enjoyed.

'In December 1988, a veterinary hospital in another county discovered that medicines from Wang's factory were useless and refused to pay for them. Wang sent two police officers that night to the home of the hospital accountant Liang Dezhi. The armed policemen kicked open Liang's door at 5am, and dragged him out of bed. They handcuffed him and handed him over to Wang's factory where he was beaten and locked up.

'Two low-level officials went to get Liang back, but Wang's police assistants locked one of them up and beat him as well. Wang released him and Liang only after getting US$700 in ransom. When the central authorities heard about the problem in early 1991, they demanded that three senior local officials make a special trip to Beijing to report on the case. Wang escorted the officials in his own car and paid for their room and board in Beijing. The officials not only denied that Wang was creating any problems, they also forged documents giving evidence in his favour. After his arrest, the county chief and party secretary were replaced.'

Smuggling is also a lucrative area for official corruption. For example, Liu Qishan, Fan Zhanwan and Liu Ning, from Rushan City, Shandong Province, were executed[23] in 1994, for this activity. Liu Qishan was head of the Rushan Municipal Commerce Bureau, while Fan was a political commissar in the frontier sub-bureau of Weihai police bureau and Liu Ning was his subordinate. They were found guilty of illegally transporting 9,000 packing boxes of cigarettes from southern China by sea, and taking bribes collectively of around half a million Yuan. Fan provided four officers armed with machine guns to protect the cargo when it landed to intimidate local customs officers who wanted to inspect the ship. A party of 20 police and three police cars were also provided to unload the cargo and take it away for sale on the black market.

Yuan Mingji, a former frontier officer in Shuhai, Guangdong Province, was sentenced to death for ordering his staff to provide armed escorts for cigarette traffickers from Macao. He was also accused of smuggling 2,300 packing boxes of cigarettes worth 5.18 million Yuan, extorting escort fees of 172,000 Yuan and pocketing 48,000 Yuan himself. Zhu Mingshan, vice-president of the Supreme People's Court, described the two cases as 'typical' with crimes characterized by the involvement of a 'considerable number' of officials, state agencies, organizations and enterprises, and huge amounts of state funds siphoned off. Another feature reflected in the crimes is the collusion between smugglers and law enforcement officers, which had played an increasingly essential role in setting up rampant smuggling activities. 'Local protectionism and departmental cover-ups are at the root of the malignant and cancerous crimes.'

Many Chinese believe the reason police are not more effective in combating soaring crime is that they sometimes have links with the underworld. One officer of the Beijing public security bureau ran a sideline business as a pimp in one of the city's most lavish Western-managed hotels. In Jiangxi Province, a restaurateur arranged for his waitresses to seduce customers on the premises. Then he would summon the local police, who would burst into the room and catch the couple in bed together. An instant fine would be levied on the man, depending on how much money he was carrying, and after he had dressed and rushed off, the funds would be divided among the police, the restaurant owner and the waitresses. The scheme was eventually uncovered and the police arrested.

As part of the anti-corruption drive, a crackdown on the luxury life-styles of Party cadres has had some success. In 1997, for example, the official media reported that local governments had saved more than $120 million by stopping construction of 80 office buildings regarded as having suspicious origins. Central government departments and local authorities also saved more than $1.2 million by cutting back on meetings.

'Cases of luxury cars used by officials were investigated and more than 40 expensive overseas tours funded by public coffers have been stopped, according to the Disciplinary Commission. In Hubei Province, 122 big-spending party officials were disciplined for their actions, and 146 units given fines totaling more than 400,000 Yuan ($48,200) for violating state rules on corruption. Zhejiang Province launched lightning checks on 1,030 luxury hotels and recreational centres, searching for cadres who were breaching regulations. More than 4,000 residential telephone lines and 6,000 mobile phones bought with public money were removed during raids in five Provinces.'[24] The country's leading official English language newspaper announced that 'Party and government departments and officials who spend public funds pursuing extravagant lifestyles will be severely punished, according to a recent regulation from the CPC Central Committee and the State Council. The regulation, dated 25 May, says the move is aimed at fostering a hard-working, thrifty atmosphere and further curbing extravagant behaviour.'

The regulation stipulated that:

- ☐ 'The construction and decoration of office buildings must be put under strict control. No office buildings of Party or government departments should be redecorated within three years starting from 1997.
- ☐ 'The number of conferences must be reduced to the minimum.[25] Spending on conferences for 1997 should be reduced by at least 10 per cent compared with last year, and news coverage of meetings should be cut. Celebratory activities must be restricted to those highly necessary. Spending public funds on extravagant meals or entertainment is strictly forbidden.
- ☐ 'The installation of telephones for individuals and the purchase of mobile phones must be put under strict control. Inspections must be restricted to those of practical necessity. The supply or change of motor vehicles must be strictly in line with related stipulations.
- ☐ 'A lid must be put on travel abroad at public expense. Travelling abroad using public funds in the name of inspection, study, training, business tendering or attending exhibitions is forbidden.'

In October 1997, it was announced that all Party and government departments would no longer be allowed to purchase 'luxury consumer goods like mobile phones or to take part in expensive recreational activities. This was announced in a national telephone conference by Wei Jianxing, a member of the Standing Committee of the Political Bureau of the CPC Central Committee and secretary of the CPC Central Commission for Disciplinary Inspection. In connection with this, statistics were released from 11 provinces, municipalities and autonomous regions showing that, by the end of September, some 1,900 Party members and government officials had been disciplined 'for their involvement in extravagant activities paid for with public funds, and a number of government-paid mobile phones and house phones have been removed'.[26]

In the new spirit of open reporting, partly one suspects designed to emphasize official determination to establish rule by law in all aspects of social behaviour, the government is now seemingly prepared to admit that Western claims of torture in order to extract confessions from alleged wrongdoers does take place. Thus, two legal officials in Wuwei, a small town in the remote far West Province of Gansu were sentenced to two years in prison with a reprieve after being convicted of extorting confessions. The case was publicized by the CPC Commission of Politics and Law, which urged judicial organs across the country to learn from it, as well as 'enhancing their professional quality and ethics, eliminating corruption, strictly implementing the law, serving the people heart and soul and firmly safeguarding people's legitimate rights'.

According to the report, three innocent people were sentenced to death over a 1992 grocery store robbery in which one person was killed, but the sentence was stayed while it was submitted to the Provincial Higher People's Court for approval. It ordered the Wuwei Intermediate People's Court to retry the case. But while it was still being re-investigated, the three real murderers were captured and confessed to the crimes. Subsequent investigations found that Wang Shouping, then deputy director of Wuwei Public Security Bureau, and Wei Yong, then director of the bureau, together with 16 others who went unnamed, had contrived to obtain false confessions 'by compulsion'.[27]

This new spirit of openness is also evident in the area of housing reform; where the sudden opportunity for quick profit has been a temptation a good many in China have been unable to resist. This seems to be a typical dilemma of modern China: laudable ambitions being corrupted by a 'fast buck' mentality. Billions of dollars are being spent on new housing construction throughout China today. This stems in part from a laudable government ambition to end overcrowding and create not only more living space per capita but better quality living space. This involves razing whole districts of sub-standard old housing and putting up new apartment blocks. The second reason for the boom is the government's desire to commercialize the housing market, ending the old system under a centrally planned economy of allotting heavily subsidized housing as a perk with a job in the State sector. Encouraging people to buy their own homes is also a way of relieving part of the heavy financial burden stemming from welfare costs for State-run enterprises as described in Chapter Two.

But the dream of home ownership can often turn sour, due to corrupt practices and shoddy workmanship in particular.[28] In the Qiao Yuan residential area of Wuhan, an 18-storey building with a construction area of 17,000 sq.m., having reached its planned height of 56.6 metres, was about to be roofed in when it suddenly began to subside in a very uneven manner. After three weeks, it began to tilt at a most alarming angle, before correcting itself and swaying the other way. Within 24 hours the angle of tilt had reached some 24 degrees and the top was off vertical by 2.8 metres. Three days later, its developer, Wuhan No.1 Construction Company, blew up the entire structure sending an investment of tens of millions of Yuan up in smoke.

Meanwhile, near the Jiaozhou cross-roads in West Shanghai, passers-by saw a lot of office and residential buildings going up, but amid all the frenetic activity, the building site of the Jingkou Mansion was silent. Having reached the 14th floor, construction work suddenly stopped. Several days later, however, the top four floors were demolished. These floors, it transpired, had used cement supplied by Sui Qi Electricity Supply Bureau of nearby Anhui Province, which had one cement manufacturing plant under its wing as a sideline business. The cement turned out to be of a dangerously inferior quality and Shanghai Construction Committee stepped in to order the high-profile demolition.

The Wuhan and Shanghai incidents are merely the tip of the iceberg, a sign of the growing quality problems facing the Chinese building industry and government regulators trying to bring some order out of the chaos that has emerged with the explosive growth of office, commercial and residential buildings right across the nation. 'At many worksites, there are big banners declaring "quality above everything". But it's mere words and doesn't seem to be practised,' lamented a source in the Ministry of Construction. Corners are being cut, it seems, and the problem is most acute in the housing sector. According to the source: 'There are many people working hard to try and save money to buy a house. But when they do so, the dreams turn to dust because of numerous quality problems.'

According to a ministry study, housing constructed in the 1950s was reckoned to need serious maintenance and structural repair after some 15 years. Now, there are many buildings which need extensive repairs even before the first tenants move in. And, asserted the official *Real Estate Newspaper*, 'Some buildings immediately after they are finished have to be condemned as dangerous housing and people cannot be allowed to move in under any circumstances.'

I can recall visiting a friend living in a 15-storey building in Beijing's northern Chaoyang district in 1991. Ill-fitting doors were hanging off their hinges; the paint was peeling off the walls; damp patches could be seen everywhere; rusty pipes protruded from cracked concrete walls; the elevator did not work. It looked like one of the prison-like high rise apartment buildings in some of the West's inner cities that, having become eyesores, are thankfully blown up these days. How old do you think this building is? inquired the host. Twenty years was the confident answer. He smiled. 'It was opened for tenancy only five months ago!'

In Luzhou, Sichuan Province, 38 families wrote a joint petition to the local authority to complain about the poor quality of their apartment building. Immediately after the building was finished, serious cracks developed in the walls. A worker was walking on the roof when it collapsed, severely injuring him in a fall. The underground waste pipe that had been installed proved to be too narrow for the amount of sewage, leading to extensive overflowing and an overpowering stench that made living there almost unbearable. On the design plans, the floor height between different storeys was 2.8 metres, but in reality it was only 2.6 metres.

A 75-year-old man named Yang, in order to take care of his semi-paralyzed wife, chose a first-floor unit. However, there were no drains on his balcony, so that after a heavy rain, water flooded the house. Another owner was closing his window when the glass fell out severing two blood vessels in his feet. The facilities offered by Chinese commodity housing are often very poor. On the southern island of Hainan, a certain Mr Wang used more than one million Yuan to buy an apartment on an upper floor of a high-rise building. But when he got the key, he found there were no light fittings, no water connection and no elevator (although one had been promised in the promotional brochure).

A developer in the northern coastal city of Tianjin built one residential block which enjoyed brisk sales. But when residents took possession of their units they found that there was no gas or heating supply. When confronted by angry tenants, the company responded: 'Oh, we have no source of gas available.' The leaking roof problem has been solved in many countries. For example, according to Chinese research, only one house in a thousand in Japan ever experiences such a problem. But in China, the rate is 53 per cent in the first year after a building is finished. And the average number of years is shrinking from the finishing date to the first leak. In the 1950s, it was 16 years; in the 1960s, 7–9 years; in the 1970s, 3–5 years. This has created a whole new industry of companies specializing in repairing leaking roofs.

But these are minor problems compared with an entire building collapsing around the ears of unfortunate tenants due to shoddy construction. Incomplete Construction Ministry figures show that in 1993, there were 23 building projects which collapsed causing the death of 52 people, and injuring a like number. In 1994, 18 buildings collapsed, causing the death of 57 and injuring 75. In 1995, there were 12 recorded incidents, including: On 6 April in Anyi County, Jiangxi Province, one seven-storey commodity house under construction collapsed, killing six people and injuring six more. On December 8, in Deyang City, Sichuan Province, an eight-storey commercial building collapsed and 17 people died, with 10 more injured. On December 10, in Qing Qi Town in Dongguan City, Guangzhou Province, an eight-storey residential block just completed collapsed. Eight people died and three were injured.

In the first quarter of 1996, different government departments around the country started to check all the commercial housing and 2,400 projects were discovered to have quality problems; 210 of them were either blown up or knocked down. The damage cannot be estimated. However, if the ministry had not published this emergency notice, if all these poor quality buildings were not blown up and people had moved in, the death toll could have been worse.

So, who is responsible for putting up all these shoddy, unsafe buildings? There seem to be several reasons that can be identified with some certainty. First, according to government statistics, 40.1 per cent of the quality problems were caused by design deficiencies. Some analysts suggest that many building designers are irresponsible. They just draw a pretty picture and that is the end of their responsibility. There are many underground architects who do not have the right professional qualifications. Many have emerged because of the rapid development of the industry. They are very quick at drawing and their costs are very low. So the developers use them because they can save money. Some students after the first or second year of study start 'putting on their stage costumes' – as the Chinese saying goes – often in collusion with their teachers.

One example concerns two schoolteachers who were moonlighting. In order to establish their bona fides, however, they had to forge the signature of the head of a design institute as well as the institute's stamp. They then began the rounds of the real estate industry seeking customers. One construction company won a contract to construct a building according to their design, and then sub-contracted the work to a private contractor. Before it was finished, however, it collapsed. The teachers are now serving long prison terms. Secondly, the poor quality construction materials can affect the housing quality. There are, for example, many problems with bricks, steel and cement.

There are 12,000 brick factories around the country, of which only about 50 have a guaranteed record of producing quality goods. In China, 500 billion bricks are produced each year. Only 50 per cent are reckoned to be qualified for use. But, of course, the other half are also used in projects and after a few years they become like powder and start cracking. Poor quality cement, steel and aluminum alloy waterproof materials are starting to come into the market. The collective township, street corner or private enterprises products are become the mainstay because they are cheap and thus attractive to builders who have to keep down their costs in order to gain any sort of a profit margin in a very competitive industry.

Thirdly, developers try to save on materials. This is one of the major reasons for poor quality housing. The *Real Estate Newspaper* quoted one sub-contractor from Hebei Province as declaring quite openly: 'Houses are long-line products. A contract once signed is dead. But raw materials are changing in price every day. If we don't save on the materials we will lose money.'

Fourthly, poor project management. In recent years, commodity house construction scale is large so the macro control is lagging badly behind. Developers and builders often use sub-contractors in order to frustrate control. Some unqualified people with no legal status are trying to break into the market with low fees, less labour and low price in general, so they can get the private sub-contract. The sub-contractors sub-contract, so that there are many layers and the market is in disorder.

The *Real Estate Newspaper* cited the case of a woman who had been a persistent failure in business. Eventually, she became the public relations manager of a construction company, but then quit after 12 months to set up her own construction company. Despite having no funding, no staff and no office, she still gave herself a title of general manager. 'Using her charm and big kickbacks, she got 18 construction projects and then sub-contracted them to 31 building companies each of which had to pay her a large management fee. After years, she became a millionaire.'

The fifth problem relates to lax quality supervision. In recent years, there are so many real estate projects being started. However, the quality monitoring system has not yet been adequately formed. According to the newspaper's investigation: 'Normally, when the project is finished, the inspection is just starting. For many projects, it is not easy to detect the problems inside no matter how much experience the inspectors have. And on many occasions, the quality evaluation meeting is not held at the worksite but in KTV [karaoke television] rooms.'

In 1994, Shenyang in Northeast China chose 192 construction projects as 'excellent' ones, citing the quality of their engineering work etc. But when the news got out, there were so many complaints from the occupants of some of these projects, that a fresh evaluation had to be carried out which resulted in only 66 meeting the required standard. Sixth, there is the issue of poor quality construction workers. The main group are farmers. There is no training; no construction technique; they do not have certificates; there is no skill, only muscle. They walk up the ladders on a building site and start building a high rise without any preparation.

Seventh, powerful money can cause so many loopholes. Commercial houses need a huge investment and approval from many different departments, opening the door to corruption. The *Real Estate Newspaper* reported on one city, where a flock of construction companies went to visit the deputy mayor concerning contracts for a 20-floor residential building. 'Each got a task according to how much he was paid,' the newspaper alleged. 'He had a list and then prioritized according to the payment. Construction firms with reputation and strength did not get any part of the job.

'If a commercial building project costs 10 million Yuan, its ultimate cost will be 13 million Yuan. The other three million goes to different private pockets. However, "the wool will still come out of the sheep" (meaning the end users will pay).'

In 1994, different inspectorates discovered 101,142 bribery cases of which 64,270 related to real estate. In 1995, the bribery related to real estate was 88.6 per cent. Ministry of Construction officials acknowledge the extent of the problem and stress that everything is being done on the government side to bring the construction and real estate industries under tighter control and regain public confidence – vital if the housing market is to be developed into an economic mainstay. A nation-wide probe into unfair competition, fraud in bidding for building contracts and shoddy building practices was launched in 1996 resulting in new procedures and regulations for supervision and management of enterprises by both local and central government. As part of the efforts to promote construction quality, the ministry is disseminating nation-wide information about procedures used in building high quality housing projects and to implement a construction inspection system in all China's major cities. Programmes are also planned for upgrading the skills of the country's 30 million building workers through education in operation, safety and quality. Whether these measures will get to the root causes of the bad practices in the building industry, however, remains to be seen. One is pessimistic given the inter-relationship with overall official corruption.

∞

Meanwhile, another problem providing the State media with a platform for social campaigning is the return of drug-taking. Between 1952 and the late 1970s, the international community widely recognized China as a 'drug-free' nation. But the country faced a resurgence of drug problems in the 1980s and has witnessed a constantly growing influx of drugs since 1990. Various overseas drug cartels have used China as a relay point for the smuggling and trafficking of drugs, with some resorting to the use of weapons to support their actions. This has led to the spread of large caches of drugs to all parts of the country. By the end of 1995, the Chinese government had registered over 500,000 drug abusers, with young people accounting for more than 70 per cent of the total.[29] The number of drug abusers and people involved in drug-related crimes has surged upwards, with large tracts of cultivated land in some poverty-stricken border areas remaining fallow as a direct result of drug abuse. An even more serious problem centres on the fact that intravenous injections of drugs have led to the spread of AIDS. Thus far, more than 1,400 people have contracted AIDS through drug abuse.

The drug scourge has spread from rural to urban areas, as well as from southern and Western borders to central, northern and eastern regions. The ranks of drug abusers have expanded from adults to youngsters, and the previously dominant practice of smoking opium has been replaced in inhalation or injection of heroin. A report from the Yunnan Province Narcotics Control and Research Center notes that China was still a 'drug transit country' as late as a few years ago, meaning that both drug production and consumption were conducted abroad. However, the situation has changed in recent years, and according to conservative estimates by experts the current annual use of heroin stands at 40 tons.

Infertile land and frequent droughts combined to reduce Tongxin, Ningxia Hui Autonomous Region, into one of the country's 200 poverty-stricken counties. Nonetheless, Tongxin has registered a record high number of drug abusers and an alarming rise in the number of drug-related crimes. Some 60 per cent of the young people in Weizhou town, for example, were identified as drug abusers in 1996. Despite consistent efforts, Tongxin's 20-member narcotics control team has failed to curb usage.

In Shanghai, there are 5,000 registered addicts, many among the migrant population, but this figure is reckoned to be far too low in revealing the seriousness of the problem. A conference on drug abuse in the city heard that the number of addicts caught in 1996 was 70 per cent higher than the year before, while another major rise was indicated by the number for the first half of 1997. About 70 per cent were poorly educated, unemployed, with criminal records and aged between 16 and 35. Meanwhile, the authorities claimed to have confiscated 2.7 times more heroin in drug raids in 1996 than in the previous year, while in the first half of 1997 the haul was six times greater the same period of the previous year.

Zhao Baotong, director of the Drug Enforcement Section of the Beijing Public Security Bureau, meanwhile, described the capital's situation concerning drug-related crime as far from optimistic. The lack of optimism is manifested by 'the growing number of drug abusers, expanding area of drug trafficking, the development of drug-related gang crimes, and the formation of trafficking and marketing networks. Some drug trafficking gangs are also engaged in the illegal armaments trade, with crimes resulting therefrom seriously endangering social security.'[30]

The government uses iron-handed measures to crack down on drug-related crimes. Trials of dealers are often conducted in public stadiums with tens of thousands of local citizens invited to attend and the execution of the inevitable death sentence, although conducted out of sight, is widely publicized. On 26 June 1996, International Narcotics Control Day, the Supreme People's Court organized 262 simultaneous sentencing courts open to the public, dealing with 1,725 offenders, and watched by an estimated 1.75 million people.

In June 1997, there was a flurry of activity on the execution grounds with at least 100 drug traffickers being shot shortly after sentencing at mass rallies. They included 27 in Kunming, capital of

Yunnan Province on the edge of the 'Golden Triangle', 24 in Chengdu, capital of Sichuan Province, and 14 each in Beijing and on southernmost Hainan island. In Kunming, 1,000 kgs of heroin was also burned after the dealers were executed, and at a rally in Chengdu, 100 kgs of drugs were burned. Such mass executions tend to arouse the concern of international human rights watchdogs, but the Chinese are adamant that the death penalty is a necessary deterrent. Talking at a meeting of the Standing Committee of the Political Bureau of the Central Committee in 1986, for example, Deng Xiaoping insisted:

> The death penalty cannot be abolished and some criminals must be sentenced to death. Recently, I have received some relevant documents from which I understand there are a great many habitual criminals who, on being released after a few years remolding through forced labour, resume their criminal activities, each time becoming more skilful and more experienced in coping with the public security and judicial organs.
>
> Why don't we have some of them executed according to the law? Why don't we punish severely, according to the law, some of those people who trade in women and children, who make a living by playing on people's superstitions, or who organize secret societies, and some of those habitual criminals who refuse to reform, despite repeated attempts to educate them. Those who have merely made mistakes in the political and ideological sphere, but haven't violated state law, should not be given any criminal sanctions, let alone the death penalty. But some of the perpetrators of serious economic and other crimes must be executed as required by the law. Generally speaking, the problem now is that we are too soft on criminals. As a matter of fact, execution is one of the indispensable means of education.'

But, the government also insists that it attaches great importance to rehabilitating drug abusers. Public security departments nation-wide have established more than 500 compulsory drug abstention centres which currently provide services to over 50,000 drug abusers. There are also 65 centres devoting to reforming drug abusers through labour.

Previously, the emphasis was on medical detoxification, an extremely unpleasant 'cold turkey' process with little sympathy shown for the sufferings of the addict. Once 'cured', the patient was released back into society with little thought given to further convalescent treatment and follow-up counseling. In the past few years, however, more attention has been given to cultivating the rehabilitated former addict's ability to maintain self-discipline and care for themselves, including dealing with social and family

144

relations, and methods for seeking employment and confronting inevitable social pressure.

At the same time, there have been calls for an American-style 'Just Say No' anti-drugs campaign in schools after it was revealed that up to 80 per cent of addicts in China may be under 18. Drug use is also cited as the main cause of juvenile delinquency in cities such as Guangzhou, where young people accounted for nearly 50 per cent of users arrested by police in 1995, for example. An official survey published in mid-1997 found young people's knowledge of the dangers of drug use was 'surprisingly naïve'. 'Many middle-school students have little or no awareness about guarding themselves against drugs,' the survey said. Experts quoted by the *China Daily* said the official anti-drugs campaign had failed to address the grassroots problems of addiction, especially among young people. According to Zhang Panshi, a research fellow with the Chinese Academy of Social Sciences, one of the primary reasons 'for the resurgence of drug offences is the lack of education.'

∞

Finally in this chapter, I would like to deal briefly with some of the other social issues that are a cause for official concern.

For a start, there has been a revival of Triad gangs, many of whom moved in from Hong Kong in the 1980s, followed by groups from Taiwan and other overseas Chinese communities. A swoop in the ShaoYuan area of Hunan Province in 1996 unearthed 1,110 underground gangs most of them with Triad affiliations. More than 3,000 of the 3,963 alleged Triad members investigated were given stiff sentences and 47 Dragonheads were executed. Triads and affiliates of the Japanese Yakuza have been very active in the Shenzhen Special Economic Zone just north of Hong Kong, involved in drugs, prostitution, smuggling, gun-running, extortion, illegal gambling and loan-sharking.

The authorities are alarmed about the large number of young Triad members, workers and students, who make up 70 per cent of new recruits in some cities. One early report revealed that from 1986–90, Hong Kong and local Triad elements set up more than 50 runs in Guangdong cities, including Guangzhou, Zhuhai, Foshan and Shaoguan. In rural areas, Triad societies have formed 'strategic alliances' with clans and underground units based on cults and feudal superstitions.

The revival of 'feudalistic clans' which are undermining the authority of the party in the countryside are a growing concern.

Clan organizations, which were supposed to have been wiped out in the 1950s, have become the centres of power in counties with low income and education levels, according to internal circulars issued by government security units. 'Some village cadres have abolished local party committees, with the clan chiefs becoming the de facto administrators,' one document said. 'In other rural areas, the election of village committees is under the control of clansmen.'

While the revival of clans began in the early 1980s, they have become larger and much better organized recently. Rural cadres complain that clan activities have siphoned off badly needed funds for agriculture and education. The security departments cited villages in Hunan as having clan units so powerful they had refused to pay taxes or implement family planning measures. At the same time, since only males can join clans, their revival has fuelled families' desires for male children in rural areas.

One clan in central China boasts more than 30,000 members from three generations. Clan members make regular contributions to Spring Festival celebrations and the maintenance of ancestral shrines, temples and cemeteries. The Education Ministry cited the case of a county in the north-West which had more than 100 clan temples. Enthusiasts there spent more than one million Yuan ($120,500) in 1994 on clan-related activities, more than the area's budget for schools. In the Hunan Province districts of Dingcheng and Hanshou districts, where there are several prominent clans, fights over territory or committee positions often degenerate into blood battles. 'Many villages turn to clan organizations instead of the police or courts to settle disputes,' a rural official in Hubei told a local newspaper.

All this adds to the impression that the central government is finding it increasingly difficult to retain the iron-fisted social control over the country it enjoyed in the Maoist era, and that an increasing number of citizens find the word of Beijing irrelevant in their daily lives.

■ CHAPTER 8

# The Status of Women: Still a Long Way to Go

Despite attempts at progress, many people's attitudes towards women still reflect traditional ideals of them as being submissive, obedient, hard-working and silent. But in big cities like Beijing at least one of the most profound changes in their society is the surge in divorce, almost a quarter of all marriages ending in this way, double the rate seen at the start of the 1990s. The national divorce rate has now moved to over 10 per cent, still far behind many Western countries, but still a remarkable increase.

For women in Beijing at least, the growing divorce rate is a reflection of a new social and economic freedom and of damaging effects from what many Beijing residents say is the remarkable increase in adulterous affairs. More than 70 per cent of divorces are now initiated by women, and the most common reason given is that the husband has had an affair. 'Only a few years ago, people would let a temple be destroyed before they would let a marriage fail,' says Pi Xiaoming, a leading divorce lawyer whose work at the East Beijing Women's Federation used to involve applying intense pressure on couples not to divorce.[1] 'We did everything possible to keep people from separating,' she recalls. 'If there was a one per cent chance of saving the marriage, we'd expend all our effort to overcome the 99 per cent of difficulty.' Now divorce is an acceptable alternative to an unhappy marriage, and a legal separation that once took years to win approval can now be processed in three days if both sides agree.

But the government's shift in attitude is only one ingredient. A larger one seems to be growing demands by women in an era of expanding opportunity. In a lament familiar to many Western

147

women, Ling Hua, a 41-year-old divorcee, recalls: 'My husband used to say, 'You have your job, your study overseas, a roof over your head, what more do you want?' What I wanted was a husband who didn't sit at home all day, watching sports on television.'

If most Chinese men still look for a stable home and a reliable mother for their children, women who used to be content with a steady family income now want more romance, sex and affection. 'My husband never kissed me, not once,' said Lan Ding, 40, a self-employed tailor who said she had divorced her husband, an air force officer, because of the way he treated her. 'We had a child, but he never kissed me. I only learned how to do that much later.' 'Before, marriage was very stable, but the quality was very low,' said Wang Xiangjuan, who listens to hundreds of complaints each month on the women's hot line she runs in Beijing. 'It was something you did and didn't think about. Now people have high expectations from marriage.' Wang also said that most Chinese women traditionally had sex only for the purpose of bearing children. But China's one-child policy has made urban women at least freer to pursue careers and to pursue sex.

Wu Liyong, a 36-year-old director of a food products company in Beijing, recalls that one of the causes of her divorce after 12 years of marriage, was an unsatisfactory sex life. 'We were taught that the man should initiate sex. I didn't say anything for a long time. But when I finally talked about it with my friends, they told me I was stupid. I feel like I wasted 10 years.' Part of the broader problem is that Chinese society does not teach men to treat their wives well. 'My husband was a good worker, a good son to his parents, a good father to his son and a terrible husband,' said Lan Ding, the woman who divorced the air force officer. 'That's what our society teaches men to do.'

The current surge in divorce is not the first in modern China. The 1950 constitution and a new marriage law, which redefined rights within families, encouraged a wave of divorces in the early 1950s.[2] Many of these were initiated by Communist army soldiers who after their victory of 1949 moved to cities and divorced wives they had married in rural hometowns but abandoned during the long years of war against the Japanese and Chinese Nationalists. In the early years of ideological struggle, many marriages were also destroyed for political reasons, with one spouse being forced to denounce the other, often in public sessions known as 'spitting bitter water'.[3]

At the start of the Cultural Revolution in 1966, when millions of lives were shattered by accusations of political incorrectness, many people were forced to divorce a spouse for this reason. For all the women who have divorced, though, there are countless more who have considered it but been unable or unwilling to do so. Lan Ding said she urged many of her friends not to follow her own example because of the economic difficulty she has had raising a son on her own and because of the hard time she had finding another man. 'A lot of people will see a divorced woman as immoral, but see a divorced man as fine.'

For a glimpse at how social pressures work, consider the case of Hai Xia, who worked in a barber shop after arriving in Beijing at the beginning of the 1990s. After marrying Zhang Haitao, a restaurant driver, she felt life had become comfortable. But, to her dismay Zhang then had an affair, even bringing the woman into his home. Her lawyer visited Zhang at work, but the latter was not interested, and even the restaurant's manager lent the driver a hand by openly commenting that it was not worth making such a fuss that a man has a lover beside his wife. Given the fact that Hai Xia disapproved of any possibility of separating from her husband, her lawyer mobilized social power to exert pressure on Zhang.

Those whose help was sought included the neighbourhood committee (the group of local worthies, often retired and elderly people who keep watch over the goings-on in every small community) and police sub-station of Zhang's community, the parents of Zhang's lover, and the police sub-station of the lover's community. This combined social power eventually knocked Zhang down. He was held in custody for a week by the police station for adultery plus bullying his wife. Then, the restaurant sacked him. The frustrated Zhang finally said goodbye to his mistress and returned home reportedly contrite.

Divorce lawyers say they often feel ambivalent facing clients who are physically as well as psychologically hurt by their husbands, but stick to 'saving the family' and refuse to consider separation and legal punishment. These kinds of women who are from every social rank – farmer, worker, government official and university professor – share the same view in marriage by saying: 'I would lose my home and be incapable of supporting a child by myself if I get divorced. So it's impossible for me to let him go.' Guo Jianmei, associate professor of the Law Department of Peking University, says: 'I am really angry and disappointed with these women when they behave so incompetently. But China is a developing country. A woman living with full self-confidence remains a slogan when their living conditions are by no means favourable and some cultural traditions discriminating against women persist today's in society. This is a fact that we have to recognize and always bear in mind.'

In fact, in spite of all the new-found freedoms, there is still official concern that the mainland's traditional family structure is under assault by tawdry Western values, in which divorce is seen as a manifestation of a new hedonism which must be controlled. In 1997, the government abruptly launched a strong attack on adultery, for example. Tabloid-quality stories about the evils of infidelity began appearing in the state-run press. The *China Women's News* said in a censorious editorial: 'Having an affair was despised 10 years ago. People who were discovered in extra-marital affairs lost face and could not survive. Suddenly, our society and views have changed from one extreme to the other.'

During the Cultural Revolution, even a warm glance in the wrong direction could bring a scolding from the Communist leader of your work unit. But the economic reforms have brought more freedoms for individuals, including in their love lives. Money, too, has become a potent aphrodisiac. Wealthy married men are chided by the official press for setting up mistresses in apartments like modern-day concubines. A new phrase has emerged: young women try to *bang da kuan* – hug a rich man.

The government's attack on promiscuous behaviour is part of a broad campaign to uplift the 'spiritual civilization' of China. By the end of 1997, the National People's Congress was expected to issue its first draft of a rewritten Marriage Law. Although policy-makers are not going to make adultery a crime – as it was as recently as 1981, punishable by up to two years in jail – they are planning to get tougher. Law professor Wu Changzhen, 68, a highly regarded expert on family law who worked on the legislation, believes the existing law was not tough enough. In a throwback to the days when the government intruded into all aspects of people's lives, Ms Wu thinks police should be able to detain the worst adulterers, such as those who abuse their spouses or neglect their children. The offenders could be held up to two weeks without trial. She also believes that if a marriage ends because one of the partners has had an extra-marital affair, the guilty party should be penalized when the assets of the marriage are divided. The adulterer should pay damages for pain and suffering, she said.

Ms Wu, like other conservative thinkers in the party, blames the West for the rise in infidelity. 'It is not the Chinese way. It's a Western way. People are influenced by the American sexual liberation so they think they can be free. They read Western novels, watch foreign films. Students go abroad and live together. In the past, if you had an affair you kept it secret. Today, people are talking about adultery or having affairs.

Such prudery may seem out of place in a country where until 50 years ago it was quite acceptable for a man to have several wives and numerous concubines, and where Mao Zedong was notorious for his sexual escapades. The big difference today, Ms Wu said, is it is no longer just men. Now, she says disapprovingly, married women are the ones having the affairs. She blames the failure of marriages for a host of social ills, from family violence to bigamy, illegitimacy, and the destitution of children and spurned spouses.

In 'Yearnings', the first Chinese soap opera televised in 1991, Liu Huifang, the heroine, experienced the bitterness side of a tragic marriage. In the end she lost her marriage, her job and her health in order to bring up her daughter. The drama became the focus of national attention. Many film critics said the heroine incarnated all the desired merits of Chinese women. A spate of press articles appeared loudly singing her praises. But the female writer Ri Li took exception to this. 'The heroine has been crowned as a "good woman" for making sacrifices for her husband, her family and her adopted daughter. I doubt that her character would have achieved the same swell of popularity if it were a male. In China, a country long plagued by the belief that men are superior, males have always been highly praised for their willingness to make sacrifices for their country and their families. They were deemed foolish to be immersed in love as family men. So it is unfair that a woman who makes sacrifices for her family is taken as a symbol of beauty and virtue.'

A writer in the official *China Daily* took up the same theme: 'Liu's greatest misfortune is neither her broken marriage nor her severe leg injury from a traffic accident. Her biggest problem is her obedient character. [She] has invited all her troubles on herself. The public debate over the TV series shows a conflict between traditional and contemporary ideas of women.' A survey conducted by the Beijing Socio-Psychology Institute found that in the capital, the show was less popular among young, well-educated viewers than among the older generation. More than 68 per cent of viewers above 50 years old liked it, dropping to 62 per cent among those in their forties and 40 per cent among teens and early 20s.

There is also a hidden message in the film and that is the subconscious desire on the part of many men for an egoless woman. The meek and amiable heroine found an echo in many hearts among the audience – many young men judge young women by comparing them to the television heroine.[4]

But that old values die hard is evidenced by the lauding of Hou Guiying as a 'virtuous daughter-in-law' in the best traditions of old China, where a girl married into her husband's family and had no avenue of complaint if she was treated as no better than an unpaid maid. Hou, we learnt from the official media, never complained about having to spend the first 10 years of her marriage caring for her husband's invalid parents and managing the household chores and the family farm while her husband worked to cover the medical expenses. This, she felt, was her duty as a good daughter-in-law. As a result she was one of 50 women awarded the title of 'virtuous daughter-in-law' by Chadian Township [population 60,000] in Henan Province.

Guo Gaihua, Hao Fengying and Wan Yinger, three sisters who married into the same family, attended to their paralyzed mother-in-law for six years. Every morning, their citation declared, they undressed her and washed her feet. They fed her three meals a day and helped her use a bedpan. Hao Fengying was quoted as saying that the honour she had won 'makes me firmly believe what I have done is right and that I should work even harder in looking after my mother-in-law. Moreover, I think this kind of activity will also serve to educate those daughters-in-law who are not virtuous'.

Li Jizeng, Party secretary of Chadian Township, said the reform and open policies had brought about many changes in China that challenged the minds of people with traditional moral concepts. 'Therefore, it is necessary to award the virtuous daughters-in-law in the township to promote the fine tradition of respect and support for the aged.'[5]

Looking at Chinese history, we find a different attitude towards women prevailing until Confucius came along and put on the bridle. The original social system was matriarchal, and traces of this were still evident in the Chou dynasty (1122–222 BC), when the marital family name was the woman's not the man's. Women enjoyed freedom in the choice of mates, and there was considerable sexual freedom for the female suggested by the folk-song in the 2,500-year-old *Book of Poems* which begins:

'If thou thinkest of me
I will lift my petticoat
And cross the River Ts'en.
If thou thinkest not of me
Why, are there not other men?
Oh, thou silly boy!'

The book, in fact, has many examples of songs of women who ran away with their lovers, for the marriage system had not yet become the severe bondage to women it was to become in a later day. Thus, could the Queen of Wei in this period force the king to summon the handsomest men of the kingdom to her boudoir. Divorce was easy and divorcees could remarry; the cult of feminine chastity had not yet become an obsession with men.

Enter Confucius with his elaborate system of social behaviour leading to the seclusion of women. According to the *Book of Rites*, married sisters were not allowed to eat at the same table with their brothers. The Confucian social philosophy encouraged the womanly woman, possessing such feminine virtues as quietness, obedience, good manners, personal neatness, industry, ability in cooking and spinning, respect for the husband's parents, kindness to her brothers-in-law, courtesy to the husband's friends – all the virtues desirable to the male.

In its purest form, however, Confucianism did honour the female. 'The wife was given "equal" position with her husband, somewhat below him but still an equal helpmate, like the two fish in the Daoist symbol of *yin* and *yang*, necessarily complementing each other.'[6] But this Confucian attitude towards women's role in society eventually came under the influence of male scholars that resulted in the gradual introduction of the basic notion that woman was inferior. Discrimination was soon evident. One flagrant example was that whereas a husband's mourning period for a wife was only one year, a widow had to undertake three years of mourning.

Typically feminine virtues, such as obedience and loyalty, were codified by Liu Hsiang in the Han Dynasty (206 BC-219 AD) into something resembling female ethics, while Ban Zhao (48–117AD), woman author of the Lessons for Women propounded the 'three obediences and four virtues' of women. The former dictated that a woman obeys her father in her maiden home, her husband once married, and her son when widowed. 'There were seven grounds for divorce of a wife, namely disobedience to parents-in-law, barren-ness, adultery, jealousy, incurable disease, loquacity and theft.'[7]

From the time of the Han Dynasty, the tradition evolved whereby men could remarry but women could not. Then came the scholars of the Song Dynasty (960–1276), who placed women in even stricter purdah and made remarriage by a widow a moral crime. 'Worship of chastity, which they so highly prized in women, became something of a psychological obsession and women were henceforth to be responsible for social morals from which men were exempt.'[8] A woman who distinguished herself by committing suicide to guard her chastity stood a fair chance of leaving her name in literature in one way or another.

In the Ming Dynasty (1368–1643), the practice was further institutionalized by a rule that women who retained their widowhood from the age of 30 to 50 received a pension and their families were exempt from official labour service. As a result, chaste widowhood became a matter of deep concern for the whole family, and any woman who sought to break the rule could expect to be subjected to intense pressure and condemnation for moral laxity. Yet at the same time as these examples of moral rectitude, we have society condoning the practice of drowning baby girls,[9] especially by poor parents who could not afford the required expensive wedding ceremonies for their daughters, and the creation of vast armies of concubines and 'sing song' girls (prostitutes) for man's pleasure.[10] With women becoming men's playthings, the way was open to the final sophistication of male fantasy: the barbaric practice of foot-binding.

At an early age, a girl's toes were bent under her sole and bound until the flesh rotted and grew into an extremely small 'golden lily' foot. It is often assumed that this practice was introduced as a means of keeping women from straying far from home, for it certainly proved difficult for them to walk far if for no other reason than the excruciating pain. And it is certainly true that to be crippled physically was to be crippled economically as well.

But, in fact, foot-binding throughout its thousand-year history was purely sexual in nature. Chinese men, it seemed, had a distinct foot fetish, and literature contains many tales of them achieving pure ecstasy in fondling and kissing the deformed body part. The small feet also influenced not only the woman's walking gait but also her entire carriage-somewhat similar to the modern body 'shimmy' in extremely high heels, although in reality looking more like a tightrope walker in action.

What is most depressing to the modern mind is that successive generations of women went along with the perversion, mothers threatening tearful daughters with prospects of being unmarriageable if they did not submit to the torture. Only peasant girls went around with unbound feet, open to social ridicule. 'Refined' ladies did not work in the fields, but stayed demurely at home, where their feet were of little use but as objects of sexual worship. Grim-faced mothers closely examined the feet of prospective daughters-in-law at the very start of any serious negotiations for betrothal.

It was not until the Taiping Rebellion in the mid-nineteenth century, when a group of Hakka women warriors with unbound feet were the most ruthless of all in the fighting that led to an estimated 30 million deaths, that the first serious challenge to foot-binding reverberated around the country. But the practice still existed well into the twentieth century. The female writer Hsieh Pingying, for example, recalled that at the age of six in the 1920s, her mother sought to bind her feet. 'Her own small feet were bound too tight, so that it was very inconvenient for her to walk. My elder sister's feet were likewise bound very small. Although they looked very nice, she could not walk more than two steps without having to support herself on to the wall. Indeed, my poor sister was no better than an invalid.'

Although her mother wanted Pingying to walk better than her elder sister, still 'she thought that if she did not start to bind my feet now, my bones would become hardened and there would be no likelihood that I would ever be able to have small feet.' A tearful Pingying tries to talk her mother out of the binding treatment. 'Mother it will be very painful. I won't be able to walk. Please do not do it to me.' In response, her mother says: 'I must bind your feet because I love you. If I do not bind your feet I shall not be doing the right thing by you. You must realize that a girl with huge feet will never be accepted by a husband.'[11]

Another twentieth-century writer has recalled that 'my feet hurt so much that for two years I had to crawl on my hands and knees. Sometimes at night they hurt so much that I could not sleep. I stuck my feet under my mother and she lay on them so they hurt less and I could sleep. But by the time I was eleven my feet did not hurt and by the time I was thirteen they were finished.'[12]

For women, the other potential tragedy was the tradition of arranged marriage, in which they had little if any say. In the country areas, in particular, the doctrine of 'predestined marriage', or 'marriages made in heaven', held sway, which led to such practices as betrothal arranged almost as soon as the child was born. Families might even agree on a match, assuming the sex of the child was right, while it was still in the womb. The arrangements were entirely in the hands of the parents and the matchmaker, and as long as the horoscopes of the pair were acceptable there was no thought of possible incompatibility.

Hsieh Pingying recalls constant battles with her mother over this pre-selection of her partner for life, whom she rejected. Hunger strikes, suicide threats, abortive escapes from home, after which she was locked in her room for weeks on end, did not move the obstinate mother. 'To commit suicide! That was a mere threat. Every young girl is liable to threaten her parents if she doesn't get a husband to her taste. To escape! When she is married she will think better of that. When a woman is in a man's hands, no matter how fierce she was before, she will become as gentle as a lamb.'[13] Pingying, however, was made of sterner stuff and eventually made good her escape on the third attempt.

Chao Wu-Chieh, however, chose a different course to escape from her marriage, arranged for 14 November 1919. As a matter of course, the match had been arranged by her parents and the matchmaker. Although Miss Chao had had only a brief ritual encounter with the young man, she disliked him intensely. But her parents refused to undo the match or postpone the wedding date. On the day of the wedding, as the girl was being raised aloft in the bridal (sedan) chair to be delivered to the groom, she drew out a dagger previously concealed in the chair and slit her throat.

Bridal suicide was not entirely unknown, and the incident might have passed off virtually unnoticed if it had not been taken up by the youthful revolutionary Mao Zedong. Mao wrote nine articles for various publications in which he took up the case of Miss Chao in the context of the broader issues of the role of women in Chinese society. They were, he declared, the unhappy depository of all old habits of thinking, typified by superstition, fatalism and slavish devotion to living authorities. He urged women to abolish the 'man-eating feudal morality . . . and sweep away the goblins [that destroy] physical and spiritual freedom.'[14]

Three months after Miss Chao's death, Li Chitsu became another media *cause célèbre* when she ran away from home in Changsha, Hunan Province, to escape an undesirable match to enroll in a work-study programme in Beijing. Her father, who subscribed to the traditional formula regarding women that 'stupidity is the only virtue', was furious that he had ever let his wife have her own way in sending their daughter to a local girls' school a few years earlier.[15] His outrage became a public issue, with the modernist element hailing Miss Li as a perfect example of how a woman could successfully struggle against the crushing environment of two thousand years of tradition.

The emergence of the Communist Party sounded the death knell for many traditional beliefs.[16] Women who joined the Party struggled alongside the men in an atmosphere of sexual equality hitherto unknown. Some rose to become famous revolutionaries in their own right, rather than because of their husband's position. This was undoubtedly helped by the simple fact that due to the harshness of life in the rural areas, it had never been possible to strictly apply the Confucian rules of gender separation, for a woman's labour was needed in the fields as much as in the home.

One problem in spreading new ideas, however, was that most of the female population was estimated to be illiterate at the turn of the century. Rates remained high for some age groups quite recently, especially when compared to men as Table 8-1 shows. The problem mainly lies in the countryside. For example, only one per cent of urban women born in 1959 were found to be illiterate in the census year, against 33 per cent of rural women. The gap widens as one goes back (e.g. 1:51 per cent for those born in the period 1951–3; moving the other way, the gap had narrowed to 1:17 per cent for girls born in 1966 or 1967).[17] In traditional China, women were denied participation in any political institutions. Leadership in the lineage and village institutions was reserved for men, since this leadership was dependent on the all-male civil bureaucracy. Chinese women lacked legal rights in family councils and in the disposal of property. The kinship structure bound women to a position of powerlessness and dependency. 'Political action mystified them, and concerted group action was unthinkable.'[18]

The third century poet Fu Hsuan perfectly encapsulates the sad fate of women in the following lines:

How sad it is to be a woman
Nothing on earth is held so cheap
No one is glad when a woman is born
By her the family sets no store.[19]

**Table 8-1** Illiteracy Rates By Age and Sex in 1982

| Age | Men (%) | Women (%) |
| --- | --- | --- |
| 15–19 | 4.2 | 14.7 |
| 20–24 | 5.7 | 23.3 |
| 25–29 | 9.6 | 36.1 |
| 30–34 | 13.2 | 40.3 |
| 35–39 | 14.2 | 43.4 |
| 40–44 | 22.4 | 57.3 |
| 45–49 | 32.2 | 74.5 |
| 50–54 | 40.6 | 85.2 |
| 55–59 | 47.5 | 89.7 |
| 60+ | 60.9 | 95.4 |

*Source:* 1982 Census.[20]

But the revolution transformed that situation. And, with Mao declaring that 'women hold up half the sky', liberation in 1949 gave women a new sense of worth and considerably more rights, including those over property and the choice of marital partner.[21] The need to bring women into the work-force in great numbers for the economic reconstruction of the country also transformed their position in society and within the family.

'In the feudal society which lasted several millennia and the subsequent century of semi-colonial and semi-feudal society, Chinese women experienced a bitter history of prolonged oppression, degradation and abasement,' declared a government document published in 1994.[22] It listed some of the achievements made over the past half century, which included:

- Land reform. In old China, poor farmers and farm labourers accounted for 70 per cent of the rural population but owned only 10 per cent of the land. Women had no right to own any land. Land reform in the early days of the PRC redistributed the land according to size of family, with men and women treated equally.
- Universal suffrage. The 1953 Electoral Law stipulated women enjoyed the same rights to vote and stand for election as men.
- Move out of the home. Along with economic rehabilitation and development, there was a nation-wide upsurge of women stepping out of the homes to take part in social production after the founding of the PRC. By 1957, around 70 per cent of rural women were engaged in agricultural work, and the number of urban women workers reached 3.28 million, a 5.5-fold increase over 1949. By 1992, some 44 per cent of the work-force were women. In urban areas, an estimated 56 million were in employment. But this must be set against the increasing difficulty women are now experiencing in finding work, and the continued problem of unequal pay with men.
- Literacy campaign. Three mass campaigns in 1952, 1956 and 1958 established numerous literacy classes, evening schools and worker's part-time schools, so that by the latter date an estimated 16 million women had learned to read.
- Women's economic independence. In new China, the share of women's earnings in total family income has risen from 20 to 40 per cent, and in some rural areas can be as high as 70 per cent. As they have become more economically independent, Chinese women have gained more management and decision-making powers in principal family and economic matters.

☐ Ban on prostitution. Brothels and prostitution, 'disgusting social phenomena left over by old China', were outlawed and the women required to undertake thought reform. 'In a very short period of time, the sale of sex, a chronic social malady [. . .] which seriously damaged the physical and mental health of women and degraded their dignity, disappeared, enabling society to take on a brand-new outlook'.[23]

Writing in 1987, Lei Jieqiong, President of the Society for Research on Marriage and the Family in China, observed: 'Given the profound social and economic changes, it would have been impossible for relations within the family to remain static. The feudal ethic code that held 'the authority of the husband is supreme' and 'the husband governs the wife' has been replaced by a spirit of equality and cooperation. 'Because women have gained access to education and jobs, they are no longer economically dependent on males. Likewise the old adage 'the man manages outside affairs, the woman inside ones' has been cast aside, and the couple shares household chores.[24]

'Financial matters used to rest completely in the husband's hands; now husband and wife decide on expenditure together. As the economic reforms in the countryside have made the family a production unit once more, women have been undertaking business ventures on their own. As they exercise the new initiatives opening up to them, their position in the family is strengthened and their husbands are more willing to treat them on an equal footing.'[25]

This is certainly true to some extent. One of the current thrusts of the national family planning campaign is the empowerment of women, especially in the rural areas, educating them to regain control over their bodies and have the crucial role in decisions on family size. But old habits die hard. One old practice doggedly making a comeback in some rural areas is the buying and selling of women to serve as wives. No one knows how common the sale of wives is, but it is almost certainly increasing. Party documents say the authorities investigated 18,692 cases of women being sold against their will in 1990 and presumably many more never came to the authorities' attention. The documents say that 65,236 people were arrested in the period for involvement in the sale of women and children, a practice which disappeared during the first 20 years of Communist rule and slowly reappeared in the 1970s.

In rural areas, a bride's family will insist on a traditional wedding ceremony and these days the cost of weddings has soared as neighbours try to outdo each other. This has created a strong incentive to buy a wife and save the cost of the festivities. A wife typically costs less than $750 compared with double that amount for a wedding, and the family of the purchased bride is obviously not around to insist on a lavish wedding ceremony.

Police arrested 24 gang members accused of abducting and selling 230 young women in southern China over a three-year period up to 1996. Twenty-five victims were rescued from the city of Lufeng in Guangdong Province, after public security officials acted on tips from distraught relatives. The police investigation showed the women were all looking for jobs in Shenzhen when they were approached by female gang members who promised them lucrative employment. They were taken to Lufeng under the pretence of introducing them to employers and resold to farmers.

In Shandong Province, a check of identity papers in the 1990 census found 14,000 women sold into bondage, according to official media reports. A subsequent crackdown in the province freed 4,000 enslaved women and led to the arrest of 2,000 traffickers. In the city of Suzhou, Jiangsu Province, the same census counted 48,100 women sold into marriage. In one nearby village, two-thirds of all married women were slaves to their husbands. This is a direct result of a strong imbalance in births created by the continued general preference for a male child. There are at least 30 million more men than women, and this shows up starkly in the marrying ages. Official estimates show that in the 25–49 age group, 15 times more men than women have failed to find a spouse. The *Farmers' Daily* newspaper predicted that by 2000, 70 million 'old bachelors' would statistically remain wifeless.[26]

There has also been an upsurge in child kidnapping. Police in the city of Handan, Hebei Province, for example, rescued 51 abducted children and arrested 61 members of a gang which had been selling them. Kidnappers pluck youngsters, usually boys, from the streets of cities and towns and spirit them far away into the country's rural vastness for sale to childless couples. An official of the All China Women's Association, said: 'Most of the kidnapped children go to childless families. Girls and young women are also sold as wives or to the booming sex industry.'[27]

The authorities claim to have caught more than 130,000 people-traffickers between 1991 and 1996, rescuing more than 70,000 women and children who had been sold. Police and government officials are reluctant to give more detailed figures or to discuss their efforts to curb the trade. But media reports put the price of a stolen child at anything from 2,000 Yuan to 5,000 Yuan ($241–$602). Official efforts to find and punish kidnappers have cut the number of cases, but failed to eliminate the underground trade, prompting police to turn their focus towards the source of demand. But it is not easy to end a trade born of desperation. Most buyers are from poor and backward areas who have few alternative means of acquiring that longed-for male heir.

Meanwhile, the preference for sons and modern labour migration patterns have left many villages bereft of women, leaving poor farmers with no choice but to buy a bride. Local authorities are often sympathetic and do little to punish transgressors, while village communities sometimes unite to fend off outside law enforcers. In some remote rural areas, parents still arrange their child's marriage in infancy, a process that is considered irreversible, even if the betrothed couple, once grown up, discover they dislike each other. But young people's attitudes are changing, and they are becoming increasingly unwilling to go along with arranged marriages and are willing to fight their families, even to the extent of going to court, to win the right to choose their own marital partner.

While the market economy being built in China has unleashed productivity to a great extent, it has also posed uncertainty for many people in their lives and careers. And women are the most challenged by the changing society. In 1991, the PRC Law on Protection of Women's Rights and Interests was passed by the National People's Congress (NPC), thus providing a legal basis for women's awareness of their rights, operation of organizations devoted to protection of women's rights and interests, and social efforts in this regard.

In 1996, the concern was whether or not enactment of the Law has exerted a positive influence on Chinese society and how it has advanced social progress and Chinese women's liberation. For two months, May and June, three teams were sent by NPC's Internal and Judicial Affairs Committee to look into the status of protection of women's rights and interests in Shanxi, Sichuan and Guangdong provinces. People's congresses of other provinces were asked to carry out their own checks. In Beijing and some large cities, seminars involving law experts and women activists were held to review the law's implementation and pointing out some existing problems.

Chen Muhua, vice-chairwoman of NPC's Standing Committee and chairwoman of All-China Women's Federation, sums up the results as follows: 'What took place in the past five years demonstrates that enactment and implementation of the law did bring about good changes to our society. The traditional belief that men were superior to women is being gradually eradicated, and women's legal rights guaranteed by law are taking root in most people's minds. 'As a result, women are able to enjoy more choices in development. Never before in history have ordinary Chinese women felt better about their rights to participate in social life, decide their own affairs and stand to protect the rights and interests of their own.'

Professor Yang Dawen of the People's University in Beijing, one of the framers of the law, adds: 'The issue of protection of women's rights and interests appears to be more complicated during the current transition period of China from a planned to a market economy. For example, in the past an enterprise had no right to recruit employees but depended on the government's personnel department for labour supply. Hence, it took on everyone sent by the government, whether male or female. Now, most enterprises have autonomy in employment, and for them, women are the last to be hired and first to be laid off. This is a problem of law, and it is an economic problem too. Given the current situation that China has not had a well-established market system yet, government interference in the protection of women's rights and interests remains necessary.'[28]

Soon after the Law on Protection of Women's Rights and Interests was promulgated, courts at each level organized training classes for judges studying the Law. And, as part of the publicity process, many courts allow the public to attend court sessions hearing typical cases related to women's rights and interests. The Higher People's Court of Qinghai Province opened such a court session in a village yard. The person who violated the Law and would be punished was a deputy of the county's people's congress. Being angry with his daughter-in-law unable to give birth to a baby because of a physical problem, this 'people's representative' had forced his son to divorce her, while ordering some people to smash his daughter-in-law's private property. The court session, attended by over 1,000 members of the public, resulted in the official being jailed and forced to pay an undisclosed amount of compensation to the girl.[29]

According to the Law, women have six prime and basic rights, among which is the right to participate in political activities. But China still has a poor record in this regard, so the government attaches importance to improving this through publicity and enforcing the Law. In the past five years, about two-thirds of the provinces have worked out regulations on a fixed rate of women deputies in the people's congress and people's political consultative conferences. In township governments, previous terms saw an average of 19.7 per cent, but in 1996, the figure rose to 22 per cent. Beijing boasts the highest rate (31.6 percent), while Shanghai, Xinjiang Uygur Autonomous Region, Liaoning and Jilin provinces reached 24 per cent.

Xu Weihua, head of the Rights Protection Department of the All-China Women's Federation, argues that, 'emphasizing an increase in the rate of Chinese women participating in government work while implementing the Law on Protection of Women's Rights and Interests is extremely important. 'That women's rights and interests were infringed or ignored in the past was to a great extent due to lack of the female voice in policy-making. Facts in recent years show that in the cities or areas which have a higher rate of women in government, protection of women's rights and interests are better handled, problems related to women's rights and interests are solved in a shorter period and, consequently, they record less serious cases of infringing women's rights and interests.'[30]

Zhongguancun is a busy commercial street in Western Beijing packed with shops selling computer and other high-tech products. Every day, young people flock to do business or just gossip in the neighbourhood branches of Pizza Hut and Dunkin' Donuts. They are representatives of a lucky group in the city, who share several similarities – good educational background, successful career, decent salary, confidence and optimism. But one office in the same street attracts an entirely different clientele: all female, deeply in trouble, stammering out their requests with constant weeping. This is the first law firm in China, providing legal aid especially for women.

Founded in 1995 by four full-time lawyers and a couple of part-time ones, as well as several young volunteers, The Centre for Women's Legal Studies and Services of Peking University was established to meet current social demands and respond to the call of the Justice Ministry to provide legal aid for people and groups who are weak or suffering through their inferior social status. It under-takes lawsuits for female litigants on a reduced-fee basis or free of charge. By collecting and studying typical cases the Centre regularly issues study reports and lobbies the government to amend or improve the appropriate laws and regulations. The consultations and lawsuits are mainly related to marriage problems, family violence, and labour disputes (management laying off female employees without reason, or forcing female employees to retire ahead of the legal age). And it is this latter aspect that I now wish to deal with.

Zhao Fengjun is a middle-aged woman worker divorced several years ago who brings up her son alone. In 1995, she was arbitrarily sacked by Beijing Huajian Iron Cabinet Factory, just because she had a quarrel with the manager. Zhao found nothing to support the family and once thought about committing suicide. In late 1996, however, the Centre undertook her case by suing the factory, which was eventually forced to re-employ her in a new post.

Gender disparity in the retirement age has become commonplace in enterprises and even government bodies in recent years. Despite government regulations that anyone in a senior technical or professional post should be permitted to work until aged 60, according to personal choice, there are many cases where senior female staff have been required to retire at the age of 55. While the majority of professional women swallow this unfair treatment, returning home to become full-time cooks and cleaners, a few have broken silence to defend their legal rights according to the law. Among them are three senior engineers with China General Company of Aquatic Products, who decided to bring the case to court after being forced to retire at the age 55 or 56.

In court, the company was disdainful, alleging that one of the implications of the modern enterprise system was that management has the right to employ or lay off staff in order to maximise company profitability. But the women's lawyer pointed out that no enterprise in any condition has the right to violate state law and regulations, thus depriving female employees of the right to work by forcing through measures discriminating against them. The three senior engineers, who were actually the technical backbone of the company, finally won their case for reinstatement. Violations of labour contracts, as well as exploitation and bad treatment in the workplace are a growing concern for many women's organizations. On occasions, even the official media has departed from the usual glowing dispatches on women's status to record abuses. One particularly harrowing report dealt with a 'diabolical' boss who locked his female workers in his factory for a year at a time.

'Landlords in the old society are said to have been notoriously cruel, but they pale into insignificance compared with Shi Mengcai and the diabolic, bloody way he treated his women workers. Shi, the owner of a jute factory in the central city of Wuhan, detained his workers for a year at a time behind heavily fortified walls, beat and tortured them for minor offences and threw into a well shaft those who died. He seized identity cards and all belongings when new workers, all from rural areas, entered the factory gates with promises of high wages and good working conditions, and then refused to pay them or let them leave for a year. 'Under Shi's violence, two workers died [in 1994] and many others who suffered severe beatings and were unable to work were thrown out of the plant without any of their salary'.[31]

His 10-year reign of terror only ended when five women escaped from their locked dormitory, evaded armed watchmen and guard dogs during a heavy storm and fled over a four-metre wall. The newspaper reporting the case pointed out that this 'prison or concentration camp', was only 500 metres from both the local government offices and the police station. 'How could Shi get away with all kinds of evil for a decade without local government officials discovering him?'

∞

In Chapter Two, I dealt with the discrimination faced by women in invariably being the first to be laid off and I wish to return to this point briefly. According to a survey in *China Women's News* in December 1997,[32] laid-off women are likely to face more challenges finding other work than men and, as the most vulnerable group, need more assistance from the nation-wide re-employment project.

The survey, carried out by the Women's Work Department of the All-China Federation of Trade Unions, covered 6,413 laid-off women employees, 413 male discharged workers and 413 firm bosses from 14 provinces, cities and autonomous regions across the country. It suggests the problem was generated by both the shortcomings in economic structure and a poor social security system. A result of an irrational industrial structure, the service sector, which is more suitable for women, still lags behind. In small cities where service industry is less developed, re-employment prospects for women are much bleaker.

A fragmented social security system is also a stumbling block to women's re-employment. Since health care, unemployment, maternity and industrial accident coverage is still small, 78.9 per cent of the female laid-off workers surveyed worry about their lives. Although the government has granted favourable policies in offering jobs, there is no operational policy for the continuation in salary and welfare benefits linking the original firm and the targeted one. Channels for job information are sometimes inaccessible, and market employment services need to expand. According to the survey, female laid-off workers made up about half the total population of female employees in 1996 in Shanghai, and Liaoning and Guangdong provinces. Fifty-one per cent of the female interviewees have never found a new job after being laid off.

Gender discrimination is another headache. The questionnaire indicated 71.6 per cent of bosses would not help even though they had positions more appropriate for women. This situation might be because female workers need time off during their childbearing years, the newspaper suggested. Private sector employers sometimes are unwilling to offer welfare, or even take advantage of women's adversity to underpay them. On the other hand, the traditional idea of State firms also hinders laid-off women from accepting reality. 'They always think enterprises are run by the government and losses are just temporary. Government and society will, ultimately, offer them jobs. The survey finds 75.9 per cent of employees still hearken to the formerly safe welfare system and prefer to be re-employed by State-owned firms. If that fails, they would rather stay at home and receive a basic living benefit of $18 per month. Those who are willing to work in the private sector often have expectations that are too high. They are inclined to refuse jobs they consider filthy, dangerous, too demanding or pay too little. Most of them reject jobs such as cleaner, housekeeper and part-time work.'

One of the problems faced by many women in the employment market is a lack of education, which makes their exploitation easier because their sole attraction is their cheapness and ignorance. The women who tend to be laid off are middle-aged and received only primary education during the Cultural Revolution, so that only about 20 per cent are ever likely to get new jobs, the survey indicated. There is an educational inequality at work, and it tends to occur in the same areas which have missed out on the opening rounds of economic reform. While the brightest girls in provincial capitals and big cities enjoy campus life, girls of the same age in remoter parts of the north-west and south-west have little chance of receiving much education. Many drop out of school, more often than not to stay at home and do housework and help support their families. For them, school is inaccessible.

About two-thirds of the country's illiterates are said to be women, a fact underlined by Table 8-1. Among 2.6 million teenage school dropouts officially counted, 67 per cent are girls. More than half are from five remote provinces and autonomous regions: Qinghai, Gansu, Tibet, Guizhou and Ningxia. The average rate of girls not attending primary schools in these regions is as high as 21.2 per cent. In the Ningxia Hui Autonomous Region, a random survey conducted in 1993 showed that 31 per cent of female Hui (Muslim) students dropped out of school or went down to a lower grade in their first two years of schooling, twice the rate of boys.

Economic backwardness is seen as the obvious main cause. In many places in Ningxia, Qinghai and Gansu, peasants retain a simple lifestyle and some are subsistence farmers struggling to feed and clothe themselves. A child is an extra pair of hands to help the family grow food. Although village schools in Gansu ask for an average annual school fee of less than $4 per pupil, this sum nevertheless is a considerable amount to a peasant family whose annual average income is only $24. Insularity is also a problem. A great number of parents, especially mothers, are illiterate and their communities remain closed to outsiders and their ideas. Daughters accept that girls traditionally stay at home to do domestic chores under maternal guidance and comply with the values laid down by ethnic tradition. 'So few of these young mothers ever completed primary school, they take it for granted that their daughters should follow suit. Hence mothers are also a big barrier hindering efforts to enroll more girl pupils in Ningxia,' says Zhou Wei, director of the Ningxia Institute for Education Research. In some Hui communities where Zhou and his colleagues did research work, they found that local tradition encouraged girls to get married at an early age. A favourable requirement to find fortunes or a good husband has always been the ability to run a household and do cooking and cleaning, rather than to have acquired knowledge.

Confucius declared that 'women are indeed human beings, but they are of a lower state than men and can never attain full equality with them'. Some 2,500 years later, Mao Zedong put forward the opposite view: 'Times have changed and today men and women are equal. Whatever men comrades can accomplish, women comrades can too.' Many women would agree with the theory, but would question whether it has yet been fully carried out in practice. Confucius still has a lot to answer for.

# CHAPTER 9

# The China that Can Say No

Politics in modern China, as in no other country, has been dominated by one question: How should relations with the rest of the world be conducted? This may seem somewhat paradoxical given the fact that for the two millennia of the empire the Chinese generally showed little interest in happenings beyond their own horizon. China was not a country, for most of her people, but a world in which foreigners impinged only peripherally. Insofar as most Chinese people thought about other countries at all, it was usually with apprehension, because of the many attacks and invasions the empire suffered from Central Asian tribes: hence the creation of one of the world's great monuments to defensive strategy, namely the Great Wall.

As long as the country was at peace, the Chinese population was generally content to live self-sufficiently off the products of their own land and within their own cultural tradition. But this long isolation is the main reason why in the twentieth century, China has been forced to make foreign policy a central theme of her statecraft. Precisely because she formerly scorned or ignored the achievements of other countries in science, technology, navigation, warfare and economic and political organization, she was weak – despite her vast size – and narrowly escaped being completely carved up by foreign powers as I have already described.

A major cause of the 1911 downfall of the Qing Dynasty was the economic decline brought about by enforced trade links with Western countries on terms of trade highly favourable to those countries, and the national humiliation caused by the loss of Chinese territory to foreign powers. China's failure to win back her lost territories and national dignity at the Versailles Conference which wound up World War I touched off the most important intellectual ferment among wide sectors of the Chinese public about what sort of society should be created and how should it deal with the outside world.

The Korean War profoundly affected China's development as a nation and her acceptability in the world community. Her exclusion from all important world forums, including the United Nations, forced her to follow a path of near self-sufficient growth, even while Soviet technicians were helping to build up her industry. The mounting quarrel with the Soviet Union over points of revolutionary principle and mutual equality led to the withdrawal of these experts in 1960 and the loss of all foreign aid. The present adult generation in the country grew up in an atmosphere of isolation, shut off from Western ideas, bombarded with xenophobic propaganda that emphasized the undesirability of any widespread contact with the outside world, aided by the West's anti-Communist stance that treated the Chinese as pariahs in the international community.

The opening of the door through economic reforms in the late 1970s, however, once again brought to the fore the key issues of foreign policy focussed on China's proper place in the world. China's leaders claim that their foreign policy over the past half-century has always been consistent. If one accepts that the foreign policy concerns of China are those of any other country – to secure its borders and preserve its sovereignty – then their claim is true. But changes in China's foreign policy have led to dramatic changes in its major alliances.

Put simply, the Chinese were closely allied with the Soviet Union in 1950s; during the 1960s, they were hostile to both the Soviet Union and the United States; in the 1970s the Soviet Union was still the arch-enemy and China considered an alliance with the United States a useful safeguard against its northern neighbour; and in the 1980s there was a drastic diminution of hostility towards the Soviet Union, leading to normalization of relations, followed in 1997 by the signing of an agreement designed to put China's relations with Russia and other parts of the former Soviet Union on a friendly footing, including a drastic reduction in military forces on their mutual borders. Now, although China still declares itself part of the Third World, its foreign policy is closely allied with its desire for economic expansion. Gone are the days when relations with fraternal Communist parties were the lynchpin of foreign policy, no matter how small and insignificant the country might be. Now state-to-state relations are of far greater importance.

The emphasis is on omni-directional diplomacy that can be summed up as being nice to everyone who is nice to China. Chinese leaders are constantly roaming the globe, while there is a steady stream of foreign visitors to Beijing, all of whom will be given front-page treatment in the official media along almost identical lines: that the 'traditional'[1] friendly relations between the two countries have never been stronger, but there is still room for further strengthening. Despite all this, there are a few key relationships that need to be examined in detail.

As China grows in strength, how will it handle its relations with the outside world? Ask any Chinese official, and even most ordinary Chinese, and one can expect a lecture on how China is a major contributor to world peace, and that any suggestion to the contrary is malicious propaganda put out by those who want to prevent China from seeking its rightful place in the sun. And yet, in the West, and even in the region immediately surrounding China, concerns still linger that keep alive the concept of the 'China threat' to world peace. Here, for example, is one American view:[2]

> For a quarter century – indeed, almost since Richard Nixon signed the Shanghai Communiqué in 1972 – a comforting and even heart-warming notion has prevailed among policymakers and experts on America's policy towards the People's Republic of China.
>
> They believe that China will inevitably become more like the West: non-ideological, pragmatic, materialistic and progressively freer in its culture and politics. According to them, China is militarily weak and unthreatening; while Beijing tends towards rhetorical excess, its actual behaviour has been far more cautious, aimed at the overriding goals of economic growth and regional stability.
>
> While this vision of China, and especially its diplomatic and economic behaviour, was largely true until the late 1980s, it is now obsolete, as it ignores many Chinese statements and actions that suggest the country is emerging as a great power rival of the United States in the Pacific.

Yes, say the proponents of this line, it is true that China is more open and internationally engaged than at any time since the Communist revolution of 1949. Nevertheless, in recent years, the leadership in Beijing has set goals that are 'contrary to American interests'. Driven by nationalist sentiment, a yearning to redeem the humiliations of the past, and the simple urge for international power, China is seeking to replace the United States as the dominant power in Asia.

> Since the late 1980s, Beijing has come to see the United States not as a strategic partner, but as the chief obstacle to its own strategic ambitions. It has, therefore, worked to reduce American influence in

Asia, to prevent Japan and the United States from creating a 'contain China' front, to build up a military with force projection capability, and to expand its presence in the South China and East China Seas so that it controls the region's essential sea-lanes.

China's sheer size and inherent strength, its conception of itself as a centre of global civilization, and its eagerness to redeem centuries of humiliating weakness are propelling it towards Asian hegemony. Its goal is to ensure that no country in the region [. . .] will act without taking China's interests into prime consideration.'[3]

The China Threat theory started in the early 1990s, a time when China's economy and comprehensive national strength experienced fast growth. In August, 1990, Tomohide Murai, a professor at the Tokyo Defence University, an article in an academic journal entitled 'On the Potential Threat of China', described China as a potential adversary in view of its comprehensive national strength and long-term development. But this did not attract much attention at the time because the world was focussing on drastic changes taking place in Eastern Europe.

In 1992, two events in China gave momentum to the theory. On 25 February, the National People's Congress adopted the Law on the Territorial Sea of the People's Republic of China, confirming a claim of sovereignty over some offshore outcrops of rock, including Nansha Islands and Daioyu Islands. Some observers interpreted this event as a sign that China was pushing for military expansionism and attempting to become a regional hegemon. The Japanese media claimed that the modernization process of the Chinese navy revealed China's marine hegemonism strategy in the twenty-first century. The US media also carried stories declaring that China was expanding outside its territory, its military might was growing fast, and that China aimed to dominate East Asia.

In the same year, the China economic threat theory also emerged following the late Chinese leader Deng Xiaoping's tour of southern China which provided the launch pad for the robust economic growth that shows little sign of diminishing. While generally showing appreciation of China's economic achievements, the Western media also worried it would become a competitor for world markets, funds and resources, and even worse, provide more resources for China's military expansion. This economic threat theory was first raised by South Korea and was soon echoed by Japan and the United States.

Harvard University professor Samuel Huntington enriched the China threat theory in 1993, when he published an article entitled 'The Conflict of Civilizations', in which he analyzed how Chinese culture challenged Western civilization. He believed that after the end of the Cold War, the ideological conflict had been replaced by a conflict of civilizations, which was the origin of international conflicts and wars. He said that world civilization could be divided into eight groups, including Confucianism. The primary adversary of Western civilization was Islam and Confucianism, which joined hands to challenge Western values and power.

Huntington made some specific suggestions for the West to ensure continued global dominance, including reinforcing interior unity and cooperation; embracing East European and Latin American countries with similar cultures to the West; promoting and collaborating with Russia and Japan; preventing regional conflicts among different civilizations from becoming real war; restricting the development of the military forces of Confucianist and Islamic countries; slowing down the reduction of military forces and keeping military advantage in East and Southeast Asia.

Before the dust had settled, Lester Brown then stepped in with his fears of China's food crisis, as discussed earlier. It will be recalled that he predicted a combination of growing population and dwindling land so that China's self-reliance in food-supply would greatly decrease and a shortage would cause a world-wide food crisis in the coming century.

In general, therefore, the 'China Threat' theories fall into the following four categories:

MILITARY. China is fast increasing its military budget and expanding its military arms, and is stimulating a new round of the arms race in the Asia-Pacific region; China sells arms and even transfers nuclear weapons technology to some countries, therefore escalating regional conflicts; China is trying to increase its military strength as the former Soviet Union has disintegrated and US military strength is contracting, attempting to fill the vacuum in the Asian-Pacific region; China prepares to use its increasingly strong navy to take control of the disputed islands in the South China Sea.

ECONOMIC. China is now the third largest economic power in the world, and will take over the leading position within the next 20 years or so. In addition, with the growing economic links between the mainland, Hong Kong, Macao and Taiwan, it raises the prospect that the coming century will be the century of China who will completely control the economy of Southeast Asia. Some critics suggest China is trying to use the economic cooperation that has been cemented by the same culture and family bonds with the overseas Chinese to harm the states where these Chinese live (e.g. Indonesia, Malaysia, the Philippines and Thailand).

OVERALL CRISIS THEORY. This includes arguments on China's food crisis, rural crisis, population crisis, resources crisis and environment crisis. These various crises will make the country a heavy burden to the entire world. The logic, as divined by the Chinese themselves, is that they should never climb out of poverty and become rich. If they do so, the world would experience shortages of food, resources and damage to the environment. CIVILIZATION THREAT. The Huntington concept merges with the China nationalism threat theory. Some US media claim an anti-Western stance is the primary characteristic of the national identity of China, which is especially strong when faced with any suggestion of an external threat.

The Chinese say the basic logic of all these theories is the same: China is an emerging monster that will threaten world security and stability and must be restrained. The theories all have the same aim: worsening of the international and regional environment that is critical to China's development so as to contain it; and inventing excuses for their interference in Chinese internal affairs so as to maintain their own monopoly over the world and ensure their utmost interests.

Many of the sentiments of the various threats were also prominent in a book published in 1996 in the United States under the provocative title 'The Coming Conflict with China',[4] which drew strong counter-arguments from China. In essence, the thesis is that if the United States, the only political, economic, military and cultural power in the post-Cold-War period, wants to maintain and develop these superiorities in the next century, it must get a clear understanding of the various challenges it faces and defeat them. One of these challenges comes from the European Union, but this is mainly economic, and is not so threatening because the EU and the United States have similar historical and cultural traditions, life-styles and value concepts.

The second challenge comes from Japan, and is also mainly economic. In addition, Japan will compromise under American pressure because it needs US military protection and because of its vast domestic market. Only China poses a genuinely serious threat because it differs greatly from the United States in cultural traditions, life-style and value concepts. Wang Jisi, Director of American Studies Institute, China Academy of Social Sciences,[5] however, is dismissive of the arguments, saying:

> The basic logic of the book is that conflict between China and the United States will be inevitable, since China's economic strength and military prowess is growing; China is refusing to copy the Western

model of democracy; Chinese nationalism is on the upsurge; and China is threatening to use force to regain Taiwan. Such an argument is neither persuasive or new. It is merely a more systematic and more dangerous version of the old 'China Threat' theory.

His belief is that such 'unfounded and biased views' are gaining popularity because of a strong sense of American nationalism, otherwise referred to as patriotism, a commodity which the United States does not like to see being paraded out by other countries.

At the same time, the American public's understanding of world affairs is often oversimplified. For more than 70 years, the US has been fighting against obvious enemies, from Germany and Japan in the Second World War to the former Soviet Union in the Cold War. After the end of the Cold War, the United States can find no enemy among the big powers and US foreign policy seems to have lost its goal. Under such circumstances, the American public is easily provoked when the media becomes excited about some alleged 'anti-democratic' big power openly challenging the leadership of the United States.

It seems to them that as soon as the United States finds an enemy, its foreign policy and military strategy will be clarified. A renowned American historian pointed out several years ago that the US people were not accustomed to having no enemy, and always wanted to find one in order to define the direction of the foreign policy.

Shi Yinhong, Professor of History at Nanjing University,[6] takes a similar line:

We might say that the current fear towards China is a normal event in history. Currently there is an Anti-China force in the United States, championing the China Threat theory and Sino-US confrontation. However, what has made this force influence the American media and politics so strongly is fear of China. The presence of such sentiment can be attributed to a host of factors, from ideology, racial sentiment, cultural psychology to geopolitics, economic interest and world power structure.

The United States is the only superpower in the world, and China is a rising developing country that has shown potential to become a big power in the future. Throughout history, the existing super powers have basically held three kinds of attitudes, or reactions toward rising new powers: coordination that results from a pragmatic and mild attitude; confrontation that comes out of fear and hostility; contradictory policies and unclear strategy, accompanied by a sense of doubt and alienation. Some Americans are afraid that the power structure will change fundamentally, their economic advantage will be hampered and their strategic sphere of influence lost. In history, most of the old powers have held such a mentality towards rising new powers, even if the latter are identical or close to them in regard to ideology, nationality and cultural tradition.

China and the United States have been through many phases of friendship and tension in recent decades. From 1949 to 1970 was the confrontation period of their relations. The US, influenced by McCarthyism, regarded New China as a scourge, refusing to establish diplomatic relations with the PRC, severed all trade and economic exchanges, imposed an economic blockade against the country, and waged war on its boundaries. During the early 1970s to late 1980s, there was a significant thaw leading to establishment of full diplomatic relations and even some forms of cooperation.

A further setback occurred in 1989 with the imposition of economic sanctions by the United States and its allies following the crushing of the 'democracy' movement in Beijing. In the 1990s, this has been superseded by a reappraisal of China's position in the world, and the implications for the global balance of power in the face of China's growing economic strength and international influence. This period has been marked by numerous ups and downs, warming and cooling, fanned at times by American policies, especially on human rights and trade matters, that have irritated China's leaders and produced a nationalistic reaction among intellectuals and ordinary Chinese alike.

At the same time, China's willingness, even eagerness, to improve the Sino-American mood is sometimes seen by American analysts as merely paying lip service to the idea of genuine friendship. Since the Taiwan crisis of early 1996, when China's decision to stage large-scale military exercises in the Strait of Taiwan during Taiwan's presidential election led the United States to deploy two aircraft carrier task forces to the region, the Chinese leadership worked hard to restore normality. This certainly reflects, in part, continued interest in the burgeoning trade and technology transfer relationship with the United States and a hope of quelling anti-Chinese sentiment in Congress and among the American public that has led to a bitter annual debate over the presidential decision to grant China Most Favoured Nation trade status.

China's goal of achieving paramount status in Asia conflicts with an established American objective: preventing any single country from gaining overwhelming power in Asia. The United States, after all, has been in major wars in Asia three times in the past half-century, always to prevent a single power from gaining ascendancy, although at a cost of declining American military prestige. Given the fact that over the next decade or two China will become the dominant power on its side of the Pacific, conflict with the United States could occur over a number of issues, headed by a Chinese attempt to seize Taiwan by force or to resolve by military means its territorial claims in the South China Sea, particularly as China's military strength continues to grow.

In approaching the Taiwan issue, however, the Chinese establishment does not see it just in terms of settling the final chapter in the civil war struggle between the Communists and Nationalists for control of the country. This is certainly an element, but it has to be seen in a wider context of a Chinese belief that dismemberment of the motherland in any shape or form, as happened in the nineteenth century, equates with weakness.

The argument can be summarized thus: the West feels heavy-hearted facing an increasingly powerful China, therefore the so-called China problem has emerged. The West thinks the best way to solve the problem is to dismember the country, as it did so effectively with the former Soviet Union, and the separatist activities on Taiwan provide just such an opportunity. If the United States, or any of its allies, does not exploit this issue, once Taiwan has been reunified with mainland China, the latter will be redoubled in might and will surely realize the rejuvenation of the whole nation within a short period, posing a threat to Western interests. Therefore, the continuing arguments over Taiwan[7] are merely a new chapter in the fight of the Chinese nation, dogged by bad luck, against the suppression and containment of the big powers and for the existence and development of the nation as a whole. This is a powerful argument that seems to be widely accepted in the country.

Even without actual war over an issue like Taiwan, China and the United States are likely to be adversaries in the major global rivalry of the first decades of the next century, with other countries in the area invited to take sides. 'Moreover, the Chinese-American rivalry of the future could fit into a broader new global arrangement that will increasingly challenge Western, and especially American, global supremacy. China's [. . .] technological and political help to the Islamic countries of Central Asia and North Africa, and its looming dominance in East Asia put it at the centre of an informal network of states, many of which have goals and philosophies inimical to the United States, and many of which share China's sense of grievance at the long global domination of the West.'[8] But what of the arguments that China's integration into the world economy will make it more moderate and cautious in its foreign policy and more open and democratic at home? Certainly, Chinese officialdom never tires of repeating the message that the country desperately needs a climate of peace and cooperation in order to carry out its economic modernization.

The alternative view, however, sees its more aggressive behaviour in recent years as a consequence of its growing economic and military strength and demonstrated through intensified xenophobic impulses. Its more modern economy and its greater economic influence, it is argued, are already giving it power to enhance its authoritarianism at home, resist international dissatisfaction with its policies and practices, and expand its power and prestige abroad in ways hostile to American interests.

Zhang Baijia, associate researcher of the History of the Chinese Communist Party,[9] asserts:

> The history of Sino-US relations since the founding of New China shows confrontation is inevitable if the United States chooses to make China an enemy. China, though unwilling to confront the United States, will not be afraid to do so if it has to; second, confrontation will hurt both sides, while cooperation will benefit both. The 20 years of confrontation in the 1950s and 1960s did both sides great harm, and the détente from the 1970s benefited them greatly.

Wang Jisi adds:

> Ordinarily, the current conflicts between the two countries will not lead to confrontation. Though they have such fundamental differences on ideology, social systems and human rights, a large-scale confrontation is unlikely unless a major national security problem occurs. The Taiwan question is, in fact, the only major problem that might ignite a major conflict. A confrontation will be inevitable under the circumstance that the central government is forced to take measures to stop the Taiwan independence activity from splitting the motherland, and the United States interferes in accordance with the so-called Taiwan Relations Act. Surely, this is merely a possibility, and not something inevitable.
>
> What is most dangerous about the China Threat theory is that the assumption of China as a strategic enemy of the United States might give the anti-China forces in the US more excuses to play the Taiwan card and encourage the separation of China.

Zhang, meanwhile, is adamant that China's development depends on a peaceful world and wide international cooperation. 'As a big country whose population makes up a quarter of the world's total, China's development is a major contribution to the world. For some reasons, however, China's development has aroused suspicion and fear among some countries. We can understand it as long as it is not malicious. 'As early as 1956, Premier Zhou Enlai said: "We understand that a rising country, especially a big country, usually cannot be fully understood in quite a short period of time, and may sometimes arouse suspicions and fears. With rumours and instigations, such misunderstanding and fear might become more intense. However, rumours and provocations cannot bear the test of facts, and misunderstanding and suspicion will be eliminated through more frequent contact." We believe history will prove that the Chinese government's pledge that it will never pursue hegemonism and never become a superpower is not empty words.'

The irony in Sino-American relations now is that when China was in the grip of ideological Maoism and displayed such ideological ferocity that Americans believed it to be dangerous and menacing, it was actually a 'paper tiger' (to quote one of Mao's favourite phrases), weak and virtually without global influence. Now that China has embarked on a pragmatic course of economic development and global trade, it appears less threatening in comparison to the height of the Cold War, but in fact has at least some wherewithal to back its global ambitions and interests with real power.

If it continues a rapid military modernization, China is seen by many Americans as the only country that will be capable of challenging their power in East Asia – and only the US will have the influence to counterbalance China's regional ascendancy. Of course, they argue, if China became a democracy, its military build-up would be far less threatening than if it remained a dictatorship. 'But while the forces pushing towards global democracy are probably too powerful for China to remain unaffected by them forever, there is no reason to believe that China will become democratic in the near future. In the first place, that would be contrary to China's political culture.'[10]

China's build-up of naval, air and amphibious forces, in the eyes of the critics in Washington, provides it with the ability to seize and control almost the entire South China Sea, now divided between Vietnam, Malaysia, Brunei and the Philippines. In fact, possession of the various islands and outcroppings stretching south would put the PLA almost within sight of Singapore and Indonesia, and astride the only viable international sea lane connecting the Pacific and Indian Ocean. If it succeeded in extending its control over Taiwan, it would simultaneously gain the two southern approaches to Japan, namely the Taiwan and Luzon Straits.

At the same time, when Korea is finally reunified, as will possibly happen at some stage, China will likely press for the withdrawal of American forces from Northeast Asia, save for troops in Japan to inhibit the remilitarization of the Korean peninsula. It will use its influence in Northeast Asia for two purposes, both of them inimical to American interests: to bring about a pro-Chinese, anti-American and anti-Japanese stance in Korea, and to perpetuate Japan's status as a non-normal country, one without the right to assume primary responsibility for its own defence. China could thus assume its predominance in Asia vis-a-vis the only country in the region with the size and strength to challenge it.

The primary American objective in Asia, therefore, must be to prevent China's size, power and ambition from making it a regional hegemon. Achieving that goal requires the maintenance of American military presence in Asia and keeping it vastly more powerful and effective than China's armed forces. Amid all the arguments for containing China, however, there are other voices declaring that these efforts are futile. Former US State Secretary Henry Kissinger, the man who negotiated the Sino-US rapprochement of the early 1970s, has said[11] that no force could hold back the rise of a new power. No matter how the United States treats China, it can never stop the more and more important role of the country in future international affairs. Kissinger also noted that Sino-US relations have been fostered and developed out of American interests, therefore, most Asian countries would think the United States was making trouble out of nothing if it took hostility towards China as the long-term state policy provoking a new Cold War.

China's concern about the direction of American foreign policy also encompasses the role of Japan, both alone and in the context of continued American Far East security strategy. In February 1995, the US Defense Department released its Security Strategy for the East Asia-Pacific Region. Subsequently, the United States and Japan took a series of steps to strengthen their alliance. Officials and scholars in both countries gave a number of reasons to reinforce their security ties: to bring US-Japanese economic friction aggravated since the Cold War under control; to cope with a potential crisis on the Korean Peninsula; and, to provide a common shield for regional security and stability. On a number of official occasions, American and Japanese officials have stressed the redefined US-Japanese alliance is not directed at China. The latter remains unconvinced.

From its viewpoint, a closer US-Japanese security alliance is cause for concern for several reasons. The redefinition of the security alliance comes at a time when the two countries are growing increasingly wary of China's development. According to several of the Chinese officials I talked to, it is tempting to infer that there is a correlation between efforts to strengthen US-Japanese security ties and the watchful attitude of Washington and Tokyo towards an alleged 'China threat'. In terms of balance of power, they argued, the United States and Japan are much more powerful than China, and the alliance between Washington and Tokyo is, therefore, a powerful one. Under the circumstances, China, the weakest in the triangle, is naturally sensitive to any move by the Americans and Japanese to seek a closer alliance. The question naturally arises: at a time when the security environment in the Asia-Pacific region has already improved significantly compared to the Cold War era, why should the United States and Japan fortify their alliance?

As one senior Beijing analyst observed: 'Although they claim they have stepped up their security cooperation to tackle possible conflicts on the Korean Peninsula, the fact is that the US-Japanese security alliance, formed during the Cold War, already constitutes an effective mechanism to check potential crises erupting in Korea. Given the increasingly distrustful attitude of the US and Japan towards China's growth and China's growing influence in regional affairs the claim that a stronger US-Japanese security alliance is not aimed at China is questionable.'

Other moves by the United States and Japan tie in with their efforts to build up their security alliance, which further aggravates China's concern. The most noteworthy issue is the Taiwan question. The US and Japan saw China's missile tests in 1995 and 1996, with dummy warheads flying over and around Taiwan, as a convincing excuse to boost their security cooperation. China, however, believed the catalyst for the missile tests (dubbed a 'warning signal' by Beijing) was the changed American position on Taiwan, which it believed negated the long-held Sino-American agreements governing the normalization of relations, that there was only one China, comprised of the mainland and Taiwan, and that the United States would do nothing to encourage separatist ideas on the island.

But the alarm bells began ringing even louder in Beijing on 17 August 1997, when Japanese Chief Cabinet Secretary Seiroku Kajiyama declared publicly that the 'surrounding areas' covered by Japan-US security collaboration should 'naturally include the Taiwan Strait'. This was described by the Chinese as 'the first time a top Japanese official has openly interfered in China's internal affairs since the normalization of Sino-Japanese diplomatic relations'.

Speaking in a Tokyo television interview, Kajiyama said: 'Since the Taiwan Strait lies to the north of the Philippines, it belongs to the Far East region. Therefore, in theory, disputes between Taiwan and China should be within the scope of Japan-US security collaboration.' A commentary published by the official media in China a few days later observed that while it was true 'the Taiwan Strait lies to the north of the Philippines, who laid down the rule that areas to the north of the Philippines should be included in the Japan-US Security Treaty? Did countries in the region give permission? It turns out that Seiroku's so-called theory refers to the sixth article of US-Japan Security and Defense Treaty signed in 1960. At that time, the world was embroiled in the Cold War, and both Japan and the United States were hostile towards China. The treaty was born under this circumstance, and thus embodied hegemonism.

Today, however, with the end of the Cold War and the improvement in Sino-Japan and Sino-US relations, what is the main purpose of applying such an old theory? What's more, as early as 1978 the then Japanese Foreign Minister declared that the article on the Far East in the security treaty has lost its legal force. Kajiyama said that if the US takes actions when a dispute breaks out between China and Taiwan, while Japan just looks on, then what use was the bilateral security pact? Besides, ignoring the fact that the Taiwan issue is China's internal affair, he said: 'We worry that China will liberate Taiwan by force'.

As is well known, Taiwan is an inalienable part of Chinese territory. Through the years, China maintains the principle of reuniting the nation peacefully under the concept of 'one country, two systems'.[12] But the Chinese government has never promised to give up using weapons, considering that independent forces exist in Taiwan and there is a possibility of foreign interference.

In April 1996, Japan and the US decided to revise the principles of their security collaboration, in regard to which Prime Minister Ryutaro Hashimoto observed that defining security scope was 'unlike drawing boundaries on a map', while an official of his Liberal Democratic Party commented that the 'surrounding areas' in Japan's view was not 'a geographical concept'. He thought an 'ambiguous' attitude should be taken on the issue, because the security scope should not be stipulated beforehand in detail. On the contrary, it should be determined when the proper time comes.

Obviously, say the official Chinese spokesmen, such attempts are directed at nobody else but China, which must remain vigilant to every move. From a global perspective, the fortified US-Japanese security alliance is part of a greater effort by the West to implement what is known as 'preventive diplomacy' against the non-Western world, including the transitional countries. Washington has observed, to its dismay, that its role in influencing non-Western powers such as Russia and China in the post-Cold War era is limited.

It subsequently adopted a dual policy. On the one hand, the United States continues to keep Russia and China engaged in the hope they will evolve in a direction favourable to the West. On the other hand, it seeks to strengthen US-orchestrated security alliances forged in the Cold War to strategically 'prevent' non-Western powers from challenging its domination; hence, the enlargement of NATO and the fortification of bilateral alliances in the Asia-Pacific region centreing around US-Japanese security cooperation.

The United States and Japan find it necessary to find some kind of 'common enemy' to maintain stability in their relations. The security alliance is the foundation for US-Japanese relations and a major adhesive for bolstering that alliance is a common enemy. The collapse of the Soviet Union eroded that foundation, and the escalating economic friction between the two countries threatened to jeopardize their overall relationship. In the Chinese assessment, setbacks in Sino-Japanese relations coincide with improvements in US-Japan security links. Since the release of the Japan-US Joint Declaration on the Security Alliance for the twenty-first century, in particular, Sino-Japanese relations have been described on many occasions as having 'sunk to their lowest ebb since the establishment of diplomatic ties in 1972'.

In Beijing, officials point to the fact that Prime Minister Hashimoto became the second prime minister since Yasuhiro Nakasone in 1985 to visit the Yasukuni Shrine where the remains of many Japanese war criminals are buried and worshipped. At the same time, Diet members had 'offered irresponsible remarks on history', such as downplaying Japanese aggression in China, along with the rewriting of history to suggest that such well-documented events as the sack of Nanjing in 1937, in which hundreds of thousands of civilians were slaughtered, either never took place or was grossly exaggerated. In addition, some Japanese rightists landed on the Daioyu Islands (known to Japan as the Senkakus) on several occasions, reviving a territorial dispute that had lain dormant for many years. Although Tokyo disowned the island landings, the Chinese remained suspicious that rightist forces were gaining ascendancy in Japan, presaging a revival of the militarism that once proved so disastrous for China and much of Asia.

Although it is more than half a century since the Japanese imperial army was ousted from Chinese territory, feeling continues to run high, fanned for each succeeding generation by constant repetition of the crimes of the invaders. New books continue to be published dealing either with the atrocities committed by the

Japanese, or the heroic fight against them waged ceaselessly by the outgunned Communist guerrillas fighting with one hand tied behind their back (due to the treachery of the Nationalist forces more intent on defeating Communism than Japanese militarism); hardly a week goes by without Chinese television showing at least one film of the anti-Japanese struggle. Comic books inculcate the new young generation with resentment against Japanese militarists, as does a 1997 revival of the Peking Opera *Shajiabang*, portraying an incident from the war, which first gained popularity in the Maoist era.[13]

The Chinese government never tires of reminding its Japanese counterpart of this particular period, or of seeking further proof that the Japanese have learnt the lesson of history. There is a strong sense of betrayal evident at times when Chinese officials contrast the magnanimity of the Beijing government in waiving the right to seek war reparations from Japan, and Tokyo's refusal to curb the anti-Chinese activities of its rightist elements, which is cited as one reason that bilateral relations can never be regularized:

> The magnanimity and tolerance of the Chinese people did not receive a positive echo from the Japanese nation. To some extent, it is really a tragedy to the former. If it hadn't given up voluntarily the war compensation, its people would surely have better living conditions today and it wouldn't happen that the Japanese time and again threaten to freeze its loans to China – a kind of compensation known clearly to both sides.
>
> Japan has always turned its back to China. The distortion of historical facts in its history books, the interpretation of invasion as 'entering and helping' [China], the repeated nonsense of some senior officials, the export of third-grade products to China (the best to the US and the second kept for itself), and the strengthening of the US-Japan security system which is aimed at China. Japan hasn't made any effort to narrow the historical gap with Asian countries.[14]

These considerations nurture China's distrust of the US-Japan security alliance, which official sources stress was previously absent. Since the early 1970s, when President Richard Nixon visited China, and the latter forged diplomatic ties with Japan, the US-Japanese alliance, as part of a global strategy to contain the Soviet threat, was not challenged by China. On the contrary, China even spoke positively of the alliance. Shortly after the end of the Cold War, even with the disintegration of the Soviet Union, the alliance still did not become a concern to China. Rather, it started to criticize only after the US and Japan sought to redefine their security alliance in a direction that China deemed detrimental to its security interests.

These changes not only invite distrust and wariness from China but may also affect adversely regional peace and stability.

The Chinese view summarized above gains some credence when set against the remarks of the authors of *The Coming Conflict With China*, that the 'growth of Chinese power has made America's overarching attitude towards Japan obsolete. The United States can no longer operate on the assumption that a weak Japan is a good Japan. If that was once true, it was only because China was poor and weak. In the post-Cold War world, it is Japan's weakness that threatens peace and stability by creating a power vacuum that the United States alone can no longer fill. A strong Japan, in genuine partnership with the United States, is vital to a new balance of power in Asia. A weak Japan benefits only China, which wants no stabilizing balance of power but Chinese hegemony, under which Japan would be little more than Beijing's most useful tributary state.

'The difficulties here are considerable. The United States cannot block Chinese hegemony in Asia unless Japan is an equal and willing partner in the process. But if it pushes Japan, the result could be an anti-American reaction there. The United States must demonstrate that it is a reliable ally, while waiting for Japan to come to grips with an increasingly threatening security environment. China's determination to achieve hegemonic status in Asia will probably facilitate this. But the United States and Japan must realize they need each other.'

The Chinese response to this can be summed up as follows:

Because of the sheer weight of the three countries in regional security affairs, it is imperative for China, the United States and Japan to establish a security relationship of mutual trust and stability. As demonstrated in the past, such a relationship serves the peace, stability and prosperity of the Asia-Pacific region. A review of recent history reveals the regional landscape exhibiting vastly different features when China, Japan and the United States choose different policies towards each other.

When the US and Japan joined forces in the confrontation with China, the region witnessed two large-scale wars in Korea and Indochina. When the United States and Japan opted to cooperate with China, however, peace and prosperity dawned, which eventually nourished an economic miracle – the rise of East Asia. This was achieved when other parts of the world were experiencing chaos and economic recession. A constructive and cooperative relationship among the three nations, therefore, is a public asset contributing to the region's stability and prosperity, an asset that should not be discarded simply because the Cold War has ended.'[15]

It is worth stressing, however, that although having Japanese troops on Chinese soil continuously from 1894 to 1945 has certainly coloured current attitudes in China towards Japan, it would be wrong to talk in terms of the two countries as being 'traditional enemies'. As neighbours bound closely together by geography and many elements of a common cultural heritage continually reinforced over the ages, they are destined to be either friend or foe. Indifference or aloofness do not seem practical for either in the long run.

If we look back over the centuries to the time when the Japanese first absorbed the literary culture of the Tang Dynasty as well as the Buddhist religion, cultural ties were close and there was little political enmity. This was the norm for most of the succeeding centuries, although the Mongol invaders of China tried to undo all the good feeling by two abortive attempts to land an invasion army in Japan; at the same time, Chinese scholars and monks fleeing the Mongols brought a fresh infusion of cultural and religious influence. In the succeeding Ming Dynasty, Chinese philosophers were widely read and studied as much in Japan as in their homeland. Contacts were sparse for much of the Qing Dynasty, however, due to the closed nature of Japan to outside trade and other influences.

Even when relations began to deteriorate, as a revived Meiji Japan, an apt pupil of the colonial and imperial European powers, began to target China in fulfillment of its expansionist ambitions, there were still close contacts in other fields. Japan became the transmitter of the modern, originally Western science and technology which backward China desperately needed. Thousands of Chinese students completed their higher education in Japan, eager to learn what had enabled that nation to throw off the shackles of feudalism and stand up against the Western powers with such evident success. If nothing else, in recent decades, Japan has become the benchmark against which the Chinese can measure their economic revival.

In many ways, particularly in the economic arena, Japan and China complement each other, so that there is much to be said for trying to restore aspects of the ancient good relationship that I have described. This, however, runs up against the seeming inevitability of the two countries becoming rivals for economic dominance in their region. And, yet, in the interests of regional security and stability, there seems little option but for the two countries to find ways to put recent history behind them and cooperate in a broad range of economic, political and social fields.

But, having digressed into the Japan issue, let me now return briefly to the over-arching theme of Sino-American relations. In seeking to help the Chinese public understand why the United States has such a 'distorted' view of China, the explanation most often offered is that a key factor is the inaccurate reporting of the American media, still bogged down in cold war rhetoric. A book entitled *Behind the Scene of Demonizing China*, published in 1997 by a group of eight Chinese scholars and journalists[16] all of whom received higher education in the United States, provided fulsome evidence of this.

The first chapter, 'Inside Story of Demonizing China', says narrow capitalist national interests, ideology formed during the Cold-War period and the racist concept based on white chauvinism are the major social and ideological roots for some US media to deliberately vilify China. The authors claim the key reason for US news organizations to act in this way 'lies in their stand to safeguard the great capitalist national interests of the United States:

These national interests are dominated by the US hegemonical inclination for foreign aggrandizement and maintenance of its position as the sole superpower in the world. Driven by such national interests, the US media employ every possible means to defame China and depict the country as an autocratic 'evil empire', so as to isolate China in the world.

Ideology first is another distinguishing feature of US media in reporting on China. Their coverage is not pluralistic, but totally parochial and exclusive. All news and comments seem to follow the same pre-set tone. This makes the United States known as a country the most ideologically tinged among all Western nations. The power culture demonstrated in the country's news reports and comments is quite compatible with its political, military and economic hegemony in the world.

Due to the strong anti-Communist sentiment of the US media and their high-handed policy against Communism in the ideological field, Americans are the most afraid of being tied up with Communism or Communist countries. Those who are accused of sympathizing with the Communists would find themselves in an isolated position in society and would even be unable to find a job. This is also the chief reason why few in the US news organizations dare to step forward bravely to report on China objectively and impartially.

In addition to the ideological prejudice, the racism giving superiority to the white is another major factor. The US media use the Western Christian human rights concept to oppose the Oriental Confucianist human rights value.[17] Their reports on the issue of

China, regardless of the Taiping Heavenly Kingdom (1851–64), Yihetuan (Boxers) Movement (1900) or New China led by Mao Zedong, all bear racist descriptions and prejudice. The US media generally demonize China by giving it the following bad names: (1) China will be the future nuclear war maniac; (2) China threatens the United States and its neighbouring countries[18]; (3) The Chinese are becoming 'increasingly nationalistic'; (4) China is stealing intellectual properties and threatening the global economy; (5) China is a police state trampling on human rights; and so on.

The authors believe that in demonizing China, the ultimate goals of the American media are to 'sabotage the Sino-US relations, scare away foreign investors in China, and divert the international public's attention from the hegemonic and expansionist activities of the United States around the world. They also aim to bolster up the Japanese militarism, advocate the US-Japanese alliance to counter China and stimulate Asian countries to form an anti-China military alliance with the United States'.

I must say that I have a great deal of sympathy with the arguments put forward. As someone who worked for many years as a foreign correspondent in many parts of the Far East for some of the world's leading news organizations, I have always been appalled at the arrogance, naïvete and narrow-mindedness of much of the American media. Superficiality, stereotypical representations and formulaic writing typify much of the coverage of the extremely complex developments occurring in Asia. If one doesn't accept the entire package of American cultural values, then one must either be backward or lacking in morality. At the same time, there is nothing new in this desire to present a negative portrait of the Chinese.[19]

It would be well to pause for a moment and consider why China generates so much passion in the United States. My feeling is that it has much to do with the strong emotional ties which Americans have had for China since the nineteenth century. China was in many ways the Westernmost point in the expansion of the American land. American movement has been from East to West away from Europe towards the Pacific. America's territorial acquisitions, aside from continental North America and Puerto Rico, have been entirely in the Pacific: Hawaii, Samoa, the Philippines, the islands of Oceania, and now Okinawa.

In the period following the Civil War, thousands of American missionaries and businessmen went Westward, and China was one of their main targets. 'Accounts of life in China formed a major part of the vast missionary literature that appeared during the late nineteenth century in America. Whatever the anti-Oriental feeling on the West Coast, to the established upper and middle classes of New England and the Middle West, China appeared to be America's special responsibility in the world.'[20] America's oft-repeated concern about the territorial integrity of China and the need to make China into a modern nation rested on a deep conviction that China was so poor and backward that it would take decades or even centuries before she could reach the levels of the great world powers, a conviction arising perhaps from the missionary writings of the period. China was portrayed as weak, degenerate, starving, disorganized, incapable of doing anything for itself, and in need of special protection.

There was a strong sense of betrayal in the United States when China fell to the Communists typified by the demand during the MrCarthy era to unmask the 'traitors' within the government who had 'lost China'. State department officials saw their careers ruined, and writers on China such as Edgar Snow, author of the seminal work 'Red Star Over China', were forced to live in exile for years.

Whatever the reasons for the American-led Western attacks on China, their affect has been to strengthen the country's sense of national pride and patriotic sentiment: exactly the characteristics the American media and some politicians find most distressing. In mid-1996, for example, two best-selling books were published in Beijing with the titles of *The China That Can Say No* and *Chronicles of Sino-US Contest*. At the same time, public opinion polls conducted by some leading newspapers showed that the number of young Chinese who thought the United States was unfriendly towards China had increased rapidly.

The US media hold that such hatred for America is whipped up by the Chinese government in its advocacy of education in patriotism. And yet, do not American schoolchildren salute the flag and sing 'The Star Spangled Banner' at the start of each day in class? If there is one nation that has brought flag-waving patriotism to a peak it is surely the United States. My own feeling is that the seeds of hatred for the United States among Chinese youths, especially the young intellectuals, have been planted by the US media themselves, although I do feel a bit uncomfortable when I hear Chinese government spokesmen repeatedly attacking the actions of other countries by saying these acts have 'hurt the feelings of the Chinese people', which creates a rather wimpish image in my mind.[21]

∞

In this final section, let me now try to pull together the main elements of Chinese thinking as expressed in conversation, through perusing official documents and reading the latest best-selling books on foreign-policy issues. I think that the following sums up the main arguments:

China's present young generation live in period most open and stable in Chinese history when the Chinese nation that has experienced 5,000 years of hardships is advancing towards modernization. Whether China will become a power in the twenty-first century relies mostly on the concerted efforts of all Chinese of today, especially the youth, to shoulder such a significant historical task. The Westernization Movement over a century ago advocated 'learning from foreign countries so as to control them'.

Today, China still needs to learn the advanced technologies and economic management experience with a different aim of peaceful coexistence and equality with the West instead of 'control'. Only by insisting on rational, not blind, nationalism and through contacts with and learning from the West can China accelerate its steps towards prosperity with a low cost. And this requires all Chinese to view the policies towards China of the West headed by the United States with reason and try to avoid blind opposition to everything foreign.

In recent years, because of the repeated mistakes of the United States in its policy towards China and due to their further understanding of American society, a kind of anti-American feeling has developed among the young Chinese intellectuals who had sought American culture in the 1980s. As revealed by a wide survey entitled 'the World in the eyes of young Chinese' made in August 1995, 87.1 per cent of the interviewees held the opinion that 'the United States is the most hostile country to China'.

In the past most of the elite in society were those that had received education in famous Western universities and absorbed Western value concepts, and therefore were deeply influenced by the West, and the common mass of society used to adhere to their native culture and never expected any change. Meanwhile, today, such relations are changing to the opposite. The phenomenon of the elite's 'de-Westernization' and 'indigenization' has appeared.

The tensions in Sino-US relations over the Taiwan Strait is a kind of test of the soul of the Chinese nation. Along with profound changes in social concepts and personal values, the Chinese pay more and more attention to practical and material reality. But taking national dignity or sovereignty into consideration, the fundamental element of the cornerstone of an integrated nation should be the biggest or most practical reality. Although Chinese leaders have time and again promised to the world that China will never be a superpower, or seek hegemony in the world, they still believe the country can be an active leader or a positive mediator in international affairs, shouldering more responsibilities for developing countries. Hence the longstanding emphasis in Chinese foreign policy since liberation to place China in the vanguard of the Third World; fighting its battles against Western interference will remain predominant.

The authors of *The China That Can Say No* suggest that fighting should not be taboo to China. Youth, they say, should be proud that 'we are ready to fight for the motherland at any time and at any cost', against anti-China forces. 'Force is a means to uphold dignity, and sometimes a measure to obtain peace. The price paid at the time will not be worth mentioning compared with the eternal price in the future. The law of interest conservation should not be adopted in trading with some Western countries. It is the cancellation of orders, instead of fair play that is an effective medicine to stubborn powers. China will never trade its national interests with foreigners. While the biggest fair play of China is to strengthen its aid and support to the poor regions and weak nations in the world.

> Despite the warning of the far-sighted Americans of not boycotting or containing China, the 'containment of China' has become a long-term strategy of the US. It tries every possible means to make China a tool utilized by itself; to realize this, the US will try to make the reunification of China an unfulfilled dream, and impose its value concepts on China for dramatic changes in the country, just like those in Eastern Europe. However, as long as the containment policy exists, anti-containment will be a long-term strategy of China, too. There are good examples already in Cuba, France, Russia, Singapore. Asia is a continent of the Asian people; China should establish solid relationships with mutual reliance and mutual trust with neighbouring countries.

Then, there is the issue of Western cultural values, which are seen as merely another weapon in the struggle to subvert China. 'Hollywood films are a good reflection of the real social life of America, full of violence, sex, murder and drugs. The burning of Hollywood film copies by France shows the anger not only of France but also of Europe, of even the whole world.

> The flame lit up a kind of confidence and conviction to uphold the dignity of the film art of France, of Europe, of culture and humanism. Individualistic heroism and pleasure-seeking as preached in films are also burned with the film copies. The introduction of Hollywood films to China has attracted bigger audiences than the cheerless domestic film industry. But to protect the essence of our own culture, we should learn something from the French people.

Self-love and ultra-selfishness are the most outstanding features of the Americans. When interfering in world affairs, it always held a banner of safeguarding global interests, which is actually the global interests of the US. The kind Chinese people should be careful and watch out: when you think you are making a non-governmental exchange with the American people, the CIA is actually by your side; and when you sincerely recommend to your friends the quality of American products, you are, in fact, an agent of the CIA. It could be well concluded that the US college students know even less about their own country than the common Chinese middle school students.

It is an effective way to attract as many talents as possible back to the modernization construction of the motherland. The great many students and intellectuals abroad, especially in the United States, are a huge potential and a great treasure for China in its competition in the world. They will help China narrow the gap with the West in science and technology.

The competition in absorbing talent resource is far more significant than grasping petroleum, minerals or gold. It is of the same importance for the whole of Asia to do so. Do not take the praise, rewards or criticism of the Westerners so seriously. China is China itself. Do not be so sensitive of the world's opinion. We should be what we are, instead of being directed by others, who don't have full knowledge of us. When exporting goods, Chinese enterprises should stop their practice of setting a lower price in the international market than in the domestic market merely in order to earn some foreign exchange. It is never good to protect the national economy or industry. The fact that the US is the sole power in the world today does not mean it can control everything on earth. It thought the China Threat made by itself could expect an echo from China's neighbours, but the East Asian countries have always been vigilant against US hegemony ambitions in the region. The successful holding of the Europe-Asian conference without the presence of the United States is really a victory for Asia and China. Asian countries can do well without the direction of the US.

The authors end their work with a defiant rallying call to their fellow countrymen and women: 'China has slept so long and the great shaking of the world has awoken it. China said No! to the opium vendors in 1839 when Lin Zixu burned the 2000 tons of opium in Humen. China has always said No! to any invaders and powers in history. China can say No! The US can control no one else. It can only master itself. Japan can master no-one and sometimes it does not even master itself. China wants to control no-one and it only wants to be master in its own house.'

The Foreign Ministry spokesman in Beijing, when asked by Western journalists for a reaction to this book, played down its significance, stressing it was 'just the work of a few young scholars, and you cannot stop the young coming up with radical ideas'. But the book did strike a chord in many Chinese, and I find its tone no different than the numerous ideological-tinged speeches of the current Chinese leadership or the lengthy diatribes against the West that one can read any day of the week in the official media.

And, after all, one cannot really dismiss these young scholars as lightly as the Foreign Ministry spokesman, given the fact that they are part of a generation that will be steering China through muddy international waters in the next century. They are far better educated than their predecessors.

They are imbued with a strong sense of justifiable national pride, underlaid with a close awareness of China's sad history when weak. They have studied in the West, and are familiar with its ways, but they are also still traditional Chinese. The tone of the current intellectual debate on China's place in the world, therefore, suggests a China just as outspoken and argumentative as that with which the West had to live throughout the Cold War era, and one whose people we will not be able to easily dismiss as 'fanatical Communists'.

# CHAPTER 10

# The Future: Groping Over the Stones

The reform process of trial and error has sometimes been described figuratively as 'groping for stones to cross the river'. Many stones have been negotiated already and the forward movement towards a discernible goal is probably not in doubt.

To review some of the key gains:

☐ The latitude for free expression of ideas has widened enormously. No longer must all publicly expressed thoughts spring directly from a small opus of Marxist classics, let alone a single collection of quotations (Mao's *Little Red Book*). In personal expression, there have been weighty gains in the areas of dress, religion, music, literature and other cultural activities. The parliament, the National People's Congress, is no longer a cypher, but an increasingly independent body ready to express its disapproval of Party policies by casting 'no' votes.

☐ The majority of working people are freer, if not yet entirely free, of arbitrary domination by State and Party officials. In rural areas, for a minority of farmers paths of upward mobility have been created to reward entrepreneurial ability.

☐ *If* China was a 'police state', as many Western commentators have suggested, it is less so now. The rule of law, although still somewhat weak, is beginning to permeate many aspects of life. Those facing criminal charges not only have the right to a defence lawyer of their own choosing, but the latter is permitted to participate in court hearings in a way unknown until a few years ago. Citizens who go to court to seek compensation for a civil wrong have a reasonable chance of winning, even if the State is the defendant.

☐ Personal income has increased rapidly. Although the gains have been distributed unevenly across the country, most Chinese are better off. Although new forms of poverty have arisen among those not able to take advantage of new market conditions, or dependent upon weakened social welfare services, they are outweighed by those who have benefited from change.

☐ The opening of free markets for private production, trade and services have significantly improved people's lives. Goods and services previously unavailable or hard to obtain because of the impossibility of handling them through central planning can now be found in the private market.

☐ Massive amounts of investment, both domestic and foreign, are being poured into housing in the cities,[1] finally reversing a long-term trend towards deterioration in urban housing standards, and doubling, tripling or even quadrupling per capita living space.[2]

Considering what they inherited in 1949, namely a country devastated by decades of foreign invasion and civil war,[3] the Communist leadership can claim considerable credit. Nevertheless, reform has given rise to a whole set of dilemmas for which all possible resolutions are costly. Reform has brought China to the point at which the interests of some large constituencies must be threatened. Official propaganda repeatedly stresses appeal to individual interests as the effective motivator of human energy. Luxury consumer goods are dangled on television before the populace, and tales of the emerging wealthy fill the media. 'Developing the forces of production' is treated at the sole criterion for choosing social policies. Belated attempts are being made to revive the old Utopian values such as solidarity, cooperation and equality, but it is an uphill battle given the teachings of the past two decades that tend to oppose and discredit these values.

It seems, in fact, that the leadership has still to find a new model and a new vocabulary to describe what they seek to create. 'Socialism with Chinese characteristics' is essentially a catch-all concept. Similarly, the idea that China is at the 'primary stage of socialism'[4] which the leadership use to lend Marxist legitimacy to reform policies, does not seriously confront the issue of preserving the core of the socialist enterprise through a long historical detour. Party ideologies go to great lengths, involving themselves in tortuous arguments, in an effort to show that any new policy is still socialism in action. Many of these policies will probably fail unless they are ready to acknowledge that this simply is not true.

It took the late Deng Xiaoping five years to begin the process of knocking Chairman Mao Zedong off his pedestal. His successor, Jiang Zemin, has wasted even less time in beginning the process of 'de-Dengification'. While Jiang's legitimacy very much rests on his being the heir of Deng,[5] he is trying to carve out his own niche at a time when his essential conservatism is ill-suited for the challenges facing the country. For a start, he has to try and keep the reform process going to satisfy the growing appetite of the populace at large for a better life, while facing up to the fact that the more the reforms bite, the more there will be people who will feel short-changed by the whole process.

I have discussed most of the main elements in previous chapters, but here briefly is a reminder of the main ones:

☐ CORRUPTION: Deng was never much of a graft-buster. His go-go reformers accepted corruption as the price for faster 'progress'. Numerous leftist ideologues have alleged that such Deng lieutenants as ousted party chief Zhao Ziyang had condoned if not coined the 'corruption is inevitable' slogan. The anti-corruption campaign that Jiang is waging serves to enhance the president's prestige by emphasizing that the post-Deng leadership upholds the traditional moralistic approach to curbing graft.

☐ EGALITARIANISM. Deng's well-known formula for speedy development was to 'let some get rich ahead of the others'. The scales are tipped in favour of the 'gold coast', urban intellectuals and entrepreneurs. Now, the emphasis is on *fupin* ('save the poor') to redress the balance. To offset the quasi-privatization that has emerged in recent years, the country's first job and social insurance programmes have been created. It is too early to know whether these will be sufficient to offset the smashing of the iron rice bowl that provided workers with such all-embracing protection from the vagaries of the real world.

☐ REFORM AND OPEN DOOR POLICY. The Dengists' single-minded quest for economic integration with the West will be fine-tuned by ideological and practical imperatives. Jiang has said the socialist market economy must not depart from 'the basic system of socialism', meaning public ownership as the mainstay. The chief source of tension here is whether it is possible to achieve the full potential of economic reforms while still clinging to vestiges of the old system in the shape of a powerful State-owned industrial sector.

Reforms will also be constrained by domestic factors such as the need to pacify peasants and workers. The post-Deng leadership is more concerned about protecting domestic markets and nascent industries. New guidelines have been spelt out to attract only those kinds of investments that dovetail with local priorities. At the same time, the leadership faces the same challenge that confronted its predecessors in trying to separate politics and economics, in seeking to have a liberalized, diverse economy, while continuing to adhere to strong centralized political power in which the Communist Party must always have the dominant role.

In some ways, this is going to mean a certain amount of backtracking. For, even while it is driving furiously towards the twenty-first century, China still hankers after some of the comforts provided by its long history. In fact, the more one reads, the more one is struck with the continuity of Chinese society, and the extent to which the Communist state resembles the Imperial China of the past. Most of the major elements of state Confucianism, as it existed in its fully developed form during the second millennium, are consistent with present-day Chinese Communist practice. The Chinese government has always been authoritarian, based on the idea that a ruling elite will emerge, and is indeed necessary. That elite could exercise unquestioned authority, and must be accorded unquestioned loyalty, provided its policies succeeded and continued to benefit the people. This concept of a government holding the Mandate of Heaven while it is successful, and conceding the right of the people to overthrow an unlucky or unjust administration, goes back more than 2000 years. The main difference today is that, even while paying lip service to the concept, the government in Beijing has up to now dealt ruthlessly with anyone who tried to put it into practice.

Confucianism itself was not a religion. It was a state ethic independent of religion, just as Chinese Communism is. The Confucian and Communist ethics both favour state, rather than private enterprise, both stress the rights of groups as more important than those of individuals, both are operated by a dedicated group of public servants who share a common philosophy and a sense of brotherhood, who are tried and tested in their loyalty. Any Western attempt to foist 'democracy' on China has to face the fact, therefore, that this has hitherto been an unknown concept in the country.

As the Australian academic Professor C.P. Fitzgerald, commented in a 1971 lecture: 'One of the first things to recognize in dealing with China is that we are encountering a very old and different tradition of political life and action. This tradition has been modified during the past century to conform, outwardly at least, with the conventions established in Western Europe and now widespread, but the thinking behind Chinese policy is often much closer to the ancient pattern than to the modern appearance.'[6] In accepting the West – whether democracy or socialism – Chinese leaders always seem to have harboured a desire to adulterate the innovation so as to make it less completely foreign. Regardless of their ideological persuasions, the great Chinese leaders have always seemed inclined to seek a new order that is thoroughly modern yet distinctly Chinese. Moreover, they have exhibited an innate desire to surpass the West in various subtle ways.

The debate continues as to how China should best be governed in order to achieve its overall economic-oriented goals. One of the most remarkable contributions to this debate came from Shang Dewen, a senior professor of Beijing University's Economic Institution, wrote an article in August 1997 calling for radical political reform. Given the frequent Western references to China as an oppressive 'police state' it seemed to suggest that either Professor Shang was a very brave, if perhaps somewhat foolish, man, or that he was better informed about the current political climate than the rest of us. His article is such a remarkable document in the context of China's political system that it is worth quoting a few passages verbatim. The proposals for change are first carefully built on solid foundations by quoting a keynote speech by Jiang Zemin to a Party conference in which he called for 'raising the great flag of Deng Xiaoping's theory of building socialism with Chinese characteristics by making efforts to deepen economic system reforms and promote political system reforms'.

According to Professor Shang, after several ups and downs in the reform of the political system, there was no denying that the process had been seriously delayed, and Jiang's speech pointed to the need to solve this principal contradiction standing in the way of China's further development:

> Some say that we need to control inflation. Some think we must carry out state-owned enterprise reform. Some suggest that we should stress spiritual civilization. I consider all these important social issues which should be solved earnestly. But I think the main contradiction of Chinese society is the contradiction between the market economic system and the political system. Theoretically, it is the friction and the collision of these two contradictory systems which generate all malpractice and corrupt and illegal behaviour. Therefore, we must speed up our pace of political reform. The main obstruction to the social and economic development of China is its retarded political system.

When our economic reforms were carried out for the third economic cycle, inflation led to political turmoil in 1989.[7] Major problems have been caused by our slow political reforms during the transition from a planned to a market economy. These problems include disorder and confusion between major systems and their sub-systems, unusual government behaviour and too much unreasonable government interference; investments remaining in the shadow of a planned economy; the rule of people being above the rule of law; and corruption of the political system.

Between 1988 and 1989, Deng and the Communist Party planned political reforms and even set up a special department – the Political System Restructuring Committee. It was aborted due to various complicated elements and incidents. If Deng were still alive he would also raise the issue of political reforms, because the market economic system reforms he launched made up only part of the package guaranteeing China's economic take-off. There must be reform of the political system to maintain the momentum of development other-wise the economic order will fall into confusion and development may slow or start to decline.

We need to create a new constitution. The worst malpractice of the present political system is its lack of a system of checks and balances. We should set up a Supreme Court and chief judge system , which should operate parallel to the parliament and presidency. We should set up a monetary and financial administrative committee, which wields a certain degree of independence. We should reform thor-oughly the current investment system and redefine the rights of central and local governments.

The central government should only exercise powers over national defence, diplomacy, posts and telecommunications, railways, under-takings of culture, education and medical care and only control a few big state-owned enterprises. The prime minister should be appointed by the president and should appoint ministers and among them the national defence minister who must be a civilian. We should greatly develop our education support and develop forcefully our high-tech industries; adopt a free press, which allows journalists to expose the slanders of government and enterprises and draft a media law in accordance with international practice. We should open wider to the world.

Anyone with even slight knowledge of China's development under Communism will recognize that these are bold proposals, which challenge the very essence of the current political system. They point out clearly the contradictions that exist in trying to graft new shoots onto an old plant. Such voices for change are beginning to be heard more loudly. Liberal economist Yu Guangyuan, for example, has expressed the hope that China can complete political reform by the late 2030s. 'If political reform is not thorough, economic reform will never be thorough.'

Yu once advised former party chiefs Hu Yaobang and Zhao Ziyang. Having sided with Zhao during the student-led democracy movement, he was expelled from the Communist Party in 1990. Since then, he has rarely revealed his liberal thoughts about China or commented on government policies until now. According to his proposed timetable, political modernization could best be completed in the next stage of reform, from 2009 to 2038, when the market system was more sophisticated. The economist argues that the Communist Party's history since 1919 can roughly be divided into three stages, each consisting of 30 years. The first lasted from the 4 May movement of 1919 until the Communist revolution in 1949 when the party fought against the Japanese and Nationalists. The second was from 1949 to 1978, when the Communist Party became powerful and struggled to find the right path to socialist construction. The country is still in the third stage, which is from 1979 to 2008, when the establishment of a market economy hopefully will be complete.[8]

As Professor Lucian Pye[9] has observed: 'It could be that no people have ever outdone the Chinese in ascribing model virtues to the state or in deprecating the worth of the individual'. Both Confucianism and the Chinese version of Leninism extol the importance of rulers and of the paramountcy of the State over individual rights. It is the extraordinary imbalance between the two that provides the most contentious issue in relations with the West, especially the United States: namely, human rights.

Yet although the massive weight of cultural inertia that favours the state and inhibits the growth of a vibrant civil society is still evident, there is nevertheless a significant change in the diminishing of the public's awe of state authority and lessening hostility towards individualism. Ever since the reforms began in 1978, the major trend in Chinese society has been the retrenchment of direct Party-State control over peoples' lives, with a few hiccups along the way. Individuals have recaptured some degree of control over their lives. Scholars, as I have demonstrated, are debating the linkages between economic and political liberalization. Some Chinese reformers are advocating 'neo-authoritism' along the lines of Singapore, for example, as a halfway house to full liberalization.

Under the reforms, China's economic, political, social and cultural systems began to differentiate from each other in classic modernization mode. The old means of coercive and ideological control and integration became increasingly ineffective. Students and intellectuals have created an autonomous sphere for themselves in the face of continued Party impotence and incompetence. Think-tanks; salons; the ability to express cultural introspection; participation in global communications networks; and the internationalization of the Chinese intelligentsia through foreign travel, and scholarships all contributed to creating bases for a civil society that continues to expand and evolve.

Anyway, government power is absolute only in theory. It is true that, in many matters, a one-party central government can be implacably determined if thwarted, particularly if an individual or relatively small group is involved. In major matters it can force everyone into line and can even control a great many aspects of its citizens' everyday lives with considerable success. But the government of a sprawling country such as China, or any other which is run by an entrenched and largely unaccountable bureaucracy, may have a difficult time indeed in securing day-to-day obedience from its civil servants. Things becomes even more pronounced the further one moves away from the capital, as petty functionaries were very much aware under Imperial rule.

Regulations are misunderstood, intentionally or not; a particular rule is conveniently considered not applicable because of supposed special conditions (a friend in higher office will protect against troubles if rules are not followed), and, with no agency outside the jurisdiction of the party to blow the whistle in any decisive way, the chances are slim that anyone can object successfully to subversion of official orders for the purpose of gaining personal power or profit. The freewheeling willfulness of officials is seen in many other aspects of life as well. The combinations and permutations of personalities, interests, opportunities, loyalties and objectives and so on can be dizzying.

Decentralization in recent years has drastically reduced the central government's monopoly of economic power and weakened its power to control. Localities are forging ahead eager for profits – typified by Shanghai, with 13 million people, determined to become an economic hub of the new Pacific era and bitterly resentful of having to send too much of its money to Beijing.[10] When the economy threatened meltdown in early 1993, the centre had to send out squads of ministerial enforcers to try and persuade recalcitrant provincial authorities to toe the line and accept a Beijing-imposed credit crunch. As far as the latter were concerned, there was no economic overheating in their area, so why should they slow down? They have been encouraged in their resistance by the fact that much of the feverish investment activity which led to overheating was perpetrated by corporations affiliated with senior cadres, military officers and their offspring.

But despite all the criticism of the Communist Party, one still has to ask: what, for the moment, is the alternative? And the answer is that in a vast country like China, with so many intra-regional rivalries there simply is no alternative. There is, in fact, probably a very good case to be made right now for a strong government. By their nature, unregulated market systems pay little or no heed to such strategic areas as basic industries, health and education, scientific and technological research, and the preservation of the environment and natural resources. China has reasons for requiring a strong central government. These include such problems as a bloated population, environmental deterioration, poor infrastructure, increasing unemployment and the widening income gaps between regions, individuals and urban and rural areas.

Advocates of maintaining a strong central authority cite the example of the fiscal responsibility system adopted in the 1980s, which invigorated local economies, but at the expense of the central coffers. The revenue element of GNP fell from 31 per cent in 1978 to 14 per cent in 1992 as a result of this, as well as massive tax evasion, cheating and what were seen by Beijing as wanton promises made by local governments to attract foreign investors. It would cost the country dear, so the argument goes, if people believed the market economy cleared them to indulge in tactics like undisciplined speculation in real estate and securities, tax fraud, regional protectionism and bad local tax policies. This is not a call for a return to a planned economy, but merely that China cannot afford to drift into a market economy without a strong hand on the tiller.

Undoubtedly, there is great debate at the heart of government over how the reform process should be handled. And not everyone is in agreement, as was evidenced by a series of attacks launched by the *People's Daily* in August 1997 on diehard Marxists blamed for slowing reform. On its front page, the Communist Party mouthpiece published a vigorous defence of the no-holds-barred experiments pioneered by Deng Xiaoping. It cited Shenzhen and Wenzhou in Zhejiang Province as two examples of Deng's reform success, arguing that the two cities would not have been built in the 1980s if the leftists had their way. Defending Shenzhen, it said: 'Years of leftist influence have made it difficult for us to shake off all at once our worries about socialism versus capitalism. We have in one way or another tried to judge the right or wrong of it [Shenzhen] using different standards. But could we imagine there would be a prosperous and developed city in southern China today had we kept arguing?'

Both Shenzhen and Wenzhou were hailed by reformists as two beacons of Deng's capitalist-style reform experiments, but attacked by the leftists as betrayal of the nation's socialist tradition. The commentary said it was unnecessary to debate whether China should have embraced such un-Marxist concepts as free markets, private enterprise and stock exchanges. The debate should stop to make way for policies 'in the interest of productivity, in the interest of boosting overall national strength and in the interest of improving the lives of the people. We must boost our productivity to become rich and strong'.

A day later, it intensified its defence of the changes to the public ownership system, arguing that turning state-owned enterprises into shareholding cooperatives would not betray the socialist tradition. Allowing workers to own shares in their firms did not equate to privatization and would not lead to losses of state assets. It rejected criticism that such steps would weaken the economic foundation of the regime and said even Deng had encouraged bold experiments in reform. The ownership changes could help raise efficiency in the use of state capital and boost workers' morale. The reforms were necessary as China was still in the primary stage of socialism, and past experience had proved a monolithic state ownership system could not meet the needs of a market economy.

Although the reform process was begun in 1978, it did not gain universal endorsement until 1993 when the Third Plenary Session of the 14th Congress of CPC finalized its blueprint for establishing a 'socialist market system'. Equally, although many breakthroughs have been made in various fields such as the structure of economic ownership, price, taxation, finance, foreign trade, foreign exchange, economic planning and investment, the reform process has repeatedly encountered fresh difficulties engendered by the process itself.

Despite the widely-recognized fact that the gradual reform that China has chosen is successful in maintaining sustainable development and social stability, it produces a prolonged transition period during which the old and new systems conflict with each other while market rules and order are absent, thus actually augmenting the cost of the reform. Reform is a process during which the old interest pattern will be adjusted and rearranged according to public opinion and policy making. This, obviously, needs time, and many Chinese analysts believe that the new system will not be firmly in place before the second decade of the next century. One key reason for this, of course, is that the process also involves a total overhaul of Chinese society, including a transformation of urban and rural management, residence registration, employment, education, income distribution, health care, pensions and housing.

The current development of the reform movement sees the establishment of a social security system lagging far behind the economic and institutional reforms, for example. If this problem was not given prime consideration and a solution found, it would be a drag on the whole effort to establish a new system based on a market economy, thus escalating social conflict by prolonging the transition period. Among the efforts to establish a new system of social security is the urgency to help those living under the poverty line. This work includes several measures such as compulsory unemployment insurance in urban areas, a minimum wage system, bottom-line living guarantee and poverty relief in rural areas, but in addition, the increasing number of urban poor has constituted a serious social problem calling for urgent solution.

All this is necessary not only to avoid social tension, but also to make the populace at large believe that socialism does work and that it is worth working hard to achieve it. Equally, it is necessary to prevent the further spread of lawlessness, for there is plenty of evidence that segments of the population now believe the only way to riches is by cutting corners. This means not just the endemic corruption, which I covered in an earlier chapter, but also an alarming upsurge in banditry by armed gangs who do not hesitate to kill to achieve their ends.[11]

Regarding industrial structural transformation, a key task is to help old enterprises in 'sunset industries', in the old industrial bases, especially in the north-east of the country – accommodating a quarter of the national iron and steel production, half of the crude oil production and one sixth or more of the coal and electricity production – to shift to newly-rising industrial sectors. Although they were the country's backbone in the past few decades, these enterprises are now poorly equipped and overmanned. It is unrealistic to demand that these industrial monsters should automatically shift to meet different market demands in a short time. Therefore, it seems the only answer is more government subsidies to speed up structural transformation. But, in order to modernize and transform themselves, these enterprises need to shed workers wholesale, and that requires the government to find other ways to create millions of new jobs – and there must surely be a limit to what it can do in this regard. And, equally, it comes back to the need to pump money into a financial safety net for those workers who are surplus to requirements.

The livelihoods of many state workers hang by a thread on bank bailouts to their enterprises. Some 20 per cent of the bank loans may be unrecoverable, making banks technically bankrupt. Massive waste in state industry is paid for by Chinese workers and peasants whose personal savings of $464 billion in banks, and $67 billion in state treasury bills, equals roughly 65 per cent of gross domestic product (GDP). What would happen if Chinese savers panicked and staged a run on the banks?

In 2020, it is likely that Chinese leaders will continue to be absorbed with making sure their people are fed and found jobs. And that bank doors stay open. Consider that the country must find jobs for 15 million people who join the work-force each year; that hundreds of millions of people still live on less than the equivalent of $1 a day; that China must feed 22 per cent of the world's people on seven per cent of its arable land; and that the population is expanding while farmland shrinks. Consider also that the gap is growing between the rich coast areas and the poor interior and between wealthy cities and underprivileged rural areas. Deep resentments are brewing, and could explode. All this is against a backdrop of the country's wrenching transition from a predominantly rural to urban society, with tens of millions of displaced peasants on the move, a restless army soon to be swelled by the urban unemployed.

Finding jobs for jobless agricultural labour is an enormous task. No government in history has ever been able to generate up to 170 million new jobs in a short space of time – and it is obvious it does not have the luxury of a prolonged breathing space. The vast army of rural migrants is pressing in on the overloaded cities competing for scarce jobs and raising the temperature in the urban areas. One answer is to encourage an exodus not to the cities but to outlying areas with potentially good land and less population. There are signs of such a movement, to areas like Xinjiang, for example, but life in these regions has to be made more attractive to encourage migration on a significant scale. At the same time, as already discussed, this has to be set against the dilemma of raising concerns among restive ethnic minorities about being submerged by the main Han grouping.

The country, on paper, has huge foreign reserves that give an impression of prosperity, but it also has to spend massive amounts to create a modern State and end centuries of neglect. The World Bank estimates, fore example, that it will need to spend $80-$90 billion in infrastructure investment alone each year for the foreseeable future to keep growth on track. And that means continuing efforts to maintain national stability that will ensure China remains attractive to overseas money as well as more of the policies that have seen such a dilution of Communism that many feel China is now a socialist state only in name.

Considering that non-state enterprises are the major job-creating source for the laid-off workers from the bankrupted or stagnant state-owned enterprises, for example, the government will have to loosen its control over the private-funded sectors. More private enterprise means the state-owned sector becoming even smaller and the government exercising increasingly less control over all business and economic activity.

With regard to the urban-rural structural transformation mentioned above, many Chinese analysts feel the answer is to create an 'urbanization drive' that concentrates on small and medium-sized cities to soak up surplus labour, rather than adding to the burden of the major cities as now. I have mentioned elsewhere the Ministry of Construction plan to create 600 new towns over the next decade or so to partly fulfil this need. But the creation of more cities, with new factories, new roads, new sprawling housing estates, also raises the prospects of further degradation of the air, water and earth, already under severe assault due to rapid economic development and huge population pressures. Although there was a time when the Chinese tried to pretend things were not too bad, in defiance of the evidence of the nose or eyes, they now admit that the picture in some respects is pretty grim.

The 1997 annual report of the National Environmental Protection Agency noted that respiratory diseases in the previous year were the joint main cause of death in urban areas, with 0.91 deaths per thousand. The cancer rate was 1.31 deaths per 1,000. The study said both respiratory diseases and cancer were attributed partially to environmental pollution, and admitted that the country's overall environmental quality was well below World Health Organization standards. Up to 70 per cent of the water in key waterways and lakes equalled or fell below the modest Chinese standards for quality. The water in the urban sections of 133 of the 138 rivers tested was polluted, mainly by petroleum and magnesium acids; lakes continued to be choked by phosphorous from soaps, detergents, fertilizers and nitrogen.

An estimated 80 per cent of the country's 36.8 billion tons of industrial wastewater and domestic sewage is dumped untreated into rivers and lakes. The consequences of centuries of neglect became depressingly evident in the late 1980s in Shanghai when an accumulation of wastes contaminated shellfish beds, causing an outbreak of hepatitis that affected 300,000 residents. The Huaihe River valley, one of the most heavily polluted waterways in the central part of the country due to uncontrolled industrial development, became so dangerously fouled that the government had to admit to a heightened incidence of cancer and intestinal diseases in an area along the river running through Shandong, Henan, Anhui and Jiangsu provinces.

Air pollution, due mainly to heavy reliance on coal with high sulfur content[12] by industry and for power generation, and the growing weight of vehicles on jammed city roads, is worsening. Major cities had an average of 309 micrograms per cubic metre of particulates in the air, with some registering as high as 618 micrograms pcm – way above the WHO standards of between 60–90 micrograms pcm. Daily average sulfur dioxide readings in 1996 averaged nearly double the WHO standards, with some readings ten times as high.

Global atmospheric tests show the five cities of Beijing, Shenyang, Xian, Shanghai and Guangzhou are among the 10 cities worldwide with the highest levels of dust pollution. The northeastern city of Shenyang alone pours out 200,000 tons of sulfur oxide a year, equivalent to a quarter of the emissions of the whole of Japan. The US-based Worldwatch Institute estimates that within a decade, China could overtake the US as the world's largest source of air pollution.

The state-owned factories are now cleaning up their act to some extent, but their place is being taken by less well-monitored township enterprises, where local officials tend to turn a blind eye to a belching chimney in the finest Yorkshire tradition of 'where there's muck, there's brass'. As a result, an estimated 40 per cent of the country is thought to be affected by acid rain, and this is also being felt in neighbouring Japan, as the prevailing winds tend to carry Chinese pollution in that direction. This has become a foreign policy issue for Japan, which became so exasperated in 1993 that it threatened to stop its aid programme unless the Chinese did something to clean up its factory wastes output.

China is sensitive to Western criticism of its environmental record and claims that it has done more to curb pollution than developed countries did in their early days of industrialization. In 1996 and 1997, it claimed it had shut down 57,000 dirty factories, mainly paper and chemical plants. And said it would be spending

$40 billion, equivalent to more than a third of its foreign exchange reserves, to cope with industrial pollution alone in the period 1996–2000.

But the Chinese also react angrily to some of the complaints against its record on environmental protection, seeing it as part of a Western attempt to curb the economic development of the Third World. Having contributed most of the global pollution in its own development, Western capitalism now seeks to use the environmental card to ensure no new rivals emerge to challenge its dominance.[13] China also insists that to be fair, the pollution figures should be calculated on a per capita basis, which, with its huge population, would give it one of the cleanest environments in the world!

More economic development, however, is going to mean more pollution and a higher clean-up bill. Where is China to find the $40 billion it wants to spend up to 2000? Where will it find the more than $100 billion that international organizations say it should be spending to cope with existing problems? If dependent on domestic sources, this could seriously derail its entire economic development, especially the vital job creation programmes. Heavy reliance on international sources will add to its existing heavy debt levels and leave it vulnerable if something should go wrong.

This, at the very least, requires the government to intervene even more strongly in industrial policy than ever before, while at the same time facing demands from within and without to pull back in the majority of areas and let the traditional 'hidden hand' of the market dictate the allocation of resources to the most efficient operations. Investors, by and large, should bear the risks without government nannying, and, it is being argued given the financial constraints imposed by a vast number of competing projects, the State should concentrate on a few prime projects needed in the overall development policy.

There is no doubt that even in the much-maligned State sector there are many very capable Chinese managers who could match their Japanese or Western counterparts in achieving business success if the dead hand of the ignorant Party hack or ministerial bureaucrat was removed.[14] But can China afford to be totally *laissez faire*? China does have some advantages for economic development in the next century. Its high savings rate,[15] *relative* stability, large domestic market, a disciplined work-force amenable to further education, the strong support of the Chinese diaspora, and good record of reform so far all bode well for the future. But all the glowing developments in economic advancement need to be put into some sort of context. Even if the present rate of rapid economic growth continues, by 2020 per capita income in China, by World Bank calculations, will only be approaching those of Portugal today but will still be less than half those of the United States.

The huge risks that China faces, which I have sought to bring out in earlier chapters, could yet take the shine off the envisaged future potential. But with resolute leadership at home and statesmanlike policies from the world's industrial powers, China has a chance of overcoming these challenges, enabling one-fifth of humanity to have within its grasp the power to break free of the shackles of poverty and underdevelopment and accomplish what could become the most remarkable economic transformation the world has ever seen.

In achieving these goals, China will not always be an easy country for the rest of the world to deal with. The Chinese watched with horror the disintegration of the Soviet Union from its own economic reform programme, and are determined that the same thing will not happen to them. Repeatedly, officials profess in public to believe that the United States and its allies are waiting for just such a disintegration to occur. The Americans saw the collapse of the Soviet Union as a vindication of the superiority of capitalist values, they tell the nation; if China suffered a similar fate, that sense of vindication would be even stronger.

A 500,000-word novel *Yellow Peril* published in 1997 and written under a pseudonym by a mainland Chinese author, gives a flavour of the kind of doomsday ideas spinning around Beijing. It describes a civil war between north and south China – with Taiwan supporting the south – ending in nuclear conflict and millions of starving refugees spilling across the borders into neighbouring states to trigger fresh unrest there. The message is that the demise of Communist ideology, and the passing of old guard leaders whose revolutionary credentials gave them a certain legitimacy, poses new problems. It also raises the question of whether the Chinese Communist Party survives to 2020. No feast lasts forever, say some intellectuals in Beijing. There is only one powerful Communist Party, and if one day it fails society will be thrown into disorder. China, they say, has only two futures: control or loss of control.

Because of this belief, the Chinese are ever alert for any sign that the United States and its allies are trying to assist the disintegration process. One of the key stumbling blocks in the negotiations with Britain for the smooth handover of Hong Kong, for example, was a

Chinese belief that the British were trying to use the territory to subvert the mainland. I referred in the opening chapter to the mainland's desire for Hong Kong to act as a bridge to the world in the economic sphere; but it is now watching out for any sign that this bridge is being used for the transport of subversive ideas. Stability and national unity, as they have always been in China's history, are the key concerns of the present generation of rulers. The opening up of China in the nineteenth century, after all, was forced upon a weak China by militarily strong powers, who 'ensured decentralization of control of their own spheres of influence',[16]a lesson in the considerable loss of power and authority by the central government which is not lost on the current leadership. They are determined not to see history repeat itself, which explains the extremely strong reaction in Beijing to any action that suggests that, say, the people on Taiwan or in Tibet have any right to independence separate from the mainland. To resist any loss of national territory, China has to be strong – economically and militarilly. But the realization of the need to go fast to achieve China's full potential is tempered by a fear that this also contains the seeds of national disunity and destruction.

Whether it is destined to be strong or weak, a superpower or under-achiever, China will exert a major influence on the world in the next century. How, therefore, should the international community deal with it? To many Western analysts, the over-riding goal is the integration of China into the network of market-based rules and institutions that make up the international financial and trade systems. China should receive benefits, as well as assuming the responsibilities, commensurate with its economic importance and level of development. This, so the argument goes, will enhance the domestic reforms and support a more open global economy. As a result, it is of crucial importance to bring China into the World Trade Organization (WTO), whose rules will strengthen the hand of the country's reformers in terms of programmes to reduce subsidies to ailing industries, liberalizing state controls, strengthening the rule of law and moving towards greater openness.

WTO membership, unfortunately, has become a pawn in the seemingly never-ending squabbles between Beijing and Washington over a host of economic, trade and political issues and at the time of writing, it is not clear how soon China will be able to add the WTO to its existing participation in such important multilateral organizations as the World Bank, IMF and Asia Pacific Economic Cooperation (APEC). But the underlying assumption here, from a Western perspective, is that China can be changed, its experiment with Communism consigned to the dustbin of history, so that it becomes a fully-fledged member of the Capitalist Club. It was just such a deeply-flawed assumption that governed the activities of Western missionaries in the nineteenth century, with the frustration at being unable to remake China in their image leading to the vilification of the Chinese and the emergence of the 'Yellow Peril' syndrome.

As I discussed earlier, this showed a complete lack of understanding of Chinese history. Even when it was conquered – by the Mongols or the Manchus – it was not China that changed, but the conquerors who became more Chinese than the Chinese. Of course, China has changed. But throughout its history it has sought to retain the right to do so in the context of its own value systems; no alien idea, even one as profound as Buddhism, has been adopted wholesale, but has always undergone a process of adaptation to enable it to fit comfortably into the existing national template. There is no reason to believe that the current efforts to Westernize China economically (and, obviously in the long term, culturally and politically) will be any more successful.

I have no doubt that in Beijing, entry to the WTO is seen as part of China's efforts to undermine and change the global capitalist system, rather than be entirely disciplined by it. One can see this in the continued Chinese efforts to assume the mantle of leadership of the developing Third World. Previous efforts, especially in the Maoist era, were clumsy and often counter-productive, and often ended up alienating the target countries. Nevertheless, there is no doubt that China does speak on behalf of a number of developing and under-developed countries who resent Western domination and Western condescension, so that such leadership ambitions are not entirely preposterous.

But Western nations have to recognize that in seeking to integrate China into their cozy club they are not getting a house-trained pussy-cat but a veritable tiger. China's emergence as an economic force will have a tumultuous impact on its neighbours and on the rest of the world. Its geographical size, roughly equivalent to the United States, and its massive population, its ever-advancing economic strength, its strong attachment to advanced education, its growing technological and military potential, and its oft-stated geopolitical goals will all impose a disruptive influence similar, if not greater, than that imposed by the emergence of the Kaiser's Germany in the nineteenth century or Japan in the twentieth century.

It is not just a question of integrating China into the system, but working out if there is room at the top for it (a factor which may be behind some of the United State's criticisms of it). And vilification, threats of military or trade embargoes, actions seen as interference in the country's internal affairs, all of which have been seen in recent times as the world reacts to China's growing might, merely exacerbate any xenophobic feelings lurking in the Chinese breast.

Let us for a moment consider the potential tensions that might surface as China steps onto the world stage in accordance with its own rhythms and aspirations.

☐ TRADE. It will undoubtedly become an export machine at potentially frightening levels. Its current pace of export growth is three times the global average. It is closing in on Japan as the country most responsible for America's growing trade deficit. Within the next couple of decades, it will almost certainly be the second largest exporter behind the United States, and far ahead of Japan. Consider how the West reacted to the huge upsurge in Japanese exports from the 1970s, and consider how much stronger that reaction will be when China moves into top gear. At the same time, its ability to produce low cost, but good quality manufactured goods will probably have an adverse effect on countries such as Indonesia, Malaysia, the Philippines and Thailand, displacing them on world markets and worsening their current economic problems.

☐ INVESTMENT. In the opening chapter, I described the explosion of foreign investment in the 1990s. There is growing evidence that it will be a bottomless pit in this regard. It is second only to the United States as a recipient of foreign investment, and already accounts for 40 per cent of all the capital being poured into developing countries. It is the largest borrower from the World Bank and the Asian Development Bank, and gets a large share of free aid and soft loans made available by countries like Japan and Germany. This process is still at a very early stage. So far, the money has gone primarily to the richer coastal provinces, leaving most of the country still virtually untouched. As the government's investment priorities change, and the emphasis shifts to the more backward interior, it is estimated that at least $600 billion will be needed over the next decade or so to put into place the physical infrastructure – roads, railways, telecommunications etc. – needed to get the development process underway. China is going to have to have to get much of that money overseas, and will probably get it because of the ever-tempting vision it dangles before investors of a massive domestic market. In the process, however, there is a very real prospect that other countries who perhaps need investment even more desperately than China will be starved of it.

□ INDUSTRY. The Chinese have learned well under Japanese tutelage as to how to bend the global trade rules. Just as Japan managed to develop its economy by pushing exports and holding down imports, the Chinese seem to be doing the same, through high import tariffs and a tightly-control currency kept advantageously weak.[17] It uses the carrot of a huge domestic market to cleverly play off one foreign company against another[18] and increasingly awards contracts only if there is a trade-off of advanced technology being supplied.

Through the creation of gigantic state-directed industrial conglomerates along the lines of the Japanese *Zaibatsu* and Korean *Chaebols*, China is getting ready to move out and take on the world with its own multinationals. If the Japanese were able to succeed so well with this policy, to the detriment of selected industries in both Europe and the United States, consider how much greater the impact could be when the Chinese do the same, from a much larger domestic base and with much greater access to resources than the Japanese!

If this succeeds, it will provide an alternative model to American-style capitalism that could prove attractive to a whole range of developing countries across the world, transforming the make-up of international bodies like the WTO and UNCTAD. Integrating China into the global community, therefore, will not be a painless exercise. The likelihood is that the West will have to change as much as China does.

This, then, is the scenario of a strong China, on the assumption that everything goes well. Equally, however, the opposite might occur. The current growth bubble might burst, the country might disintegrate into squabbling regional fiefdoms. Yet the impact of this will be just as great as if China continues to grow in strength. Given its geographical position, a disunited China will be a major source of political and economic tension, and a strong destabilizing influence on Pacific and Central Asia.

Could it all go wrong? China has enjoyed an unprecedented, virtually unbroken, period of rapid economic growth since the late 1970s. Apart from the occasional political hiccup (e.g. the international economic sanctions following the 1989 Tiananmen Square incident), the graph shows a continually upward curve. So far, the Chinese have denied gravity, and have yet to experience the roller-coaster effect that normally applies to economic activity. This surely has to come at some stage, especially with the country now steadily being integrated into the global trade and economic systems.

A warning sign that the bubble could burst came in October 1997 as this chapter was being written. By the time these words are being read, all may be well again; but a warning has been issued and needs to be taken into account in considering China's future. It may be recalled that over a very short space of time, counted in days, the Hong Kong Stock Exchange lost around a third of its value, a staggering collapse that created panic on stock exchanges around the world.

After massive intervention by the authorities, including temporarily raising overnight interest rates by a massive 200 per cent, the market did recover some, but only some, of the lost ground. Six months later, the economy was still hurting. Half of the 12 Japanese department stores had closed down; hotel occupancy rates collapsed as Japanese and Southeast Asian tourists stayed away in droves, also forcing the flagship airline Cathay Pacific to drop many regional flights. Media criticism of the new government for its handling of the crisis raised hackles in Beijing and caused the first concerns to be expressed about Hong Kong's supposed independence from central government interference. These events demonstrated that neither Hong Kong nor China could isolate themselves from the turmoil that had gripped the 'boom economies' of Southeast Asia – namely, Indonesia, Malaysia, Singapore and Thailand – in which the local currencies and stock exchanges experienced serious declines in an economic domino effect.

These countries had contributed much to Hong Kong's rapid development in recent years as a trading and banking centre, as well as a popular tourist destination. At the same time, as all this was happening, the big two Asian economies – those of Japan and South Korea – were also undergoing severe recessionary traumas. If it can happen to the Japanese and the Koreans, one might ask, why should the Chinese be immune? As Asia's financial markets and currencies unravelled in a remarkably short space of time, China did seem to be standing apart from the turmoil and immune to contagion. Admittedly, it had many of the same symptoms that had brought down its neighbours – an oversupplied property market, an indebted banking system, manufacturing industry struggling with massive over-capacity and rising fixed costs, and an economy generally hampered by corruption and cronyism.

But it had some factors going in its favour. The foreign capital inflows into the country are mostly long-term fixed investments, rather than short-term lending – the type of 'hot money' that destabilized Thailand, for example. Foreign portfolio investment at the time of writing was still only 0.5 per cent of the gross domestic product and even the fledgling foreign currency markets are largely driven by local investors. Foreign commercial lending has grown, but with external debt at around $130 billion at the end of 1996, the debt-to-gross national product ratio, at 20 per cent, is estimated by the World Bank to be the lowest in Asia.

The currency is not yet convertible on the capital account (only on the current account for business purposes), and the exchange rate remains strictly government-controlled and defended by huge foreign exchange reserves. In fact, with exports soaring, the currency is probably undervalued and would appreciate if freed from controls. The stock markets are carefully controlled so that foreigners have access only to a few selected stocks which they must buy with foreign currency. Thus, on the surface, they would be hard pressed to mount a serious assault on either China's currency or stock markets.

But the upheavals in Hong Kong did offer some reminders of the weaknesses in the Chinese economy and how turbulence in the special administrative region can have inescapable implications for the mainland. Hong Kong's own vulnerability stems in part from the determination of the local authorities, backed by Beijing, to defend the system in place since the early 1980s of pegging the Hong Kong dollar to its American equivalent – a move which provided a strong element of stability so attractive to international investors, as well as providing the mainland with a 'hard currency' channel on its doorstep. Without this peg, Asia's sole formal currency link, there was every reason to suppose the Hong Kong dollar would join its regional counterparts in devaluation, destroying a key element in the mainland's plans for the region as I discussed in the opening chapter. This might well be a good thing, for there was ample evidence that the currency was over-valued and needed a solid devaluation to restore its competitiveness.

Any move in this direction, however, faced the risk of a huge loss of international confidence in Hong Kong and a flight of foreign capital. The peg is widely seen as a guarantee of Hong Kong's financial autonomy from the mainland. If the mainland intervenes to prop up the Hong Kong dollar, it runs the risk of running down not only the area's estimated $80 billion in foreign exchange reserves and its own $130 billion, but, more importantly, of undermining the whole concept of 'one nation, two systems' by which it places so much store – especially as a formula for peacefully welcoming Taiwan back into the embrace of the motherland. Hong Kong, effectively, could then become just another mainland city.

The BBC's Asia correspondent, in describing the frightening events of mid-October 1997, observed that the greatest significance lay in the fact 'Fortress Hong Kong suddenly realized it has become too expensive for its own good. The post-handover honeymoon is ending in despair. Money is the lifeblood of this tiny territory [. . .] and prolonged financial crisis could lead to the end of Hong Kong as we know it.'[19]

Here, then, is yet another of those appalling dilemmas facing China today: risk a destabilizing haemorrhage of foreign capital or risk pricing Hong Kong out of the Asian market.[20] De-linking the currency from its American counterpart so soon after handover would involve considerable loss of face. Hong Kong's attraction as a regional business centre, and vital conduit into the mainland, is also under threat as a growing number of foreign firms are moving their headquarters to 'cheaper' Singapore, which is playing up its own close ethnic and business links with China.[21]

The issue also has to be considered in light of Hong Kong's current crucial role as the biggest 'foreign' investor in the mainland, on which the booming areas of southern China are so heavily dependent. Many of the big property tycoons in the territory, who lost so heavily in the October crash, were those also most active in creating the massive property glut on the mainland, for a start.

Uncertainty in Hong Kong could also exacerbate the problems of mainland banks, whose non-performing loan portfolio is estimated to be as high as $200 billion, a quarter of all outstanding loans. In some cases, at least, the banks' losses have been offset by profits and appreciating assets in Hong Kong.[22] The panic selling on the stock exchange also had immediate impact on the growing number of mainland companies who see offering share issues in Hong Kong as an important way of raising much-needed investment capital.[23] These so-called 'red chip' stocks, so much in demand when they first appeared, suffered badly in the October panic selling, with an estimated 50 per cent being stripped off their value.

Well, it may eventually all be put down to a temporary attack of nerves, and no more. But I think it does require some reconsideration of the basic premises on which the assessment of China's golden future have been made. After the first euphoria of Hong

215

Kong's liberation from 'British slavery' subsides, it may well be seen that the special administration region has a potential to be China's Achilles' heel. At the same time, one has to look at China in the total Asian context. The fact that its currency is regarded as undervalued, and would appreciate if the authorities lifted the present tight controls, has to be set against the fact that the fast-developing economies of Southeast Asia, have been forced into a series of competitive devaluations which will tend to make their products more competitive on world markets head-to-head with those of China.

As these economies, not to mention those of Japan and South Korea, seek to recover their former growth pattern, there is going to be ferocious competition in the trade and investment areas from which China cannot hope to remain immune. Thus, it needs to put its own house in order. It needs to deal ruthlessly with all the social and economic problems I have outlined in previous pages factors that threaten to impair its ability to compete in an exacting market. The question that must be raised here, however, is whether the Chinese leadership has the will to take the harsh measures that are needed, and whether the Chinese people still have the fortitude to make the necessary sacrifices in order to give these measures a chance of succeeding.

One worst-case scenario suggests that a serious economic down-turn could exacerbate already prevalent corruption, along with extreme social inequality and injustice, serious economic imbalances, huge regional disparities and social disorder. 'Rich regions like Guangdong and Fujian might attempt to break away from the centre to form a South China state with Hong Kong and Taiwan in order to maintain their economic prosperity, while poor regions would become poorer with the possibility of social unrest and even civil war.'[24]

It may seem far-fetched, but I believe it is important to understand how much economic self-interest is vital for holding together such a large, geographically and ethnically disparate country as China. If nothing else, it demonstrates just how crucial China is to the continued peace and stability of the entire Pacific Asia region. Good or bad, the rest of the world has to learn to cope with it because it cannot be ignored.

China also faces this crisis at a time of leadership transition. The larger-than-life revolutionary figures that dominated the political stage for the past half century, Mao and Deng, are gone. In their place are leaders with none of the charisma or perhaps even the vision of these two great men. Essentially, they are bureaucrats and accountants, faceless, conservative. But, maybe, that is exactly what China needs as it feels its way gingerly over the stones towards the creation of a modern, industrialized state living in harmony.

Mao was constantly worried that the people he led would become soft, content with the fruits of the revolution that brought the Communist Party to power and not willing any more to make the sort of sacrifices that typified The Long March and other legendary events of the civil war era. Thus, he sought to keep the country in constant revolution, inflicting on it such destructive campaigns as the Great Leap Forward and the Cultural Revolution.

If he returned today, he would certainly feel his worst fears have been realized. All the social evils he sought so hard to eradicate have returned. Many of the most pernicious aspects of capitalism have crept back in.[25] And yet, surely, there can be no going back. The new leaders may want to hark back to earlier, purer times through campaigns for 'spiritual civilization', but the world and China have moved on from those halcyon revolutionary days when everything was seen in clear black-and-white terms; like the Yellow River, the revolutionary waters have become muddied.

Nobody knows where the great experiment in Chinese-style socialism will end up. There will be many twists and turns; many false starts and perhaps even temporary u-turns. But the best thing the rest of the world can do is to let China work this out for herself, rather than trying repeatedly to impose alien ideas on it. Whatever happens, whichever direction the country moves, the Chinese people will draw on their long history to survive, while the outside world can do little but stand aside and watch. Whatever emerges, it will, in the oft-quoted words of Napoleon, 'surprise the world'.

# Notes

## Chapter 1 – Defining a Superpower

1 If it does, it will confound the predictions of Sir Halliday McCartney, who worked for the Manchu Government in China for 14 years and was Secretary of the newly established Chinese Legation in London at the end of the nineteenth century. He once wrote to a friend: 'There is a danger [. . .] in allowing China to think that her rottenness is her strength, lest she defy you and presume, like a woman or a priest, to brave you in the protection of their petticoats. But is it certain that China must go to the Wall? Would it not be possible for her to discard her traditions and accommodate herself to the conditions of the times and live? I doubt it. History does not give us a single instance of a people who had ever declined from a high position among the nations of the world and again resumed their place among them. The very greatness of their traditions being hostile to the grafting of a new civilization prevents this. The old ideas prevent the ingress of the new, stand as insulators, breaking the circuit and preventing the pulses of the world from being felt' [Quoted in Martin, p 59].

2 Grasso et al, p ix.

3 A flavour of the growing affluence in China can be gained from the following two tables:

**Rates of possession of key consumer durables in 1997 (%)**

| | | | |
|---|---|---|---|
| B & W TV | 40 | Motorcycle | 14 |
| Colour TV | 51 | VCR | 12 |
| Refrigerator (Urban areas) | 69 | Air conditioner | 6 |
| Telephone | 52 | Mobile Phone | 6 |
| Washing Machine (urban areas) | 81 | Personal computers | 4 |
| Pager | 15 | Air conditioner | 4 |

**Key Items For Future Family Spending Within Specified Period (%)**

| Item | Buy Within Two Years | Longer Term Purchase |
| --- | --- | --- |
| Colour TV* | 34 | N/A |
| Refrigerator* | 28 | N/A |
| Car | 1 | 11 |
| Mobile Phone | 3 | 5 |
| Computer | 4 | 16 |
| Home | 17 | 19 |

*Includes replacement purchases
Source: Gallup China's Nation-wide Study of Consumer Attitudes and Lifestyle Trends, February 1997.

4 Through the Mongols, who conquered and briefly ruled China in the thirteenth century, for a time the empire stretched as far as Eastern Europe as far as the Danube.

5 Li, p 04.

6 Pye, p 32.

7 Ibid., p 33.

8 '. . . fully one-half of all the world's books printed before 1750 were printed in China.' Guisso et al, pp 3–4.

9 Kennedy, p 5.

10 Grasso et al, p 4

11 James, P.E. and Martin, G.J. *All Possible Worlds: A History of Geographical Ideas.* New York, Wiley, 1981, p 60.

12 In fact, the Roman Empire and China knew something of each other, and Chinese silk was being imported into Rome by the early second century AD. Hsu (1970), p 7.

13 Kennedy, pp 8–9.

14 Lord Macartney, the English envoy sent out to try and put relations with China on a proper footing in 1792, found a 'state of scientific and medical knowledge, the indifference of the literati class to material progress, the backwardness of the army which still used bows and arrows and lacked modern firearms, the poverty of the masses, and the widespread graft and corruption in the government.' [Hsu, p 207]. In a most prescient observation on what actually occurred in the current century, he wrote at the time: 'The empire of China is an old, crazy, first-rate Man of War, which a succession of able and vigilant officers have contrived to keep afloat for these hundred and fifty years past, and to overawe their neighbours merely by her bulk and appearance. She may, perhaps, not sink outright; she may drift some time as a wreck, and will then be dashed to pieces on the shores; but she can never be rebuilt on the old bottom.' [Ibid., pp 207–8] eighteenth century German philosopher Johann Herder wrote along the same lines: 'The empire is an embalmed mummy painted with hieroglyphs and swaddled in silk;' its circulation has a sluggish vitality of animals in hibernation. . . .' [Wiethoff, p 13].

15 Used in his speech declaring the founding of the PRC on 1 October 1949.

16 Known in China as the 'War to Resist US Aggression and Aid Korea.'

17 Research by Hao Yufan and Zhai Zhihai [*The China Quarterly*, March 1990] puts the figure at 360,000 killed and wounded and a further 20,000 captured.

18 I have an estimated 300,000 words in my computer on the Beijing case for claiming Tibet has 'always' been part of China, but I will not inflict them on readers of this volume. Suffice it to say that China bases its claim on the fact that Tibet was conquered by the Mongols in the thirteenth century and incorporated into their Chinese empire, where Beijing considers it has remained ever since. The present Dalai Lama is represented as having acquiesced in the 'peaceful liberation of Tibet' by the PLA in 1950, only to renege on the agreement subsequently, leading to the 1959 abortive rebellion. Tibet's other religious leader, the Panchen Lama, traditionally has been selected by China and the various reincarnations remain loyal to Beijing to this day.

19 Michael Leifer, Professor of International Relations at the London School of Economics and Political Science, writing in the *International Herald Tribune*, 20/1/96. Former Singaporean Prime Minister Lee Kuan Yew also observes: 'Many medium and small countries in Asia are uneasy that China may want to resume the imperial status it had in earlier centuries and have misgivings about being treated as vassal states having to send tribute to China as they used to in past centuries.'

20 Announced by President Jiang Zemin in his keynote speech at the 15th Party National Congress 12/9/97.

21 None of the world's satellites today weighs more than 4,500 kgs, and the Chinese have another version of the Long March rocket that can carry a payload of up to 9,500 kgs.

22 Eighteen months earlier, the rocket's maiden flight ended in disaster due to sudden change in its guidance system just after take-off. It crashed 22 seconds after launch, and the government eventually admitted that six people on the ground had been killed. The Chinese had begun to corner a respectable share of the international satellite launch business against stiff competition from the Americans and Europeans, due to largely to their much lower prices. Combined with an earlier failure of the Long March 3A, China's space ambitions began to look a bit rocky. But that was forgotten with the launch of the Philippines satellite.

23 Neither the navy nor the air force existed until after the Communist take-over. However, Chinese pilots flying Russian jet fighters acquitted themselves well in aerial combat against the Americans in the Korean War, although suffering heavy casualties, including a son of Chairman Mao.

24 Studies by the US Government Information Service and the International Institute for Strategic Studies have concluded that

actual spending is at least several times Beijing's official figure. Much of the spending is hidden away under other budgetary items. Based on purchasing power parity, real annual defence spending is 10 times the given figure – $87 billion, or roughly a third of the United States and 75 per cent more than Japan's. Moreover, the figure was 11.33 per cent higher in 1996 than 1995, and 14.6 per cent higher in 1995 than 1994. Even adjusting for inflation, that is still an exceptionally high rate of growth.

25 The *China National Defence News* in January 1996, for example, asserted that in the eyes of US-led Western forces 'the prosperity of a socialist China will pose a severe threat to the Western system. Therefore, some have decided China must be contained'. The containment issue is linked to recurrent tensions between China and the United States over Taiwan. The Taiwan question is not one over which Beijing can afford to show any weakness. However, the ways in which it has displayed its strength – in clouding acts of military intimidation – were noted with concern elsewhere in East Asia and gave the US a chance to demonstrate its continued military muscle in the region by deployment on occasions of elements of its Seventh Fleet in the Taiwan Strait.

26 $85.5 billion at the exchange prevailing when this book was being written in late 1997.

27 $494 billion.

28 $1,036 billion.

29 Speaking at the IMF/World Bank summit in Hong Kong 22/9/97.

30 The 1996 World Investment Report, issued by the United Nations Trade and Development Conference.

31 Total assets of the country's top foreign-funded industrial enterprises declared in December 1996 surpassed 350 billion Yuan, up 39 per cent over the previous year, according to the Ministry of Foreign Trade and Economic Cooperation.

32 Ignoring the import of capital equipment, the import and export balance of such firms nationwide in the 1990s turned from long-term deficit to favourable balance. Statistics in 1996 for the largest 500 foreign-funded firms indicated that 90 per cent prospered, with a profit of 30.2 billion Yuan, or a 6.3 billion Yuan more than the year before. These businesses have become an engine of foreign trade growth. In 1996, the import and export volume of foreign-funded firms nation-wide reached US$137.1 billion, representing a 24.8 per cent increase over the previous year and 448 times greater than 10 years ago, and accounting for 47.3 per cent of the country's total foreign trade. The export volume of these businesses had an annual average increase of 50.8 per cent over the five-year period. Due to the fact the foreign enterprises are already geared to the world, the domestic market situation and government policies had less affect on their export growth than their domestic counterparts. [Source: State Statistics Bureau].

33 'China Engaged: Integration with the Global Economy.' World Bank, 1997.

34 This is an even more impressive performance when one considers that over the whole of the Maoist era, China's share of world trade fell from 1.4 per cent in the mid-1950s to just 0.4 per cent in the mid-1970s. [Xu, p 168]. 'Under Mao [. . .] international markets were regarded as economically anarchic systems from which China's domestic economy should be insulated.' [Nolan and Dong, p 8]

35 'China 2020: Development Challenges in the New Century.' World Bank, 1997.

36 $3 billion in 1996 and total of $28 billion since the early 1980s.

37 Part of the agreement for Hong Kong's return was that it would retain a separate identity, and not simply be swallowed up by the mainland, as well as retaining its current capitalist economic system -under a formula devised by the late Deng Xiaoping, 'one country, two systems' – for at least 50 years. The Chinese government says that the same formula can be used to handle the reunification of Taiwan with the mainland.

38 For a start, Hong Kong will retain its role as the principal bridge for trade across the Taiwan Strait, according to an analysis by the Hong Kong Trade Council. In the October 1997 issue of its magazine *Trade Outpost*, the Council noted that Taiwanese laws rule that Hong Kong is still a third-country port despite its return to mainland control, and ships from Hong Kong and Taiwan can berth freely at ports of the two regions without political problems cropping up. At present, about 1,900 Taiwanese businesses have offices in Hong Kong, mainly in the sphere of international trade. The Council also believes that direct shipment across the Taiwan Strait would not undermine Hong Kong's position as an intermediate trade centre. Nearly half of Taiwan's exports to the Chinese mainland are bound for the Pearl River Delta or regions adjacent to Guangdong Province. Therefore, even if direct shipment across the Strait is given the go-ahead by the two sides, most goods will still have to be transported through Hong Kong to reduce transportation costs. Furthermore, the Beijing-Kowloon Railway has expanded Hong Kong's business network into the Chinese hinterland.

39 China still has more than 100 million illiterates. Three-quarters of the population is still rural and some 70 to 80 million people still live below the poverty line. Per capita gross domestic product is very low, between $400 and $500 a year. On a new World Bank calculation of per capita national wealth, including unexploited natural resources, China ranks 162nd of 192 countries, with $420,000 to the $6.6 million of the United States.

40 Deng (1987).

41 The ruler who founded the Chinese race (the Han).

42 Mao, p 298.

43 Ibid. p 301.

44 Ibid. p 305

45 Ibid. p 313.

46 In 1996, per capita income in rural areas was 1,926 Yuan ($240), while that of urban residents was 4,377 Yuan ($540).

47 'China Changes Shape: Regionalism and Foreign Policy,' written by Gerald Segal, a IISS senior fellow.

48 Professor Li Jingwen, in predicting a 'relatively long period' in which the gap between the prosperous coastal areas and poorer inland regions will continue to 'grow larger', also predicts the emergence of six distinct economic regions in China. These were: A South China economic sphere with Guangzhou at its centre and linked with Hong Kong, Macao and Taiwan; a Yangtze River economic sphere focused on Shanghai; a Bohai [Sea] rim centred on Beijing and Tianjin; a North-West sphere based on Harbin; a North-West China sphere bordering central Asia; a South-West region with Kunming, capital of Yunnan Province, as its focus and linked to Southeast Asia.

49 World Bank (1997), op.cit.

50 Grasso et al, p 92.

## Chapter 2 – Contradictions in Economic Reform

1 7/7/97.

2 Ministry of Labour figure.

3 'Redundant workers planted two bombs', *South China Morning Post* 30/5/97.

4 At the prevailing rate of exchange, these two figures represented US$21.69 and US$12.04 respectively. To put this into some sort of Western perspective, the latter figure would buy at McDonalds restaurant in Beijing, for example, approximately two Big Macs, along with matching fries and soft drinks.

5 Ministry of Labour figure.

6 The authoritative monthly magazine *Outlook* published its own estimates of the unemployment rate in mid-1997 which were higher than the official figure: 7.7 per cent in urban areas and 34.8 per cent in the countryside.

7 *China Labour News* 7/11/97.

8 Ibid.

9 *China Labour News* 5/8/97.

10 Ibid.

11 Interview.

12 Made available to the author.

13 Typical of the silver lining approach is the publicity given to Tian Guiqin, declared 'a star of the laid-off' by the Beijing Municipal Government. The third generation of her family to work in a match

factory, she lost her job when the plant closed in 1993. She became a bus conductor, although it means getting up at 3am and cleaning out the bus every morning. The state-run broadcasting network made a 16-part television soap opera about five women who overcome the shock of being laid off to find new jobs.

14 Even the once secretive defence industry is opening up to foreign investment. Chen Genfu, director of the Defense Department of the State Planning Commission, told the author that now that many military factories were being encouraged to switch to production of products for the civilian market, 'foreign investors are encouraged to get involved and they will enjoy the same treatment as when they launch joint ventures with non-military partners'. According to statistics from the State Planning Commission, China had approved 576 joint ventures co-invested by China's military and foreign investors involving a total of $948 million by mid-1997. These joint ventures are mainly in sectors like nuclear power, aviation, satellite launching, telecommunications equipment, shipbuilding, machines, electronics and instruments and meters. The Commission of Science, Technology and Industry for National Defence and the Equipment Department of the General Staff of the People's Liberation Army (PLA) announced that parts of the defence electronics sector would also be opened to foreign investors in 1998.

15 Between 1978 and 1990, for example, the average annual growth rate of the total output value of non-state industries was 20.1 per cent, and that of state industries 7.6 per cent. During the period 1991–5, the average annual growth rates were 31.1 and 8.3 per cent respectively. During the period 1978–1980, the proportion of total State industrial output value in the total output value of all industries saw an annual average reduction of one percentage point, with the reduction rate accelerating after 1981 to four percentage points on average, reaching a high of 10 percentage points in 1994. The proportion of industrial fixed assets in the State economy went down from 88.9 per cent in 1981 to 80.7 per cent in 1990, and then plunged to 68.8 per cent in 1995. The proportion of employees with industrial enterprises in the state economy fell from 51.5 per cent in 1978 to 45 per cent in 1990 and down to 40 per cent in 1995.

16 At the end of 1997, all but three were reported to be prospering [*China Daily* 16/12/97].

17 The banks have incurred a heavy burden of bad debts from the many years of being forced by the State to lend money to enterprises regardless of their operating performance or financial standard. However, among the reforms of the banking system has been the adoption of new rules that allow the State banks to lend purely on commercial principles. This abrupt turning off of the financial tap has been one of the factors that has hurt the State sector most in its efforts to revive or even survive.

18 In his keynote policy speech to the 15th Party Congress 12/9/97.

19 The *People's Daily* [1/5/97] urged managers of state-owned mines,

mills and factories to assign loafers to meaningful jobs. 'State-owned enterprises must reduce the number of employees and increase efficiency,' it said. 'It this issue cannot be resolved, other reforms cannot be achieved. Enterprises must change the situation of one man's work being done by three and three men's meals being shared by five. It is the most fundamental task, in deepening enterprise reform, to reduce the number of employees.'

20 *China Daily* 18/10/97.

21 But at same time, it is tackling another sore point with workers: rampant mismanagement. Less than two weeks after the Mianyang demonstration with which this chapter began, authorities sacked four executives of the Great Wall Special Steel Co. in Sichuan after the company lost more than $36 million, a move clearly intended to soothe anger among the company's 28,000 workers.

22 Interview.

23 Interview.

24 Homes for the elderly and cleaning service companies are two popular choices.

25 $361.40 at the prevailing exchange rate.

26 The implications of this will be discussed in the next chapter on rural migration.

27 Market Orientation, Decision-Making Power and Enterprise Performance – A Statistical and Analytical Report on the Sample Data of 795 State-Owned Enterprises. Liu Xiaoxuan, Economic Institute of Chinese Academy of Social Science.

28 In 1995, only 0.38 per cent of excess workers were dismissed, the report said.

29 Figures cited by Chan, A. and Senser R, 'China's Troubled Workers' Foreign Affairs, March/April 1997.

30 This in some ways resembles the great debate during the Mao era over 'red' versus 'expert' with revolutionary credentials and the right class background placed above technical expertise. It would seem the priorities have now been reversed.

31 'We Can't Take It Anymore', *Workers Daily* 17/4/96.

32 Investigation by Chan and Senser, op.cit.

33 Writing in the July 1996 issue of *China Journal*, an Australia-based publication.

34 As already noted, the rural migration issue will be dealt with in detail in the next chapter.

35 Chan and Senser, op.cit.

## Chapter 3 – Contradictions in the Countryside

1 During the period 1985 to 94, the per capita income from wages in the urban areas increased from 685 Yuan to 3,179 Yuan ($82.5 to

$383), while the per capita net income of farmers increased from 398 Yuan to 1,221 Yuan ($47.95 to $147.10), the gap widening from 1.7:1 to 2.6:1. During the same period, the contrast between the urban and rural areas in consumption level broadened from 2.3:1 to 3.6:1, not forgetting the subsidies and preferential treatments the urban residents enjoy in housing, health-care, welfare and price. In 1994 for example, State expenditure on price subsidies was 31.4 billion Yuan (US$3.78 billion).

2 Nolan, P. 'China's New Development Path: Towards Capital Markets, Market Socialism or Bureaucratic Muddle?' in Nolan and Dong, p 129.

3 As an example, Shanghai has enjoyed the highest per capita GDP in the country in recent years, 9.8 times that of Guizhou Province in the Southwest. The per capita consumption level in Shanghai, also the top in the country, is 5.7 times that of Guizhou.

4 For example, Xinjiang in the far north-west, where an independence movement has been brewing for some time among the Muslim Uygur population, who feel far more affinity with their ethnic brothers in the neighbouring states of Central Asia than they do with the Han Chinese.

5 During the period from 1991 to 1995, the urban population rose from 310 million to 350 million, and the nation's urbanization level improved from 26.37 to 30 per cent. During the same period, the labour force devoted to agriculture dropped from 340 to 310 million, a decline from 59.8 per cent to 52 per cent of total employment.

6 '1991–2010: Policy Choices of China's Economic Development'.

7 The percentage of criminal offences committed by transients has nearly doubled to 44 per cent from 1990 to 1993 in Beijing. Eighty per cent of the people arrested in the southern Pearl River Delta and other coastal regions came from other provinces. In Shenzhen, cases involving transients jumped from 26 per cent of total criminal cases in 1980 to 93 per cent in 1993. *China Daily* 17/5/94.

8 'Population flow into big cities'. *Beijing Review* 18/7/94.

9 Grant (1958).

10 Ibid. A graphic, if somewhat emotional account of poverty in both rural and urban China in the 1930s is also contained in Agnes Smedley's 'Battle Hymn of China' published in 1944, which is well worth reading.

11 Etheridge (1988).

12 There were an estimated 600,000 of these around the country, but in 1958, at the height of the drive, three million tons of the 11 million tons of steel produced 'was pronounced as unfit for industrial use'. Hsu (1970), p 754. 'Steel from the backyard furnaces was virtually useless [. . .] This ill-conceived projected wasted resources on a vast scale, not only the iron ore and household pots and pans and other iron implements gathered in the exhaustive search for raw materials, but also the trees that were cut down to fuel what turned out to be useless contraptions.' Grasso et al (1991), p 183.

13 Joffe, E. 'Between the Two Plenums: China's Intraleadership Conflict 1959–62'. Michigan Papers In Chinese Studies no.22. 1975, p 5. Ann Arbor. Center For Chinese Studies. The University of Michigan.

14 A favourite Chinese folk tale, much quoted by Mao, concerned a 'foolish old man' who did not like having to walk up and down the mountain that faced his house, so he decided to move it. He led his children and grandchildren to begin the task of chipping away at the rock, and carrying away the debris in baskets. When others laughed at his foolishness, the old man replied: 'When I die, there will be my children [to carry on the work], and the children will have grandchildren, and the grandchildren will again have children, and the children will again have children and so on and so on. So my children and grandchildren are endless, while the mountain cannot grow bigger in size. Why shouldn't it be levelled some day?' Finally, the gods took pity on him and removed the mountain. As the Christian church also declares: 'faith can move mountains'.

15 Although it should also be noted that some Chinese cadres still insist the Great Leap Forward was a success in that it introduced the peasantry to hitherto unknown industrial skills which helped lay the foundations for the current boom in rural industry, especially the so-called township enterprises.

16 Ibid, p 24.

17 Bloodworth (1966), p 207.

18 Grasso et al, p 187.

19 Leeming, p 10.

20 For a fuller account of Dazhai's fraudulent rise to fame see chapter 29 of Salisbury (1992).

21 *Beijing Review* 10/5/93.

22 Ibid.

23 World Bank 1986, quoted by Nolan and Dong, p 20.

24 Quoted by Riskin, C. 'Where is China Going?' in Nolan and Dong, p 43.

25 In the 1980s, Deng Xiaoping warned against political instability emerging from malcontents in the countryside. 'If economic trouble occurs in the 1990s, it is very likely to be in agriculture. If there is agricultural trouble, the country will not recover for many years and the development of the overall economic and social situation would be severely affected,' he predicted.

26 *Legal News*, 8/6/93.

27 The Battle of Matian Marketplace, as it has become known, was the latest chapter in a bitter clan feud between Matian villagers surnamed Liu and Jinggang villagers surnamed Li that dated back at least to the 1920s. *The Canton Evening News* reported that Matian and Jinggang had been at war since 1928, when a Matian landlord 'massacred 27 innocent Jinggang villagers in the name of eradicating

Communism', launching decades of unceasing disputes of various kinds.

28 *South China Morning Post*, 7/7/97.

29 Figure quoted by the official weekly magazine *Outlook* 28/6/97.

30 Some Chinese experts claim, however, that the provincial separatism will die out as the economic reforms continue to bite. Under the heading: 'State effective in curbing "Duke economy"' the official *China Daily* reported on 11/09/97. For example, that: 'For many centuries China has sought to control its runaway "Duke economies" of different regions. And now, success is within reach. The "Duke economies" have gained new ground since the late 1970s when the central government delegated more economic and financial power to localities. This once led to world-wide concern that China may have a difficult time formulating a national policy. If that is the case, China will only have a symbolic central government unable to pass its decisions effectively to regional ones. 'But I believe the "Duke economies" will fade away over time as China deepens its economic and political reforms,' predicted Liu Rongcang, a senior expert at Chinese Academy of Social Sciences (Cass). He said one of the main forces behind the growth of the 'Duke economies' was a financial system in the late 1980s which allowed local governments to have more revenues in their own pockets. Thus, different regions formed their own economic blocs to earn more from profitable projects, such as cigarette and alcohol factories. These blocs tended to be exclusive and the projects repeated themselves in different regions unconcerned about efficiency. From the national perspective, the blind construction of profitable projects finally led to saturation in the market and a worsening of central financial power. Liu said, however, the new financial system introduced in 1994 has put a lid on the freewheeling expansion of local economies. Besides financial reform, the emergence of a buyer's market is also becoming an 'invisible hand' that regulates local economies, Liu explained. 'As the market value gains momentum, "Duke economies" based on a planned system will have little room to stay.' He said a growing combination of enterprises from different regions and the emergence of a national market are also challenging the narrow provincial interests.

31 Work on a more scientific demarcation of borders did not begin until the early 1990s. Beijing announced in 1995 that after six years of hard work, six segments of disputed boundaries between three provinces and regions had been fixed. Work on 59 other hot spots is continuing.

32 Adapted from a table in Goodman and Segal (1994), p 162.

33 Speech to the Third Senior Policy Forum of Economic Development, Beijing, 27/5/97.

34 US$63.85 at the prevailing exchange rate.

35 Speech to Communist Party Meeting on Poverty Alleviation in Beijing in September 1996.

36 'Poorest of poor villages should move, says official.' *South China Morning Post*, 10/5/97.

37 Figure given by Feng Qiang, Vice-Director of the State Council Leading Group Office for Poverty Alleviation and Development.

38 Or abroad, because export of labour is now a flourishing industry. Chinese labourers can be found primarily in Pakistan, the Middle East and parts of Africa, sometimes working on construction projects paid for by Chinese aid.

39 While most analysis concentrates on the negative aspects of the migration on urban areas, there is also some concern about what it is doing to the countryside. Duan Chenrung, a population expert at the People's University in Beijing, for example, has predicted that it could exacerbate the aging population in the countryside, since the rural areas will not have sufficient medical and social insurance to support them. The decision by young and relatively well-educated people to leave their hometowns could pose a threat to local economic development. In addition, when they leave their children and spouses behind, family ties become more fragile. There is anecdotal evidence of an upsurge in divorces blamed on migrant workers finding a new 'wife' in the city and forgetting about the family left at home.

40 Those with a keen sense of history recall that over the centuries, migrations by landless, desperately poor peasants have often been the first move in a bloody uprising against imperial rule. 'In the rhythmic pattern of China's millennial history, peasant revolt has regularly played a leading role [. . .] A period of prosperity under a strong and energetic ruler was usually followed by a period of economic recession and court intrigues under weaker rulers. A period of anarchy would then ensue during which the country became divided among contending factions or even thrown open to foreign invasion or popular uprisings. Eventually, a new ruler would emerge to restore order. Popular discontent and peasant unrest usually stemmed from the heavy demands of the tax collector, compulsory military service and the forced labour or corvee, which most Emperors eventually imposed on their subjects.' Wilson (1971), p 25. Mao, meanwhile, declared: '. . .The Chinese bourgeois-democratic revolution is in essence a peasant revolution . . . the basic task of the Chinese proletariat in the bourgeois-democratic revolution is therefore to give leadership to the peasants struggle.' Mao, Selected Works, Vol.1V, p 190.

41 A Chinese folk-song circa 2,500 BC summed up the isolated existence of the peasant thus: 'When the sun rises I work/When the sun sets I rest/I dig the well to drink/I plough the fields to eat/What has the Emperor to do with me?' Contemplating the vastness of China and the attitudes this created in the remote countryside, one writer has recorded that: 'Within the Empire, an elaborate system had grown up of rule by family groups and guilds and village communities, but there was little or no sense of nationhood. Any call for action from The Son of Heaven in Peking passed through so many viceroys,

governors, mandarins and officials before it reached the village elders, and then the heads of families, that the individual could hardly have any feeling of loyalty to the remote Emperor, though he might fear the power officials exercised in the name of royalty. [Martin, p 99].

42 Grasso et al, p 11. In urban society, apart from government officials and a class of large landowners, the two remaining lower orders were artisans and merchants. Below them was a mixed bag of people whose occupations excluded them from membership of any of the four orders, including soldiers, actors, prostitutes and those whose work was considered menial and disreputable.

43 Ibid, p 12.

44 Estimate by Xian Zude, Deputy Director of the Rural Social and Economic Survey of the State Statistical Bureau.

45 Xinhua News Agency 18/10/96.

46 Ministry of Labour figures.

47 *China Daily* 18/4/93.

48 Professor Emeritus of Chinese Studies at the Johns Hopkins School for Advanced International Studies.

49 Barnett, p 573.

50 Ibid., p 576.

51 Interview.

52 Typical of the hardships faced by rural populations in areas not well-blessed with good conditions for agriculture is a programme now underway in a mountainous area of Guizhou, where local people are blasting away rock to create arable land. By mid–1998, the target was for 667 hectares of land to be cleared in this way. According to local officials, every $100 donated from non-governmental sources to buy explosives helps create 0.15 hectares of arable land, enough to give two people a lasting means of making a living. The rocks that are blasted away are used by the local people to build terraced fields.

53 The International Symposium by Experts on Helping the Poor in Villages During the Economic Transformation Period sponsored by the UN Asia-Pacific Economic and Social Council and the Institute of Economics, Chinese Academy of Social Sciences, 25–28 March 1997.

54 *Beijing Review* 24/3/97.

55 This is particularly so in Xinjiang, an area where Muslim-inspired instability from secessionist forces is seen as highly dangerous to national security. The Chinese army has an estimated 12 army divisions, six air bases and most of its nuclear ballistic arsenal posted to protect a long and vulnerable border in the area. The central government believes that economic development is the best antidote to local nationalism. But growth has been a two-edged sword, since it has stimulated migration of Han Chinese from the more crowded parts of the country. Since 1949, Chinese in Xinjiang have grown from about 300,000 to an estimated six million. They

often take better jobs from the less-educated and linguistically disadvantaged Uygur ethnic minority. The Han tend to settle in the cities, while the Uygurs remain in backward rural areas. Most of the jobs in the growing oil industry in Xinjiang, have been snapped up by migrating Han. A similar situation prevails in Tibet. The Tibetan 'government-in-exile' headed by the Dalai Lama alleges that there is accelerating Han population transfer into Tibet, which has reduced the Tibetan people to a minority in their own land. Today, it claims, 'there are over 7.5 million non-Tibetan settlers in Tibet including Chinese and Hui Muslims, compared to six million Tibetans. As the Chinese control over all spheres of economic, social and political life is tightened, the Tibetan people are further and further marginalized. Tibet, once a peaceful buffer state between China and India, has been transformed into a vast military base, holding between 300,000 and 500,000 troops and one-quarter of China's 350-missile strong nuclear force.' The population transfer at least is rebutted by the Beijing government, which says the only Han Chinese living in Tibet are specialists who have gone there voluntarily and temporarily to help in the region's development. The State media carries a steady diet of stories showing the immense benefits that the Tibetan population has obtained through the benefice of the central government, in raised living standards, considerably improved health standards and life expectancy, and in the elimination of illiteracy – contrasting this with the medieval conditions prevailing before 'liberation' – thanks to the 'selfless Han volunteers.

## Chapter 4 – Population Control and the Pressures of Aging

1 Yang Zihui, an associate research fellow in the Population Research Institute.

2 Hsu (1970), pp 83–4.

3 Ibid., p 169.

4 Yung Wei, p 47.

5 Chinese Statistical Outline, 1986.

6 Nolan and Dong, p 5.

7 Interview.

8 This is reflected in the fact that the gender imbalance in China – at one time as high as 125 males for every 100 females – has narrowed considerably in recent years in most areas. While most Chinese parents would still prefer to have a boy, in most cases they will accept the inevitable if the only child they are permitted is female. Couples will perhaps try and cheat by having a second child in such cases, but there is now little incidence of the most common practice of female infanticide. The thinking behind this was that apart from ensuring the family lineage, a male child would be able to work to bolster the family fortunes. A female, however, was a virtually

useless investment as her labour would eventually be lost to another family upon her marriage.

9 Especially with her mother-in-law. Chinese literature contains numerous tales of the appalling treatment of women marrying into another family and being treated as a virtual slave by her domineering mother-in-law and sisters-in-law, without a word of protest from the husband. If conditions became too oppressive, suicide was usually the only way out. A daughter-in-law who failed to produce a son and heir could expect the worst vilification of all.

10 Author's research based on a visit in 1996.

11 Many of these secret breeders in the urban areas are the rural migrants of which I wrote about in the preceding chapter. In a 1994 local government survey among 80,000 itinerant labourers in the Fengtai District in Western Beijing, about one-third of the married women had given birth to their second, third or even fourth child in defiance of family planning policies. The youngest mother was 16. A local official estimated these women had had some 4,000 babies more than the district target, adding: 'Part of our success in population control has been offset by these itinerants. They only care about having sons as heirs.' Demographer Yang Zihui estimates that 10 million babies more than the control target were delivered each year between 1985 and 1995, mostly in rural areas.

12 *Chinese Society Gazette*, June 1995.

13 Quoted in the Sichuan provincial newspaper *Gaige Shibao* (Reform Times), 10/3/96.

14 Figures provided by the China Aging Research Centre.

15 Based on analysis by Hong Guodong, Director of the China Aging Research Centre.

16 A government survey in Beijing found that 34.6 per cent of children of senior citizens frequently work overtime, 21.4 per cent take self-study courses and 43.9 per cent may need to spend time tutoring their own children. Approximately 39 per cent said helping their aged parents caused inconvenience in their daily life, and 34.4 per cent found the financial burden nearly unbearable. Some 25 per cent said they had to get their own children to help them take care of the older generation [*Beijing Review* 12/2/96].

17 One area of conflict is that attitudes towards the remarriage of elderly people, especially women, are rather restrictive and usually shared by the adult children of the couple involved. It has been the custom since time immemorial in China that widows should not remarry, a prohibition whose contravention is regarded as 'shameful and immoral' [see chapter 8]. The government sees this as a remnant from the feudal past and has tried to encourage remarriage for both practical and humanitarian reasons. The Chinese media often lauds successful second marriages and the attitude of the adult children involved for giving their support. But there are also reports of

marriages that have not taken place because of the fierce family opposition.

18 One extremely sad case occurred in Tianjin where an elderly man sued his son for alleged abuse. In court, it emerged that the older man simply felt lonely and neglected due to the fact his son rarely visited him. In the full glare of publicity, the latter was shamed into making a public apology and promising to take better care of his father in future. A growing number of similar cases have been reported in the Chinese media of late.

19 Murray (1993), p 108.

20 Estimate made by the bimonthly magazine *Management World*, sponsored by the State Council's Centre for Development and Research, September 1997.

21 *Labour News*.

22 According to statistics from the People's Bank of China, at least 76 per cent.

## Chapter 5 – Who Will Feed China?

1 'Food supply is a growing nightmare' contributed by Mr Brown to the *South China Morning Post* 7/10/95.

2 Ibid.

3 Interview.

4 The mu is a peculiarly Chinese way of measuring land, with 15 mu equal to one hectare; one mu equal to or one-sixth of an acre.

5 Speech at an international economic seminar in Switzerland, 20/3/97.

6 'Self-sufficiency Supplemented by Adequate Imports – A proposal for Ensuring China's Food Supply in the 21st Century' by Hu Angang, Chinese Academy of Agricultural Science, published in the official weekly magazine *Outlook*, Vol 35, pp 15–17, 26/8/96.

7 In 1980, China exported US$3 billion worth of farm products and imported $2.9 billion. After 1983, exports moved further ahead of imports, and in 1994, the country exported $10 billion worth of farm products, compared with $3 billion of imports.

8 1996 Annual Report on the Development of Rural Economy in China and Analysis on the Trend of 1997 Development, Academy of Social Sciences.

9 At the time of writing, the central government had begun a nation-wide investigation on how much farmland had been used to build golf courses, factories or other developments not stipulated in land-use regulations. In early 1997, a one-year freeze on land use for anything other than agricultural purposes was announced by the State Land Administration, the country's top land use and control authority, pending the working out of a more efficient land use system in both rural and urban areas. SLA officials were convinced the freeze would not interfere with China's economic development,

arguing that much of the land lost in recent years was either left idle by developers (often due to lack of money to proceed with planned construction) or was being used inefficiently.

10 Reported by *China Daily* 30/4/97.

11 'The prolonged drought in the north and northeast will have a severe impact on the country's main autumn harvest. In Shandong, a large grain producer, the river has been dry for more than 130 days, threatening 7.4 million hectares of crops and drinking water supplies for 52 million people. A brief rainy spell last week caused the lower reaches to flow, but it stopped again after only 56 hours and was insufficient to affect agriculture.' [*China Daily* 12/8/97]

12 Interview.

13 The Yellow River is not the only waterway to suffer this problem. The Grand Canal between Beijing and Hangzhou, the world's oldest, was also reported to be drying up in 1997, especially in the Suzhou section after an exceptional summer which saw the water level dropping about 10 centimeters a day. More than 100,000 ships which use the canal were reported to be grounded in Shandong Province. The central government responded by pumping around $181 million into a project to clean up decades of silt and get the water flowing more freely by 2000.

14 Estimate made by the Chinese Academy of Sciences in 1996.

15 Interview.

16 Calculated by Riskin, in Nolan and Dong, p 51, and based on various editions of the Statistical Yearbook of China.

17 Ibid., pp 50–1.

# Chapter 6 – Chinese Society: Dealing with a 2,500-Year-Old Legacy

1 Bonavia, 1980, p 2.

2 Quoted in Spence, p 720.

3 Lin (1936), p 41.

4 Ibid., p 42

5 Ibid., p 44

6 Ibid., pp 46–7.

7 Ibid., p 50

8 Ibid., p 55.

9 Ibid, p 65. I must admit that one of the surprises of living in China for me was the way ordinary Chinese poked fun at the latest political campaign, which they did not seem to feel impinged on their lives at all.

10 Warner (1966), p 299

11 Interested readers can find a full description of these in Murray (1995), pp 234–241.

12 Young, Stephen. 'Theories of Justice' in *The Concept of Justice in Pre-Imperial China. Moral Behavior in Chinese Society* in Wilson et al, p 40.

13 Ibid. pp 42–3.

14 *The Analects* 17,23.

15 Ibid.1,14.

16 Ibid, 4.11. The last three quotations can be found in translated form in Chen, p 181.

17 *The Analects*, 16.13, quoted in Chen, p 185.

18 Chen, p 25.

19 Ibid, p 23.

20 'The limits of the Confucian world view, the smugness, its self-centredness, its non-inquisitive approach to all that lay outside its immediate concerns, became dramatically self-evident once it confronted the dynamic spirit of modern science and technology' [Pye, p 52].

21 Young, op.cit., p 47.

22 Ibid, p 51.

23 Lin (1949), p 23.

24 According to historical accounts, Lao Zi was riding out of the city on a donkey, intending to say goodbye to the world, when he was prevailed upon to return long enough to write this document for all posterity. Once it was completed, he remounted the donkey and rode off into the mountains and was never heard of again – a most practical demonstration of his doctrine.

25 In direct contradiction to the typically Confucianist idea of exalting the wise in government.

26 Lin (1949), pp 28–9.

27 Ibid., p 31.

28 Ibid., p 81.

29 It would be interesting to explore further the links between Chinese folklore and Western religious and literary classics. As an example, consider this story which appeared in Fengshutung, written by Ying Shao in the second century AD. 'In Yingchuan [in present-day Hunan Province], there were two brothers living in the same house, and both sisters-in-law were expecting. The elder woman had a miscarriage, but did not let anyone know about it. When both women were in confinement and the younger sister-in-law was delivered of a boy, the elder one stole her child at night and, for three years, the dispute could not be settled. When the case was brought before the Chief Minister Huang Pa, he ordered the baby to be placed ten steps away from the two mothers. At a signal, the two women rushed for the child and it seemed the baby was being torn to pieces and neither would give it up. The baby was crying desperately, and the mother was afraid he might be hurt and let him go. The elder woman was very pleased, while the younger woman

looked very sorrowful. The Huang Pa declared: 'It is the younger one's child.' He indicted the elder woman and she was indeed found guilty.' [Translated by Lin [1944], pp 163–4]. The resemblance to the biblical story of Solomon's judgement is very striking.

30 Madsen, R. 'The Maoist Ethic and the Moral Basis of Political Activism in Rural China', in Levenson, p 154.

31 Quoted by Lifton, R.J. 'Thought Reform' – Group Psychotherapy To Save Your Soul', in Schurmann and Schell, p 143.

32 And yet, it seemed that the Chinese people could only be pushed so far in abandoning their cultural traditions. Referring to the era of the 1950s and 1960s when communization was being pushed hard, Wright (p 41) has observed that 'despite the mistaken Western view that the Chinese lack individualism, they came to hate the sudden destruction of their family units. I recently asked the great Chinese anthropologist Fei Xiaotong how it had been possible to impose the commune system on a society in which, or so one had always been led to believe, the family unit was of central importance. He replied that the Chinese family had traditionally been a productive and reproductive unit, in which affection played a very secondary role, and in which the authoritarian family head had great power. The commune system was an extension of that mode and as long as the commune leader, like the family head, could successfully organize people's lives and provide them with food, then they would accept the new pattern. But when he failed in that role, the trouble started.'

33 Sharman, p 36.

34 Remarks to leading members of the Central Committee 30/12/86 regarding student unrest.

35 'The Party's Urgent Tasks On The Organizational And Ideological Fronts.' Second Plenary Session of the 12th Party Congress 12/10/83.

36 29/1/97.

## Chapter 7 – The Cement Begins to Crumble

1 Jiwei (1994).

2 To be discussed in the next chapter in relation to the status of women, as they now initiate most of the divorce actions.

3 Under the headline 'Coping with teen angst – the paradox of lucky kids', the *China Daily* 1/10/94 carried the following report: 'Zhang Chunya had everything a 15-year-old in China could want when she tried to kill herself. Her mother and father adored her. Anything she wanted they would get for her. They lived in a nice home in Shanghai and Chunya had her own room. Her parents even took the trouble to clean up after her. 'I do everything for her because she's my only child. She should know that I love her and want her to live a far better life than me,' Zhang Youshang said as his daughter lay on a hospital bed in a coma. Chunya studied in a key school and was admired and well liked by her classmates. Neighbours pointed to her

as a role model for younger children in the community. But Chunya's mother, Yang Yuedi, couldn't believe what she read when she found her daughter unconscious after swallowing 30 sleeping pills. She still clutched the suicide note in her left hand. 'I don't understand how she can claim to hate the family,' Yang said. 'What else could I have done for her?' None of the other adults who knew Chunya could understand what prompted her to take her own life. 'Why should a lovely girl want to die?' they asked, adding, 'It ought never have happened.' Like Chunya, teens throughout China are having trouble living up to their parents' expectations of them. For parents, the key issue is how to provide their only child with the best possible upbringing. But for the Chunyas of China, their immediate crisis is how to lead a life of their own. 'I know you love me,' Chunya told her mother when she woke up from her coma. 'But I couldn't stand all the pressures that you put on me. I want to live a life of my own.'

A nationwide survey of teenagers in 1993 showed few youths listed their parents as one of the 10 people they admired most. Five out of 1000 students in a Nanjing middle school said they admired their parents. Most placed pop stars and celebrated businesspeople on their honour rolls. More than 90 per cent of the teens in the school complained that their parents meddled too much in their lives. Many said they did not want to live with their parents. They wanted more free time to pursue their own interests. And many students in Chunya's school were sympathetic to her suicide attempt.'

4 The official media in recent times has carried a number of studies on this phenomenon. One of the most striking was a case in the port of Tianjin in 1996, where an elderly man living alone sued his son for failing to pay him a regular maintenance allowance. In court, it emerged that the motive was not money: the older man was lonely and simply wanted his son to visit him more often. Media accounts said court officials eventually were able to persuade the younger man 'to fulfil his social responsibilities.'

5 Sun Puyuan, a Beijing primary school teacher, surveyed 48 first grade pupils in her class and only one of the six to seven-year-olds had not suffered a beating for failing to meet parental high standards. The Zhejiang Provincial Academy for Social Sciences conducted a survey of 200 seven to eight-year-olds and found that 60 per cent faced beatings if their school achievements were regarded at home as sub-standard. [*Beijing Review* 3/1/96].

6 Amy Wu, 'Burger 'N Fries, Hold the Democracy', *Asian Wall Street Journal* 10/6/97.

7 This is a gross distortion. BMWs are very thin on the ground in China today.

8 Pye, p 83.

9 Ibid.

10 According to one senior market analyst I spoke to at the time most private investors 'don't know about earnings per share. They don't

understand companies' performance reports, much less have the ability to analyze investment values. Most do not prepare for large losses. All they understand is that it's possible to make money share trading than leaving their money in the bank. This has increased the volatility of the stock market and aggravated speculation. Some people are going to get badly burned if this goes on unchecked.' He was right.

11 Company President Shen Taifu was executed. Former Vice Minister of the State Commission of Science and Technology, Li Xiaoshi, the highest level government official involved in the case, was sentenced to 20 years imprisonment and deprivation of political rights for four years. Li was accused of accepting bribes of over 40,000 Yuan from Shen for recommending positively on the illegal fund-raising activities and for instructing his staff to support the activities. Apart from him, the list of those prosecuted for accepting bribes or dereliction of duty included a government official at the deputy bureau director level, four reporters, three bank clerks, and three accountants. For instance, Cao Yuanjiang, a reporter from the Central People's Broadcasting Station, and Sun Shuxing, a reporter of Science and Technology Daily, were accused of taking bribes of over 50,000 Yuan each to write favourable stories about Shen. Cao got six years jail and Sun seven.

12 Li Peilin, as note 28.

13 Openly acknowledged by the government and the subject of repeated campaigns, in which the central authorities publicize their determination to crack down on wrongdoers no matter how senior their position.

14 Pye, p 74.

15 In first creating a professional civil service through competitive exams, regular evaluations and systemized promotion, the Han Dynasty regularly transferred officials from place to place and never allowed them to serve in their home district, so as to reduce cronyism and opportunities for corruption. While this had some advantages, some scholars have suggested a drawback in that officials never built up any long-range interest in the welfare or economic development of the region where they served.

16 'Sharpening the sword against corruption', Beijing Review, 1/4/96.

17 In mid-1995, the city's Liberation Daily reported that corrupt local officials were laundering their kickback money in the Shanghai stock exchange and stashing some of their wealth offshore.

18 Procuratorial Daily 12/8/97.

19 Xinhua News Agency 16/10/97.

20 People's Daily 26/11//97.

21 Beijing Review, 28/9/97.

22 Ibid., 4/5/94.

23 At least 55 offences carry the death penalty, and the categories were

extended some years ago to include economic crimes such as embezzlement and production of counterfeit goods. It is estimated that more than 1000 people are executed each year with a bullet in the back of the head.

24 *South China Morning Post* 20/6/97].

25 In Beijing, a spokesman for the Disciplinary Inspection Committee under the municipal Party committee revealed that 90 conferences above the county level were reduced, saving 1.37 million Yuan, and 391 conferences above county level were cancelled, saving 6.19 million Yuan. Local government curbed 89 delegations with 610 members to other countries and saved 23.22 million Yuan in the first half of 1997.[*China Daily* 11/7/97].

26 Xinhua news agency, 10/10/97.

27 *Legal Daily* 17/10/97.

28 The information in this section depends on a mixture of author research and information appearing at various times in 1996 and 1997 by the *Real Estate Newspaper*, published by the Ministry of Construction.

29 'Continuing War on Drugs', *Beijing Review* 2/9/96.

30 Interview, June 1997.

## Chapter 8 – The Status of Women: Still a Long Way to Go

1 Unless otherwise stated, the material in this chapter is based on personal research and interviews.

2 Vincent Chen, admittedly writing from the anti-Communist viewpoint of someone who 'fled from China when Communist troops surrounded Shanghai' to live in America, argues, however, that there was nothing new in these reforms. 'The main features of [the Marriage Law], such as prohibition of child betrothal, concubinage, polygamy, and interference with widows' remarriage, [. . .] and equal rights in divorce, were publicized as a bold, revolutionary liberation of the downtrodden people from the practices of a decadent society. It happens that all the points had already been initiated by the Nationalists in their Civil Code of 1931, and many Chinese had already availed themselves of these rights. Others, mainly the peasants, had failed to do so because of their own conservative attitude.' [Chen, p 128].

3 Official figures show there were 186,000 divorces in 1950, rising rapidly to a peak of 1,170,000 in 1953. After that, the rate tapered off [figures quoted by Chen, p 129].

4 Murray (1993), pp 99–100.

5 Ibid., pp 100–l.

6 Lin (1936), p 133.

7 Cotterell, p 121.

8 Lin, op.cit., p 134.

9 Although female infanticide is now regarded as a thing of the past, there are repeated stories suggesting that in some remote rural areas it is still practiced. Government sources in Beijing say it is very difficult to categorically deny that none takes place. However, the country's top planning official says infanticide is no longer needed as modern medical technology allows a woman to determine early on the sex of her unborn child and abort it if it is a girl. 'This is one reason for the growing imbalance in reported births between boys and girls,' claimed Ms Peng Peiyun, Chairwoman of the State Family Planning Commission. The ratio of roughly 113 boys to every 100 girls is far above the international norm of 106:100 and cannot be considered natural, she added.

10 'It is impossible to exaggerate the romantic, literary, musical and political importance of the courtesan in China. Because men thought it improper for decent family girls to handle musical instruments, which were dangerous to their virtue, or to have too much literary learning, which was equally subversive to their morality, and but rarely encouraged painting and poetry for them, [male scholars and officials] did not, on that account, cease to desire female company of the artistic and literary type. The sing-song girls cultivated these things because they did not need ignorance as a bulwark to their virtue.' [Ibid.,p 153].

11 Hsieh (1943), pp 42–3.

12 Pruitt, p 22.

13 Ibid., p 180.

14 Writing in the magazine *Hsiang-Chiang Pinglun* (New Culture), issue 3, July, 1919.

15 Quoted by Witke, R. 'Mao Tse-tung, Women and Suicide', in Young (ed.), p 26.

16 However, until quite recently, many marriages were forbidden because applicants came from different classes in a supposedly classless society, or were from a bad background (e.g. offspring of a rich landlord in the old society). This was possible because all marriage applications had to be submitted to the local government for approval. Although there is now more freedom, the Party still controls all marriages of its members.

17 Lavely, W. and others, 'The Rise of Female Education in China: National and Regional Patterns', *China Quarterly*, March 1990, pp 67–8.

18 Ibid., p 65.

19 Taken from a translation in Waley, A. Chinese Poems, p 84.

20 Salaff, J.W. and Merkle, J. 'Women and Revolution: The Lessons of the Soviet Union and China', in Young (ed.) op.cit.,p 159.

21 The Marriage Law of 1950 established the right to marry the person of one's choice, prohibited polygamy, affirmed equality of the sexes

and set out various measures to protect the interests of women and children. Article 3 of the law declares that 'marriage upon arbitrary decision by any third party, mercenary marriage and any other acts of interference in the freedom of marriage is prohibited.' The measures were further strengthened by a new Marriage Law in 1981. One change was that the minimum age for marriage was raised to 22 for men and 20 for women, from the earlier mark of 20 and 18 years respectively. This, combined with encouragement of late births, has done much to slow down population growth.

22 'The Situation of Chinese Women', published by the Information Office of the State Council, June 1994. Full text carried in *Beijing Review*, 6 June 1994.

23 The vice trade has made a spectacular comeback in recent years. Apart from large numbers of Chinese women recruited into the business, a booming trade has sprung up, especially in southern China, involving the kidnapping of young girls from neighbouring countries such as Vietnam, Thailand and Burma.

24 A number of urban working women I know would give a wry smile on reading this statement. Semi-feudal attitudes still linger and 'new man' is still somewhat thin on the ground.

25 In a preface to 'New Trends in Chinese Marriage and the Family', published by *Women In China*, 1987.

26 *South China Morning Post* 11/5/93.

27 Ibid 24/6/97.

28 Interview.

29 *Beijing Review*, 12/3/97.

30 Interview.

31 *Shenzhen Special Economic Zone Daily* 22/9/95.

32 Reproduced in *China Daily* 18/12/97.

## Chapter 9 – The China that Can Say No

1 A formula used even for countries did not exist until a few years ago.

2 China I: The Coming Conflict with America' by Richard Bernstein and Ross H.Munro. Foreign Affairs, March/April 1997, pp 18–32. Bernstein was *Time* Magazine's first Beijing Bureau Chief, while Munro was Beijing Bureau Chief of the *Toronto Globe and Mail* and is now Director of the Asia Program at the Foreign Policy Research Institute.

3 Ibid.

4 By Bernstein and Munro, as above.

5 Interview.

6 Ibid.

7 It is interesting to consider what might have happened to Sino-American relations if the Cold War in general and the Taiwan issue

in particular had not hardened attitudes. Some American sinologists believe a great opportunity was lost in the late 1940s due to a wrong policy towards events in China. In a 1971 television documentary, John Service, one of the State Department's leading experts on pre-war and wartime China whose career was destroyed in the 1950s by McCarthyism, recalls that following a mission to the Communist base at Yanan in 1944, he and others had put forward a recommendation that the US should avoid a total commitment to Nationalist leader Chiang Kaishek, given the obvious strength of the Communists, their demonstrated organizational superiority and the growing support of the Chinese masses. They were overruled, however, by American ambassador Patrick Hurley, who was staunchly pro-Chiang. Many disasters flowed from the decision to back the wrong side to the hilt which were to dog the United States and its allies for years. Service claims that but for this mistake, 'we would have maintained our relations . . . there would never have been any break. There wouldn't be any exile government in Taiwan; and probably there would not have been a Korean War. Very likely, if you follow things through, there might not have been a Vietnam War.' [Fitzgerald and Roper, p 44].

8 Bernstein and Munro, op.cit., as 1.

9 Interview.

10 Bernstein and Munro, op.cit..

11 Article contributed to the *New York Times* 2/4/96.

12 The formula used with success to bring Hong Kong back into the fold.

13 In the early days of the Japanese war, Chinese 'puppet' troops arrive in Shajiabang village looking for 18 wounded soldiers left behind by the Communist New Fourth Army to recover. Their efforts are thwarted by a brave farmer's wife. The opera contains an overture in praise of Chairman Mao and the Communist Party leading the people to fight the Japanese and save the nation, and the Red Army's marching song is a recurrent theme: Red Flags Fly; the bugles sound/ Hills and rivers echo/Drive out the Japanese invaders/Wipe out the traitors. Another popular Peking Opera, *Red Signal Lantern*, tells the story of a railway signalman, his mother and daughter, all working for the partisans, who are captured and tortured until the women die.

14 Quoted from 'China Can Say No – The Political and Mental Choices in the Post Cold War' by Song Qiang, Zhang, Zangzang and Qiao Bian. Beijing, All China Industrial and Commercial Union Press, May 1996.

15 I have distilled various statements made by Chinese officials at various times to produce this brief summary.

16 One of them was described as having worked for a year on the *Washington Post*, enabling him to obtain internal documents allegedly dictating how China should be covered by the newspaper.

17 The two countries are far apart on human rights issues because they have different interpretations of the words. The Americans appear to place a narrow, political definition on human rights, meaning the right to be governed by a 'freely-elected' government in a multi-party system. The Chinese see things differently. Human rights, they insist, mean the right to sufficient food and clothing, the right to be free of poverty, the right to education, the right to enjoy good health through access to an efficient health service etc. In all these areas, officials repeatedly stress, China has a very good record.

18 As to whether a stronger China really is an inexorable threat to the United States, the Chinese say this fear is based on a complete misunderstanding. China, they insist, has never been an aggressive country in history, even during its strongest period in the Han (206 BC–24 AD) and Tang (618–907 AD) dynasties. The only time it has taken up arms has been to resist outside invasion, and that includes the Korean War. If it had been attack-oriented, as some Americans claim, it would never have built the Great Wall.

19 A few examples from 1996 might help in understanding why the Chinese feel aggrieved with the media coverage of their nation. The New York Times has described China as the 'fifth enemy' of the United States following Nazi Germany, the Soviet Union, Japan and Iraq, in American history, therefore, it is quite natural for the United States to defeat China as it had done to the other four foes by military and comprehensive means. An article entitled 'Why Must We Contain China?' in *Time* Magazine by Charles Krauthammer likened China to Germany of the late nineteenth century in pursuit of power. He also put forth a specific suggestion to restrict China by establishing diplomatic relation with Vietnam and prolonging the alliance with Japan, adding that 'it's high time to exert and maintain pressure.' Business Week, in using China as its cover story, called it an 'Unrestrained Giant', and warned of the threat to world trade by a nation 'that never acts in accordance with regular rules'.

20 Schurmann and Schell, p 285.

21 James Sasser, the US ambassador to China, has expressed concern about the US media's narrow coverage on China, and its obsession with negative aspects. Speaking on Sino-US ties at the Committee of One Hundred in Washington on 26 April 1996, he complained at being unable to see from the US press any information about China's progress in the fields of protection of human and intellectual property rights, prohibition on nuclear proliferation and democracy. At a symposium held in Beijing on 5 September 1996, former US President George Bush also expressed his concern: 'There is too much China-bashing in the United States of America. Some people have little understanding of China and how to deal with Beijing.'

## Chapter 10 – The Future: Groping Over the Stones

1 The government's target by 2000 is for investment in 'national urban and township residence construction' to make up around five

per cent of the gross domestic product, with total residential construction of some 1.2 billion square meters over the Five-Year period, with the annual level not falling below 240 million square meters, although part of the money will also be spent on updating existing housing to meet higher standards of living (e.g. every apartment to have a toilet and kitchen). The government is also pledged to try to improve the proportion of commercial housing being built (i.e. that available for sale rather than for renting to employees of State-run enterprises), with a target of 60 per cent by the turn of the century. But this depends on the further development of the current fledgling mortgage system, as rising costs have placed owning their own home out of reach of millions of urban residents in recent years.

2 Millions of Chinese families still live in extremely cramped conditions with three generations forced to sleep together in one room and share cooking and toilet facilities with other residents. A number of official studies have said that this has become a major cause of social tension in overcrowded cities and has led to a rapid rise in marriage breakdowns. According to a Construction Ministry study, at least 5.5 million urban families now occupy less than 45 square meters of living space. But this number is expected to grow to eight million by the year 2000, as more young people get married and start families, especially as rapid social change, and the new freedom to move around the country with the abandonment of the residential permit system, is breaking up the traditional extended family. Until recently, the average Shanghaiese was used to sharing a bathroom and kitchen with at least 10 others. A 'Comfort Housing Project' was launched in 1995 to provide a total of 150 million square meters of low-cost apartments, each with 60 meters of floor space. This will help realize the government's goal of providing eight square meters of living space for each Chinese resident by the year 2000.

3 In 1949, heavy industrial production had fallen to 30 per cent of the previous peak level, while agricultural and consumer goods output was only at 70 per cent of former peaks. Hyperinflation had ruined the value of the currency and barter trade dominated economic exchanges. The transportation system was in ruins and the country's most important industrial base, Manchuria, had been looted of all its modern equipment by the Soviet Union, claiming war booty after defeating the occupying Japanese. [Selden & Lippitt, p 4].

4 The weekly magazine *Outlook* 17/12/97 commented: 'China is in the primary stage of socialism and will remain in this stage for a long time to come. It has made notable achievements in its construction of the socialist market economy since the 14th Party Congress in 1992 and is stepping into a golden period of economic development and social progress. However, the basic national conditions – a large population, a poor foundation to begin with, uneven regional development and underdeveloped productive forces – have yet to be fundamentally improved.' It identified 'the primary stage of

socialism' as an 'historic stage in which China should gradually put an end to underdevelopment and realize socialist modernization.' The interesting thing here is that socialism is seen purely in economic and not political terms.

5 The ritual formulation, used in every major speech, is of a collegiate style of rule, 'the first generation leadership with Mao Zedong at the core, the second generation leadership with Deng Xiaoping at the core, and the third generation leadership with Jiang Zemin at the core'.

6 Quoted in Mason, p 127.

7 The pro-democracy movement that led to the bloodshed in and around Tiananmen Square.

8 'Economist sees political reform hope' *South China Morning Post* 9/8/97.

9 'The State and the Individual: An Overview Interpretation', *China Quarterly*, September 1991, p 443.

10 Shanghai has benefited from the fact that its leaders in recent years have graduated onto the National People's Congress, including President Jiang and Prime Minister Zhu Rongji, the economic tsar. This leads to grumbles in the rest of the country about the existence of a 'Shanghai mafia' running the show.

11 After the founding of the PRC, strict controls were imposed on firearms and ammunition to maintain public security. And, apart from armed confrontations during the Cultural Revolution, this seemed to work until the 1980s when crimes involving weapons began to reappear once again as a significant factor, including highway robbery, attacks on banks and cash-carrying armoured cars. Although private ownership of weapons is still virtually forbidden, criminals have been able to circumvent this by smuggling in guns from neighbouring countries, especially Vietnam. Thefts from military bases and illegal manufacture supplement this trade.

12 Old, inefficient technology means that China must burn 50 million tonnes of coal more than a developed country would have to for the same amount of energy. And 50 million tonnes of typical Chinese coal produce 1.4 million tonnes of sulfur dioxide.

13 This was very much the argument put forward at the environmental conference in Kyoto, Japan, in late 1997, when China led Third World attacks on the 'hypocrisy' of the United States in seeking to curb their development in order to meet targets for reduction of so-called greenhouse gases while planning to use its own wealth to 'buy the right' to go on fouling up the planet. This was also the line taken by the official media in telling the Chinese public what happened in Kyoto.

14 A perfect example is Changhong, the country's leading television manufacturer. Founded in 1958 as the State Changhong Machinery Factory, it was one of the key military industrial enterprises in China. But in 1973, with military orders beginning to dwindle, the company began to manufacture monochrome TV sets for the civilian market to stay alive. By 1985 even this lifeline was not

enough. With orders dwindling for an outdated product, the factory was on the verge of closure, until Ni Rufeng, then 41 and one of the youngest major factory directors in the electronics industry, took a bold step. Faced with stagnant domestic demand in 1988, Chinese colour television manufacturers reduced their production of the prevailing standard 14-inch set one after another, leaving suppliers of cathode ray tubes with massive inventories. But from his vantage point in Sichuan province, Ni saw things differently. His logic was that farmers would obviously increase their income as the government had raised the price of grain and cotton. Few rural families then had a colour TV, but that was bound to change when they got more money. Thus, he went out and bought all the stocked 14-inch colour tubes from the country's largest producer at bargain prices. And, he expanded his production. At the time, other TV manufacturers were vying with each other in the cities for the sale of 28-inch colour televisions. Not until Ni had begun placing 14-inch sets in the hands of farmers in a steady stream, did other factory directors realize the potential of the large rural market. And by then, 14-inch CRTs were in short supply and the prices soared. With money borrowed from the provincial government, Ni also imported colour TV technology and production lines from the Japanese company Matsushita (National Panasonic). The injection of new Japanese technology was an instant success, combined with the right marketing instincts. As a result, Sichuan Changhong Electrical Appliances Co. Ltd. went from strength to strength and in 1997 accounted for a third of domestic colour TV set sales. This year, it may well be one-third, and Ni is now quite seriously considering the not-too-distant day when Changhong enters the Fortune 500 list of the world's biggest companies. [Author's research].

15 About 40 per cent in recent years, although likely to decline somewhat to perhaps 35 per cent in the foreseeable future.

16 Cook and Li, p 201.

17 Although these are practices that are supposed to end, or at least be gradually phased out, with WTO membership.

18 See Murray (1995), chapter 9, for the strategies used.

19 Matt Frei, writing in the Sunday Telegraph 26/10/97, and repeated in his report on the Money programme BBC2 27/10/97.

20 An important factor is a vastly overpriced property market – second only to Tokyo's crazy price levels – which has placed buying office or residential properties out of the reach of all but the richest. Sixty per cent of the money circulating on the local stock market is in property-related shares, so a fall was inevitable.

21 Readers interested in learning more about the Singapore-China connection are referred to Murray, G. and Pereira, A. *Singapore: Global City State*. London, China Library, 1996.

22 For example, the Bank of China, one of the four largest state banks, reported that $1.6 billion of its $2.3 billion profits in 1996 were

generated by operations in Hong Kong and Macao (the Portuguese colony on the other side of the Pearl River due to return to China in 1999).

23 Much of the current road construction on the mainland is being funded in this way. Hong Kong is also being used as a stepping stone for the big mainland companies with ambitions to have their shares listed on the world's leading stock exchanges, such as New York and London.

24 Cook and Li, p 213.

25 As Deng Xiaoping used to remark: 'When you open the front door inevitably a few flies will enter.'

# Bibliography

Anonymous. *Forty-Five Years of Successful Economic Development (1949–1994).* New Star Publishers, Beijing, 1994.

Anonymous. *The Prospects For China's Economy 1996–2010.* New Star Publishers, Beijing, 1996.

Anonymous. *Capital Iron and Steel Corporation - An Archtype for Enterprise Reform in China.* New Star Publishers, Beijing, 1993.

Ansprenger, F. *The Dissolution of Colonial Empires.* London, Routledge, 1989.

Barnett, A.D. *China's Far West.* Boulder, Westview Press, 1993.

Bauer, W. *China And The Search For Happiness. Recurring Themes In Four Thousand Years Of Chinese Cultural History,* New York, The Seabury Press, 1976.

Bernstein, R. and Munro, R.H. *The Coming Conflict with China.*

Bloodworth, D. *The Chinese Looking Glass.* Farrar, Strauss & Giroux, New York, 1966.

Bloodworth, D. and Ching Ping. *The Chinese Machiavelli. Three Thousand Years of Chinese Statecraft.* London, Secker & Warburg, 1976.

Bonavia, David. *The Chinese.* New York, Lippincott & Crowell, 1980

Breslin, S. 'Centre and Province in China' in Benewick, R. and Wingrove, P. *China in the 1990s.* London, McMillan, 1995.

Brugger, B. *Contemporary China.* London, Crook Helm, 1977.

Buchanan, A. (ed.). *China and the Peace of Asia: Studies in International Security.* London, Chatto and Windus, for the Institute of Strategic Studies, 1965.

Bukharin N. and Preobrazhensky E, *The ABC of Communism,* Harmondsworth, Penguin, 1969.

Cameron, N. *From Bondage to Liberation. East Asia 1860–1952.* Oxford University Press, 1975.

Cannon, T. and Jenkins, A. (eds). *The Geography of Contemporary China; the Impact of Deng Xiaoping's Decade.* London, Routledge, 1990.

Chen Jingpin. *Confucius As A Teacher.* Beijing, Foreign Languages Press, 1990.

Chen, Jerome. *Mao and the Chinese Revolution.* London, Oxford University Press, 1965.

248

Chesneux, J., Le Barbier, F. and Bergere, M. *China From The 1911 Revolution to Liberation*. London, The Harvester Press Ltd, 1977.

Chu, V. *The Inside Story of Communist China*. London, Allen & Unwin, 1964.

Cohen, A.A. *The Communism of Mao Tse-Tung*. Chicago, The University of Chicago Press, 1964.

Cole, J.P. 'China and the former USSR: A Comparison in Time and Space,' in Cook, I.G., Doel, M and Li, R. *Fragmented Asia: Regional Integration and National Disintegration in Pacific Asia*. Avebury Press, 1996.

Cook, I.G., Dole, M. and Li, R. (eds). *Fragmented Asia: Region Integration and National Disintegration in Pacific Asia*. Avebury Press, 1996.

Cotterell, A. *The First Emperor of China*. London, Macmillan, 1981.

Cotterell, A. *China. A History*. London, Pimlico (Random House), 1995.

Croll, Elisabeth. *Feminism and Socialism in China*. London, Routledge and Kegan Paul, 1978.

Davin, Delia. *Woman-Work. Women and the Party in Revolutionary China*. Oxford University Press, 1975.

Dawson, R. *The Chinese Chameleon*, London, Oxford University Press, 1967.

Deng Xiaoping: *Fundamental Issues in Present-day China*. Beijing, Foreign Languages Press, 1987.

Dickinson, G.L. *Letters From John Chinaman*. J.M.Dent & Sons, 1906.

Dwyer, D. (ed), *China: The Next Decades*. Harlow, Essex, Longman, 1994.

Elvin, M. *The Pattern of the Chinese Past*. London, Eyre Methuen Ltd., 1973.

Etheridge, J.M. *Changing China*. Beijing, New World Press, 1988.

Ferdinand, P. 'Russia and Soviet Shadows Over China's Future', *International Affairs*, Vol.68, No.2, April 1992.

Fitzgerald, C.P. *Revolution In China*. London, The Cresset Press Ltd, 1952.

Fitzgerald, C.P. and Roper, M. *China: A World So Changed*. London, Thomas Nelson Ltd, 1972.

Fleming, P. *Bayonets To Lhasa*. London, Readers Union,. 1961.

Garthoff, R.L. (ed). *Sino-Soviet Military Relations*, New York, Frederick A.Praeger, 1966.

Gao Shangguan and Chi Fulin (eds). *Several Issues Arising During the Retracking of the Chinese Economy*. Studies on the Chinese Market Economy Series, Foreign Languages Press, Beijing, 1997.

Gao Shangguan and Chi Fulin (eds). *China's Social Security System*. Studies on the Chinese Market Economy Series, Foreign Languages Press, Beijing, 1996.

Gao Shangguan and Chi Fulin (eds). *Development of China's Nongovernmentally and Privately Operated Economy*. Studies on the Chinese Market Economy Series, Foreign Languages Press, Beijing, 1996.

Gold, T.G. *A Nation State. China After Forty Years*. Institute of East Asian Studies, University of California at Berkeley 1990.

Gompertz,G.H. *China in Turmoil. Eye-witness 1924/1948*. London, J.M.Dent & Sons, 1967.

Goodman, David and Segal, Gerald (eds). *China Deconstructs: Politics, Trade and Regionalism*. London, Routledge, 1994.

Goodman, D. *Deng Xiaopeng and the Chinese Revolution*. London, Routledge, 1994.

Goodmaan, D. (ed). *China's Regional Development*. London, Routledge (for The Royal Institute of International Affairs), 1989.

Grant, P. Celestial Empire. *China In The 20th Century*. London, Queen Anne Press.1988.

Grasso, J., Corrin, J. and Kort, M. *Modernization and Revolution in China*. London, M.E.Sharpe Inc., 1991.

Greene. F. *The Wall Has Two Sides. A Portrait of China Today*. London, The Reprint Society, 1962.

Gullain, R. *The Blue Ants*. (English Translation), London, Secker & Warburg, 1957.

Guisso, R., Pagani, C. and Miller, D. *The First Emperor of China*. London, Sidgewick & Jackson, 1989.

Han Suyin, *The Crippled Tree*, London, Cape, 1965.

Han Suyin, *The Morning Deluge*. Mao Tsetung and the Chinese Revolution. Vol.1.1893–1935. *St. Albans*, Panther Books, 1972.

Harris, Nigel. *The Mandate of Heaven. Marx and Mao in Modern China*. London, Quartet Books, 1978.

Hensman. C.R. *Yellow Peril? Red Hope?* London, SCM Press, 1968.

Hibbert, C. *The Dragon Wakes: China and the West 1793–1911*. Newton Abbot, Readers Union, 1971.

Hinton, W. *Fenshan: A Documentary of Revolution in a Chinese Village*. New York, Vintage Books, 1966.

Hinton, W. *Shenfan*. London, Secker & Warburg, 1983.

Hogg, G. *I See A New China*. London, Victor Gollancz Ltd., 1945.

Hsieh, Pingying. *Autobiography Of A Chinese Girl*. London, Allen & Unwin, 1943.

Hsu, C.Y. *The Rise of Modern China*. London, Oxford University Press, 1970.

Hughes, E.R. *The Invasion of China by the Western World*. London, Adam and Charles Black, 1937.

Jiwei, C. *Dialectic of the Chinese Revolution: from Utopianism to Hedonism*. Stanford, Stanford University Press, 1994.

Joffe, E. *Between the Two Plenums: China's Intraleadership Conflict 1959–62*. Michigan Papers In Chinese Studies no.22. 1975. Ann Arbor. Center For Chinese Studies. The University of Michigan.

Kallgren, J. (ed). *Building A Nation State. China After Forty Years*. Institute of East Asian Studies, University of California at Berkeley, 1990.

Kennedy, P. *The Rise and Fall of the Great Powers*. London, Fontana Press, 1989.

Kubek, A. *How The Far East Was Lost. American Policy and the Creation of Communist China 1941–1949*. New York, Twin Circle Publishing Co. Inc., 1972.

Leeming, F. *Rural China Today*. London, Longman, 1985.

Levenson, J.R. *Modern China. In Interpretative Anthology*. London, Macmillan,. 1971.

Li Jingwen. *1991–2010 Policy Choices of China's Economic Development*. Beijing, Chinese Academy of Social Sciences, 1994.

Li Peilin. *New System Initiatives and the Challenges Encountered*. Beijing, Foreign Languages Press, 1997.

Li Zhisui. *The Private Life of Chairman Mao*. London, Chatto & Windus, 1994.

Lin Yutang. *My Country, My People*. London, William Heinemann, 1943.

Lin Yutang, *The Vigil Of A Nation*, London William Heinemann, 1946.

Lin Yutang. *The Wisdom of China*. London, Michael Joseph, 1949.

Lindsay, M. *China and the Cold War*. Melbourne University Press, 1955.

Liu Xiaoxuan. *Market Orientation, Decision-Making Power and Enterprise Performance - A Statistical and Analytical Report on the Sample Data of 795 State-Owned Enterprises*. Economic Institute of Chinese Academy of Social Science, 1996.

Loewe, M. *Imperial China. The Historical Background to the Modern Age*. London, Allen & Unwin, 1966.

Ma, H. (ed), *Modern China's Economy and Management*. Beijing, Foreign Languages Press, 1990.

Mackeras, C. *Western Images of China*. Oxford University Press, 1989.

Mannix, W.F. *The Memoirs of Li Hung Chang*, Houghton Miffin Co., 1913.

Mao Zedong. *Selected Works on Foreign Affairs of Mao Zedong*; edited by the Foreign Affairs Ministry of the PRC and the Document Institute of the Central Committee of the CPC; Beijing, Central Document Press; 1994.

Martin, B. *Strange Vigour. A Biography of Sun Yat-Sen*. London, William Heinemann, 1944.

Mason, C. *The View From Peking. An Account Of The Chinese People Today*. London, Angus & Robertson, 1977.

Mehnert, K. *Peking and Moscow*. New York, G.K.Putnam's Sons, 1963.

Mende, T. *The Chinese Revolution*. London, Thames and Hudson, 1961.

Mi Zhenyu. *Megatrends China*. Beijing, Hualing Publishing House, 1996.

Millard, T.F. China. *Where It Is Today And Why*. New York, Harcourt, Brace & Co., 1928.

Murray, G. *The Rampant Dragon*. London, Minerva Press, 1993.

Murray, G. *China: the Last Great Market*. London, China Library, 1994.

Myrdal, J. *Report from a Chinese Village*, London, Heinemann, 1965.

Nolan, P. and Dong Fureng (eds). *The Chinese Economy And Its Future*. Cambridge, Polity Press, 1990.

Ono, K. *Chinese Women in a Century of Revolution 1850–1950*. 1989, Stanford University Press.

Peck, S. *Halls of Jade, Walls of Stone. Women in China Today*. New York, Franklin Watts, 1988.

Ping, C. China. *New Age and New Outlook*. Penguin Books, 1960.

Pruitt, I. *A Daughter of Han. The Autobiography of a Chinese Woman*. Stanford University Press, 1967 (first published in 1945).

Pye, L. *China An Introduction*. Boston, Little, Brown and Company, 1972.

Roxby, P.M. *China*. Oxford United Press, 1942.

Salisbury, H. *Orbit of China*. London, Secker & Warburg, 1967.

Salisbury, H. *The New Emperors. Mao & Deng, A Dual Biography*. London, Harper Collins, 1992.

Selden, M. and Lippit, V. (eds). *The Transition to Socialism in China*. New York, M.E.Sharpe. Inc., 1982.

Sharman, L. *Sun Yat-sen, His Life and its Meaning*. John Day, New York, 1934.

Schram,S. (ed.) *Authority Participation and Cultural Change in China.* Cambridge University Press, 1973.

Schurmann, F. and Schell, O. *China Readings 1: Imperial China.* New York, Random House, 1967.

Schurmann. F. and Schell, O. (eds.). *China Readings 3: Communist China.* New York, Random House, 1967.

Schwartz, B. *Chinese Communism And The Rise Of Mao.* Cambridge, Harvard University Press, 1951.

Sen, N. C. *Rural Economy and Development in China.* Beijing, Foreign Languages Press, 1990.

Sit, F.S. (ed.). *Chinese Cities. The Growth of the Metropolis Since 1945.* Oxford University Press, 1985.

Smedley, A. *China Fights Back.* London, Victor Gollancz Ltd., 1938.

Smedley, A. *Battle Hymn of China.* London, Victor Gollancz Ltd., 1944.

Snow. E. *Red Star Over China.* London, Victor Gollancz Ltd, 1937. Revised and Enlarged Edition, Penguin Books, 1972.

Snow, E. *The Other Side Of The River.* London, Victor Gollancz Ltd, 1963.

Song Qiang, Zhang, Zangzang and Qiao Bian. *China Can Say No – The Political and Mental Choices in the Post Cold War.* Beijing, All China Industrial and Commercial Union Press, 1996.

Spence, J. *The Search For Modern China.* London, Hutchinson, 1990.

Spence, J. *The Gate Of Heavenly Peace. The Chinese And Their Revolution 1895–1980.* London, Faber and Faber, 1982.

Strong, A.L. *China's Millions. Revolution in Central China, 1927.* Beijing, New World Press, 1965.

Stuckl, L. *Land Behind the Walls.* (English translation), Ampersand, 1965.

Sun Yat-sen. Sun Min Chu I [English title: *The Three Principles of the People*], Calcutta, Frank Price, 1942.

Terrill, R. *The White-Boned Demon. A Biography of Madame Mao Zedong.* New York, William Morrow & Co., 1984.

Waley, A. *Chinese Poems.* London, Allen and Unwin, 1946.

Wang, C.F. *Contemporary Chinese Politics. An Introduction.* Fourth Edition, New Jersey, Prentice Hall, 1992.

Warner, D. *Out of a Gun*, London, Hutchinson & Co, 1956.

Wenley, A.G. and Pope, J.A. *China.* Washington, Smithsonian Institution War Background Studies Number Twenty, 1944.

Wickert, E. *The Middle Kingdom. Inside China Today.* London, Harvill Press, 1983.

Wiethoff, B. *Introduction to Chinese History.* London, Thames and Hudson, 1975.

Wilson, D. *The Long March.* Penguin Books, 1971.

Wilson R and others (ed). *The Concept of Justice in Pre-Imperial China. Moral Behaviour in Chinese Society.* Praeger, Connecticut, 1981.

Wright, E. *The Chinese People Stand Up.* London, BBC Books, 1989.

Xu, Dixin (ed). *China's Search For Economic Growth. Beijing,* New World Press, 1982.

Young, J.R. *The Dragon's Teeth. Inside China's Armed Forces.* London, Hutchinson, 1987.

Young, M. (ed). *Women In China. Michigan Papers in Chinese Studies.* Center for Chinese Studies, University of Michigan, 1973.

Yung Wei (ed). *Communist China. A System-Functional* Reader. Columbus, Charles E.Merrill Publishing Co.,1972.
Zhang, W.W. and Zeng, Q.N. *In Search of China's Minorities*. Beijing, New World Press, 1993.

**Other sources**
*Beijing Review*
*China Daily*
*China Population Today*
*China Securities News*
*Economic Information Daily*
*Financial Times*
*Foreign Affairs*
*Guangming Daily*
*Liberation Daily*
*People's Daily*
*South China Morning Post*
*The China Quarterly*
*Xinhua News Agency*

# Index